Race in the Schoolyard

The Rutgers Series in Childhood Studies

Edited by Myra Bluebond-Langner

Advisory Board

   Joan Jacobs Brumberg

   Perri Klass

   Jill Korbin

   Bambi Schieffelin

   Enid Schildkraut

Race in the Schoolyard

Negotiating the Color Line in Classrooms and Communities

Amanda E. Lewis

Rutgers University Press

New Brunswick, New Jersey, and London

Ninth paperback printing, 2011

Library of Congress Cataloging-in-Publication Data

Lewis, Amanda E., 1970–
Race in the schoolyard : negotiating the color line in classrooms and
communities / Amanda E. Lewis
p.   cm. — (Series in childhood studies)
Includes bibliographical references and index.
ISBN 0-8135-3224-8 (cloth : alk. paper) — ISBN 0-8135-3225-6 (pbk. : alk. paper)
1. Discrimination in education—United States.   2. Students—United
States—Social conditions—21st century.   3. Race relations—United States.
I. Title.   II. Series.
LC212.2 .L49 2003
306.43—dc21

                                                                2002012281

British Cataloging-in-Publication data for this book is available from the
British Library

*To all the children and adults I know
who are trying to surpass the given*

Contents

List of Figures and Tables

Acknowledgments

The intellectual work involved in a project such as this book is a collective enterprise. A number of people contributed in small and large ways. First and foremost I must thank the teachers, children, parents, and community members who let me into their classrooms, their lives, their homes, and their hearts. Were it not for their generosity I would have nothing to say. It is risky business to allow someone to watch you teach, to ask you about subjects you have not mastered. Those who might judge them should first sincerely ask themselves whether they too would have permitted such scrutiny. The people whom I write about have done a service to us all in helping us to understand how educational institutions work so that they may work better. Though I cannot name them all here without breaching promises of confidentiality, I thank them again as I have before.

Throughout my graduate school career at the University of Michigan I was lucky to have some great mentors. Müge Göçek, Tomas Almaguer, Karin Martin, Sally Lubeck, and Alford Young Jr. provided crucial help throughout my time in Ann Arbor. Donald Deskins was generous in more ways than one. Perhaps most important, by funding me for much of my last year of graduate school through his Spencer mentoring grant, he gave me precious time to write. Many thanks also to the Spencer Foundation and the Rackham Graduate School at the University of Michigan for providing resources during the research and writing of this book.

Linda Levine was my first real mentor. She served as a model of an engaged human being. In designing and then implementing the Urban Education Semester at Bank Street College she provided the opportunity for me to expand my horizons, to find new hope and new excitement. She was also the person who first taught me to think ethnographically, to see what is not immediately apparent, and to pay attention to the details.

When I was an undergraduate at Brown University, Kevin Gaines, Ashley Smith, and David Rapkin (all graduate students at the time) each, in their own way, taught me what it meant to be a serious and committed intellectual. During my brief stint at the University of California, Berkeley, I had limited but significant contact with several inspiring scholars. Both Pedro Noguera and Lily Wong-Fillmore offered their highly sought-after time, thoughts, and assistance and encouraged me to pursue my degree.

Dr. Eduardo Bonilla-Silva has been kind, generous, and rigorous as a friend and mentor. If I could offer one piece of advice to anyone thinking about going to graduate school, it would be to find a Mark Chesler. Mark was always supportive and encouraging. He is a model of an action researcher, one who acts on behalf of justice in multiple venues. Mark was also crucial in the completion of the manuscript for this book. From the beginning he gave me the time and attention I needed to explore my ideas, narrow them into a viable intellectual project, and troubleshoot the research plan. In the midst of the long and arduous writing process I often drew on his belief in me and in the work to keep my own faith.

Many Michigan colleagues supported me, laughed with me, and sweated it out with me. Though I don't have the space to do them justice, they all know that without them this book would not have been possible. These colleagues include Gianpaolo Baiocchi, Sherri-Ann Butterfield, Prudence Carter, Gilberto Conchas, Patrice Dickerson, Elena Gutierrez, Tom Guglielmo, Michelle Harris, Frances Hasso, Regine and Katani Jackson, Nicholas Jones, Moon-Kie Jung, Nadia Kim, David Kinney, Rachel Lucas, Gloria Martinez and Armando and Roberto Ramos, Sylvia Orduno, Nicole Pagan, Parna Sengupta, Lori Stark, Geoffrey Ward, Deb Willis, and Mina Yoo. A special thanks to my dissertation group: Gina Bloom, Tom Guglielmo, Jonathan Metzl, and Parna Sengupta. Because of them I never felt as though I was working alone. Iberia Todd, Debbie Harris, and Jessica Vanderlaan all helped with transcribing. Jessica was invaluable in interviewing Spanish-speaking parents.

Other great friends beyond Ann Arbor provided perspective, humor, and support along the way. These friends include Chris Bischof, Janice Bloom, Johanna Fernandez, Stephanie Keyser Keller, Carryl Lee, Bernadine Mellis, Nancy Reiter, Marciel Rivera, and Tiana Wertheim. A number of students, including John Miyata, Aaron Aahlstrom, Darin Gibson, and Carlos Velez, provided good conversations and, most important, hope for the future.

Since I moved to the University of Illinois at Chicago, a number of colleagues have read and provided feedback on various parts of this book. Much thanks to

William Ayers, Cynthia Blair, Sara Hall, Maria Krysan, Bryant Marks, Tony Orum, Beth Richie, and Laurie Schaffner.

Nothing this long or this labor intensive would have been possible for me without the support my family. My brother Josh and the Herz family regularly emailed and fed me during trips to California. The Van Deusen family, particularly my Aunt Nancy and most especially my cousin Betsy, provided support, warm meals, and friendly faces during my time in Michigan. My Aunt Idonea at key moments offered her own special brand of hospitality. To my great sadness my grandfather Jim Lewis did not live to see me finish this book, but he has been a presence nevertheless throughout.

My sister, Rebecca Lewis, is a true blessing. Over the years I worked on this project she called, visited, listened to, and inspired me. Knowing she is there has given me immense strength and fortitude and helped me to keep my perspective. She is, quite literally, the greatest.

My father, Robert, was an early hero of mine. I learned from him that a life lived well, with principle and integrity, is not always comfortable or easy. My mother, Barbara, taught me what it is to be generous of spirit. In her belief that every living thing should be treated well, she nurtured my commitment to making sure everyone has the chance to live safely and well. She also played a special role in the writing of this book as one of the few people who read, and read carefully, every word that follows. She copy-edited the entire document, providing along the way some carefully chosen and exceedingly warm words of appreciation. I had always hoped that this document would be accessible—she was always my measure of that; her reassurance down the stretch that I was managing to write a book she found to be not only readable but engaging and moving proved deeply heartening at a time when I was beginning to run out of steam.

One person was with me when I decided what kind of life I wanted to live and, to my great joy, has been with me in one way or another ever since. He has loved me more than I could ask for and made me laugh more times than I can count. He has taught me to care less about the things that don't matter and to be more strategic in pursuing the things that do matter. He has regularly reminded me not to settle for less than I deserve and encouraged me to be more ambitious in my expectations. In his own often irreverent, sometimes silly, regularly brilliant, and always driven way Tyrone Forman has been a wonderful partner and a true friend.

This book honors the children who shared their jokes, who struggled to make sense of long division, who beat me at Connect Four, who hugged me daily, who came to school everyday, and who continually exude their optimism for the future. I do this work in the hope that they all get a fair chance to become the people they already are.

Race in the Schoolyard

One

Examining the Color Line in Schools

Five years after leaving a teaching-credential program and a commitment to teach in urban public schools, I walked back into elementary schools to begin the research for this project. What drove me out of urban schools or perhaps what drove me into graduate school is captured by one moment, one day, in a third-grade classroom.

Those who have spent time in classrooms know that despite our best efforts we sometimes forge deeper and stronger connections with some children than with others. These are often not children we choose but ones who choose us— those who because of temperament, interests, or karma attach themselves to us and capture our minds and hearts. These are not teacher's pets; at least in my case they have often been children who are always on the verge of mischief, who are bright and occasionally bored. After two and a half months of student teaching in this particular third-grade classroom, I had developed that kind of connection with a tall, articulate, sometimes mischievous African American boy named Kendrick Jefferson. I watched him daily, a bright child trying to keep up with his peers, who were the children of faculty members at the world-famous university nearby. He was clearly as able as they were in all areas, but it was hard to compete with their access to computers at home and summer enrichment programs. Nevertheless, Kendrick spent his classroom "free time" with me playing a math game in which we challenged each other with word problems. He was, at the risk of understating it, a curious and inquisitive child.

A detailed description of the school and class is unnecessary here, but a few details are important for this story. The classroom teacher was a charismatic and authoritative white woman who had a reputation as a successful teacher and who also, occasionally, did things that seemed supremely unjust. The midsize student body of this elementary school was approximately half white and half black. As is not unusual in this kind of desegregated space, the white children came from primarily middle- and upper-middle-class homes, while the black children were from primarily working-class or poor homes. The particular classroom where I was working had six African American boys, each of quite different appearance, temperament, family background, achievement level, and disposition. As I have said, Kendrick was tall, athletic, extroverted, and bright. Jesus was short, quiet, bookish, amiable, and round. Antoine was boisterous, fidgety, charming, and part of a program to mainstream children with special educational designations (in this case a severe emotional impairment). Taureen, Richard, and Percy were equally different.

One day near the end of the school year, I sat in the lunchroom with the teacher and principal while they talked about disciplinary referrals they had processed thus far that year. By the time they got to Jesus I was dumbfounded, realizing that they had named every single black male in our class. When I casually asked whether that was all the referrals, they declared proudly that it was (it was a relatively small total for the year), unaware that they had named all and only the African American males. "Even studious little Jesus?" I thought.

Several days later Antoine threw a tantrum. It happened during an afternoon of activity; students were working in different parts of the room in small groups to finish an extended art project. What followed Antoine's tantrum was perhaps a series of small moments in the life of the class, but these events illustrate the complicated way race shapes understandings and interactions and also the real impact that it can and does have on students' schooling experiences. A series of children asked to go to the restroom—not unusual during post-lunch class time. Over an hour or so, every ten to fifteen minutes, several white students who asked were allowed to go to the bathroom, while the two black children who asked were told to wait. Throughout this time the teacher was carefully managing Antoine's temper, doing her best to keep the room and him under control.

After Gerald, the white son of mathematicians, returned, Kendrick asked to go to the bathroom. He had asked to go fifteen minutes earlier and had been told, like Taureen earlier, to wait. From ten feet away I watched his startled response as he was told, once again, no. His protestations and "buts" were cut off as he was sent back to his group. I witnessed his surprise and indignation, and as he walked back to his table, glancing sideways at Gerald, he swallowed so hard his Adam's apple moved visibly from the edge of his chin to the base of his neck. In an effort not to cry as tears accumulated at the edges of his eyes, he swallowed the incident whole.

Again, it was just a moment, and a relatively small one, in which the troubles of one black male—Antoine—became trouble for all of them. It was fairly clear at the time (and I asked some indirect questions about it later) that this was an unintended consequence. The teacher was busy managing the classroom moment to moment as teachers do. But watching that eight-year-old contend with too many moments of inexplicable injustice, watching his protests fall on deaf ears, and watching him literally swallow back his tears was in many ways the last straw for me. The series of events was so subtle that I do not think I would have noticed had I not been especially attuned to Kendrick. My response was one I would never recommend to any student teacher. I walked over to him and whispered in his ear to wait two minutes and then ask me whether he could go. Though it addressed his immediate needs, my action had the dual effect of undermining his teacher's authority (and in some ways mine) without necessarily confronting the heart of the injustice. I could not think what else to do at the time.

Drawn from my student-teaching experiences, the preceding story is one of bearing witness. It depicts racialized moments in a setting where race is purported to—is supposed to—not matter. The exchange between teacher and principal in the lunchroom was troubling because of the clearly racialized pattern in discipline it revealed, and it was especially troubling because of their total unawareness of the pattern they had just laid out. The classroom story helps us begin to understand how such patterns can emerge and make themselves felt—how race shapes classroom practices, how race is part of the daily experiences of students of color in school, how even the most well-meaning adults can perpetuate inequities without any awareness that they are doing so. This vignette also captures the usefulness of a particular kind of research methodology. These moments I had witnessed were not depicted, could not be described, in the statistics. Here was the process of disaffection in action. Here I had seen, in minute-by-minute school interactions, the generation of unintended consequences—evidence of the ways schools might not be serving all students equally. In this and similar interactions, I never perceived that the teachers involved were doing less than what they thought was best for the children involved. Why then was the outcome less than what they hoped for?

Researching the Role of Race in the Schoolyard

My own research has sought to find explanations for these paradoxical outcomes. Although much educational research has looked at race in relation to gaps in achievement, differences in discipline patterns, or disparities in test scores, these numbers do not capture the reality of race as a product of schooling, as part of the process of schooling. When studies ask why black children and white children achieve differently, they fail to ask what it means to be black or white in different contexts. These formulations miss the fact that for children like Gerald and Kendrick race is not a fixed characteristic that they bring to school with them and then take away unaffected and intact.

Something happens in school, especially in elementary school, that forms and changes people in racial terms. Further, racial identities, both those assigned to children and those they choose, affect their schooling experiences. How does this happen? Why, for instance, are there racial gaps in achievement? Given that racist theories of genetic inferiority have been thoroughly disproved, we must go beyond theories about innate abilities or capacities. Given a growing body of literature that shows racial minorities value education as much as their higher-achieving white peers,[1] if not more, theories that suggest that gaps are due to family values are also inadequate. What goes on inside school buildings and in schoolyards? What kind of messages do students give and receive? What kinds of practices and institutional cultures and structures lead to these differences in outcomes?

This book explores how race (in terms of meaning and identity) and racial inequality (in terms of access to resources) are reproduced in day-to-day life in schools. It is about the racialization of people and schools and also about schools and people as racializing agents—as forces in the reproduction and transformation of race. Schools are arguably one of the central institutions involved in the drawing and redrawing of racial lines. Though they do not explicitly "teach" racial identity in the way they teach multiplication or punctuation, schools are settings where people acquire some version "of the rules of racial classification" and of their own racial identity (Omi and Winant 1994: 60). Drawing on ethnographic data collected during a year in which I spent time in school classrooms, yards, and lunchrooms, I found that not only does the curriculum (expressed and hidden) teach many racial lessons, but schools and school personnel serve as a location and means for interracial interaction and as a means of both affirming and challenging previous racial attitudes and understandings.

Although clearly not the only social institution that does so, schools are involved in framing ideas about race and in struggles around racial equity. They serve as a sorting mechanism, providing different students with access to different kinds of experiences, opportunities, and knowledge, which then shape their future opportunities. This relationship is particularly true for disfranchised and poor students, who are likely to have access to important tools, information, and skills only in school. Far from functioning as the "great equalizer," schools too often perpetuate existing inequalities.[2]

One conceptual framework that is particularly useful for understanding how schools perpetuate inequality is Pierre Bourdieu's notion of "capital."[3] As Bourdieu defines it, capital is essentially a resource that serves to advance one's position or status within a given context. Several kinds of resources are at play in shaping educational opportunities and outcomes: economic resources, social connections, cultural knowledge, and symbolic status.

Capital is an important concept because it helps explain the mechanisms and processes whereby "meritocratic" organizations like schools reproduce social inequality. Understanding that issues other than individual merit and effort shape school outcomes challenges meritocratic narratives that suggest that people are successful solely because of their individual abilities and that schools reward effort and talent so that those who "deserve" to excel in fact do so.[4] Absent from this story are the vast inequities in the types and quality of schooling experiences. Children arrive at school with different socially acquired resources, and they generally leave school with similarly differentiated rewards. These inputs and outcomes are not solely (or even mostly) related to individual effort or innate ability. That is how social reproduction works. As MacLeod (1995: 14) argues, the entire process is mystified and justified through the illusion that schools are rewarding merit and skill rather than merely "converting social hierarchies into academic hierarchies." This is not to suggest that effort and talent do not contribute to school outcomes but that economic, social, cultural, and symbolic capital do as well.

As an analytic tool, capital provides a way to understand how unequal social positions are reproduced in a manner that makes the inequality appear to be the result of meritocratic and democratic practices. In many ways, education plays a key role in these processes of reproduction and in their mystification. Especially in the United States, which purports to offer everyone an equal opportunity to succeed, one cannot overestimate the importance of reproductive mechanisms that appear to be open and fair but that are in fact inequitable. This insight is particularly important when trying to understand racial differences in school outcomes, as it enables us to challenge theories that ignore structural factors and suggest that only individual or family factors matter in educational success and failure. These individualized narratives ignore both history and structure as they remove social actors from their larger context and imply that, for instance, educational outcomes in a low-income, under-resourced elementary school in the Mississippi Delta are comparable to educational outcomes in a wealthy school in Westchester County, New York.

Race as a Social and Educational Construction

Important in addressing these questions is a clear understanding of what race is and how it works. In both educational discussions and social scientific research more generally, race is too often included in analyses only as a variable, used to partially explain variance in a range of social outcomes (e.g., achievement levels, income, health, incarceration rates) with little regard for the racialization process itself (Zuberi 2001). As Almaguer and Jung (1999) have argued, we need to shift some of our theoretical focus from the powerful effects of the color line to the constitution of the color line itself—that is, to examine how and where racial lines are drawn. "Although the vast majority of sociologists and other social scientists no longer view race in biologistic terms—that is, as biologically 'real' and trans-historically constant—this consensus has not had a uniformly sweeping impact on how they carry out social scientific research, much of which still employs racial categories as if they were biologically given and fixed. The straightforward way in which normal social science continues unreflexively to study race obscures the continual ambiguities and contestations over how racial lines have been drawn historically and are being re-drawn today" (213).

The danger in this tendency to treat racial categories as fixed entities is that the categories then appear to be natural or permanent. As Bulmer and Solomos (1998: 822) state, "Race and ethnicity are not 'natural' categories, even though both concepts are often represented as if they were. Their boundaries are not fixed, nor is their membership uncontested." Racial categories are not merely sociological abstractions but are potent social categories around which people organize their identities and behavior and that influence people's opportunities and outcomes. In this way, though not natural or biological entities, racial classifications are socially "real" and thus are powerful in their consequences for people's lives: they result in objective, measurable differences in the life circumstances of different racial groups.

Race is not something we are born with (in that it is not a genetic or biological fact) but something that is mapped onto us from the first moments of life (with the listing of race on the birth certificate). Racial identities do not automatically follow from these early external racial assignments. They take shape over time, through multiple interactions with those who are the same and those who are different. We learn ways to categorize ourselves and others, what the available options are, what the boundaries between categories are, what it means to belong to one race rather than another.[5] Race then is not a real or innate characteristic of bodies but a set of signifiers projected onto these bodies—signifiers we must learn about and negotiate in order to successfully move through the social world.

Racial identifications are not merely individual achievements but are formed in relation to collective identities within racialized societies. These identities are products of social and political struggles: what it means to be black was not the same in Oakland, California, in 1975 as it was in Selma, Alabama, in 1950. Both racial categories and racial identities are socially and historically specific. For example, in the 1980s a South Asian immigrant to Great Britain would have been categorized as black, a South Asian immigrant to the United States would have been categorized as Asian American, and the same person would have been categorized as Colored in South Africa. Understanding racial relations, racial realities, and racial identities then requires that attention be paid to the specifics of various racial contexts. As historian Thomas Holt (1995: 9) argues, "Human experience, motivations, and behaviors must ultimately be understood as grounded in social processes and framed by historical moments. Thus models of human thought and behavior deduced from the premise of an isolate individual . . . are inadequate at best; at worst, simply false." Race is about who we are, what we do, how we interact. It shapes where we live, whom we interact with, how we understand ourselves and others. But it does so in specific ways based on our social and historical location.

Recognizing that racial meanings shift across time and space, however, does not mean that they come to matter less in daily experience. One challenge is how to recognize race, as Phoenix (1998: 860) talks about it, as "fluid, multiple, relational, socially constructed and intersecting with other social positionings," while also recognizing it as socially "real" and determining of life chances. Any attempt to imagine or represent people's daily struggles to make sense of their own lives and identities must be undertaken with close analytical ties to the broad social, cultural, political, and economic context. Racial understandings are built not only in relation to the people and communities one has contact with but also in relation to the social divisions, real inequities, images, representations, and discourses one encounters in a local, national, and even global context. This is not a unidirectional process. How people understand the world and their place in it necessarily affects how they operate and thus shapes the world in which they live.

To comprehend how race shapes social experience and educational outcomes requires a focus on everyday practice. Determining how racial narratives and understandings shape people's lives, how their social location shapes their life chances, and how they understand these processes requires both speaking with people in depth about their lives and spending time with them in their real-life contexts.

The Process of Discovery

To address the issues outlined above, I conducted ethnographic research in three school communities.[6] All three schools were located in Hillside, a metropolitan area in Southern California. During the 1997–1998 school year, I spent upward of seven hours a day in one or more of the schools (e.g., attending a preschool staff meeting at one school and then spending the rest of the school day at another). I was located primarily in one fourth-/fifth-grade classroom in each building but spent a great deal of time in other classes as well as in the schoolyard, the lunchroom, the main office, and staff meetings, PTA meetings, and other school events before and after school and on weekends. I conducted formal and informal interviews with school personnel, teachers, parents, and students and collected site documents from each place.

The schools where I spent time, Foresthills, West City, and Metro2, were selected with several criteria in mind.[7] I sought to find three different kinds of schools: a fairly typical and diverse urban school (West City), a fairly typical and homogenous suburban school (Foresthills), and a school that structurally and culturally was a bicultural or nonwhite space (Metro2). By using the terms *bicultural* and *nonwhite*, I am signaling more than the racial composition of the students; these terms also reflect the racial composition of staff, the explicit and implicit focus of the curriculum, and the schools' culture and expressed values and goals. Thus, for the biracial or nonwhite setting, I looked for a place where, in contrast to the other two settings, whiteness was less likely to be the dominant force and influence and where the current racial-formation and racial-meaning system might get challenged. All three were small to midsize elementary schools and were neither the best nor the worst schools in their respective districts. Members of each of the school communities were generous with their time, energy, and insight as they welcomed me into their classrooms, homes, and play groups.

My role in each school varied in response to the different school climates and cultures (for more detail see the Appendix). In each setting my presence was welcomed at least in part because my past experience as an elementary school teacher promised the possibility of assistance in an institution that was all too often short on help. I did indeed provide assistance in each place; it ranged from performing small tasks such as covering a classroom for five minutes so a teacher could talk to a parent or taking students to the office when they were feeling ill, to more involved projects such as working with small groups over several weeks or substituting for a day when a teacher went home sick. These were responsibilities that I negotiated with school personnel continually throughout the year as I balanced the roles of participant and observer.

Also key in the research process was my own subjectivity. My status as a youngish, white, middle-class woman who had grown up in Hillside and attended public schools had a different meaning in each school community.[8] As Peshkin (1982) argues, subjectivity operates during all parts of the research endeavor. Like a "garment that cannot be removed," subjectivity is at play in all researchers whatever their methodology, the "nature of their research problem," or their "reputation for personal integrity" (Peshkin 1991: 286). The only way to deal with this "garment" is to be aware of it and to try to manage it consciously during the research process. I attempted to keep an eye on my own emotional involvement partly by keeping a personal journal during the entire period of data collection. This practice allowed me to get onto paper, and thus onto the table, when and how I was getting particularly wrapped up in a situation or in an aspect of the research. At times, for instance, I found myself especially interested or uninterested in a phenomenon or a person. In such cases I took time late in the evening to think through the situation and strategize about it—to determine whether this interest (or lack of interest) was a result of good research instincts or was likely to cause me to miss something important or overplay something relatively unimportant. In this way I agree with Peshkin (1991: 287) that subjectivity is not merely a "biasing" factor but "can be seen as virtuous." Some of my instincts were born of substantial experience in schools and extensive thinking, reading, and talking about racial dynamics. As a result, I was often able to notice things that a person with less experience might have missed. The self-monitoring I did often helped me to see what I might have missed otherwise.

In almost every setting I was at once an insider and an outsider on many different dimensions (Collins 1991; Merton 1972). As Alarcon (1981) and other feminists of color have suggested, our subjectivities are always contextual and never simple (Collins 1991; Glenn 1992; Zavella 1996). For instance, in race and class, I was similar to the white middle-class majority in the suburban Foresthills setting. This similarity enabled my easy access and facilitated conversations about race with those who might not have been so forthcoming if my race had been different. However, I was geographically and politically quite distinct from many in this suburb. In many ways I was clearly an outsider from the city, raising topics that people didn't regularly consider to be part of polite conversation.

Likewise in other contexts I was simultaneously (though differently) insider and outsider. For instance, at West City I lived in and experienced a world apart from the world of low-income children of color, and there is no question that this difference had an impact on our interactions and on the data collection. Yet our mutual interest in things such as music and basketball and the outcome of the NCAA tournament allowed various kinds of connections that might not have been possible otherwise. In another example, issues of difference clearly came up in interviews with low-income African American parents, with definite effects on the nature of our conversations. Yet my close relationships with their children enabled a certain level of trust that might not have been possible if a white (or black) stranger had walked into their living rooms. This is not to say that race differences did not affect the interviews, but their impact was not simple or straightforward.

My inability to speak or understand Spanish was a clear marker of "outsiderness" in some important ways at Metro2, a Spanish-immersion school. However, my meager and stumbling efforts to learn were received with laughter from children in the yard and led to an acknowledgment of a certain kind of mutual vulnerability with Latino children. In other ways, I was quite the insider with the middle-class staff and children. My Spanish-language skills had a limited impact on the central parts of my data collection, as instruction in the room where I was located and discussions at the staff, PTA, and other school meetings I attended were all conducted in English. Moreover, students almost without exception used English as the informal language outside the classroom.[9] However, in certain ways my language limitations highlighted my outsider status. Sometimes teachers or paraprofessionals forgot and addressed me in Spanish. When I looked baffled, they normally laughed, gave me an affectionate squeeze of the arm, and restated what they were saying in English. In this sense I was never able to participate as a full member of the community (though I felt almost immediately accepted and welcomed by all). It was not always possible to tell experientially all the effects that my language deficiency had, but my role would surely have been different had I been bilingual. To address this gap as best I could, I regularly asked various members of the Metro2 community what they thought I was missing and conducted regular member checks with them to test the data and findings.[10]

What Is to Come

In this book I draw on the wealth of powerful data I collected during a year of daily participation with adults and children interacting and making meaning in public schools. Some of the stories included are disheartening if not disturbing; some are heartbreaking. They describe a world of continuing inequity.[11] Other stories are hopeful and may begin to help us imagine different kinds of outcomes. I have made every effort to be true to those who gave their time and energy and who opened their schools, classrooms, and living rooms to me. This book describes some troubling incidents, often involving people whom I firmly believe were trying to do the right thing. Throughout, despite my concern for these less-than-flattering descriptions, I have remained committed to an analysis, and thus a narrative, that is as true and accurate as I can make it. Because of my deep commitment to a more just world, I have made painstaking efforts to accurately describe the ways in which race takes shape and itself shapes and influences the daily lives of those I describe.

I offer in-depth descriptions of the racial logic, racial practices, and racial understandings operating in the three different school communities. By initially looking at each of the schools separately, with their diverse demographics and expressed commitments, we can see how race matters both similarly and differently in each setting. I have drawn on participant observations of daily life in classrooms, on long conversations with teachers, parents, staff, and children, and on examples of the material culture of each place. As a member (to varying degrees) of each school community, I grappled with both success and failure, good intentions and questionable results, heartbreaking inequities and hopeful challenges. These are not stories of good or bad people; there is no recipe for doing race correctly. The only choice is to acknowledge the elephant in the schoolroom and to struggle openly with the ways race influences much of what transpires.

I also analyze issues across all three settings. I begin by examining the ways racial meaning and racial identity are reproduced in schools, focusing on the way race is learned and lived, constructed, and negotiated in the everyday. I then turn to issues of inequality; I look at the social reproduction of racial inequality, including examples from all three schools along with more macro data, to understand the production of unequal schooling experiences and opportunities.

Finally, I offer concluding thoughts, summarizing the overall issues that need to be further debated and engaged. I suggest practical ways in which educators can use the findings from this book to improve schooling experiences for all students and steps school systems can take toward becoming the great equalizers we have imagined them to be. I also suggest that racial theorists need to take educational institutions more seriously than they now do as central places where race is made and remade in the everyday.

Overall, this book is as much about race and racial equality as it is about schooling and as much about schools as institutions of social reproduction as about the reproduction of racial categories. How are race and racial inequality reproduced in day-to-day life in schools? How does race shape schooling experiences and educational outcomes?

Race in the Schoolyard is an effort to see and to bear witness. The racialized moments I describe, acts that took place in a setting where race is purported not to matter, are moments that cannot be captured in educational statistics. Through such descriptions we can begin to understand how race works in classrooms to shape the experiences of the children who show up every day. Race not only is relevant during black history month but insinuates itself into the very fabric of classroom life. *Race in the Schoolyard* emanates from a faith in the possibilities for schools to act as forces for equity and justice and from an understanding that they often fall short.

Two

There Is No Race in the Schoolyard

Color-Blind Ideology at Foresthills

Although much research has been done with regard to race in urban educational settings and in schools populated predominantly by students of color, much less work has examined how race operates in all-white or almost-all-white settings. There is some wonderful research on multiracial or desegregated schools; these studies are nevertheless part of a tradition that acknowledges the importance of race only in settings where racial minorities are present.[1] As Carby (1992: 193) argues, too much of this work has marginalized the processes of racialization and given them meaning only "when the subjects are black. . . . We should be arguing that everyone in this social order has been constructed . . . as a racialized subject." In this sense it is important to study the construction of whiteness and white racial identities (perhaps especially in white settings). Most white students in the United States are still attending schools that are almost entirely white (Orfield 1993; Orfield and Monfort 1992). In fact, most live in highly racially segregated neighborhoods and have little regular, substantial contact with people of other races (Massey and Denton 1993). Understanding how white students develop their racial subjectivities and understandings is crucial to understanding future possibilities for racial equity in the United States. In this chapter I examine the racial meanings and messages operating in Foresthills, a (mostly) white, suburban school. I look at not only the explicit curriculum in the school but the multiple lessons about race, racial difference and sameness, and racial equity offered in both overt and implicit ways by staff, parents, and children.

——— *Table 2.1.* ————————
Racial and ethnic make-up of Sunny Valley

Non-Hispanic white	82%
Asian American	9
Native American	1
African American	1
Hispanic	8

Source: 2000 U.S. Census.
Note: Total equals more than 100 percent because of rounding.

The Setting

Foresthills Elementary is located in Sunny Valley, a predominantly white suburb like many others. Situated in the diverse metropolitan area surrounding the city of Hillside, Sunny Valley and the Foresthills neighborhood itself are notably homogeneous. Almost 80 percent of this suburb's more than thirty thousand residents are white (Table 2.1). Families in Sunny Valley are mostly middle-class and upper-middle-class; according to the U.S. Census, in 1990 the median family income there for households with children in residence was over $50,000, and only 2 percent of families lived below the poverty line. The demographic composition of the school (Table 2.2) mirrors that of the surrounding town.

——— *Table 2.2.* ————————————————
Racial and ethnic make-up of Foresthills students and school personnel

Race	Students[a]	School personnel
Caucasian	90%	88%
Hispanic (of any race)	7	4
Asian American	7	6
African American	1	2
Filipino	2	—

Source: School report card, January 1997.
[a] Total of column equals more than 100 percent because Hispanic students are counted twice—both as an ethnic group and within one of the other racial categories.

Surrounded on one side by much wealthier suburbs and on the others by more diverse and marginally lower-income communities, Sunny Valley sits along a freeway corridor that carries hundreds of thousands of workers into Hillside each day. Though companies from the city have begun to relocate to the suburbs around Sunny Valley, Sunny Valley itself remains primarily residential. The parents of Foresthills students commute daily to the city.

Neighborhoods around the school are filled with single-family detached homes on moderately sized grassy lots (the median housing cost in the town in October 1998 was over $200,000).[2] Though the community has some newer and fancier neighborhoods with palatial homes as well as large, dense apartment and townhouse complexes, a long drive through Sunny Valley reveals street after street of one- and two-story, single-family, ranch-style homes.

The Foresthills Elementary School building was constructed in the 1950s; in 1997–1998 the school accommodated close to 450 students. Each upper-grade classroom had enough single-person desks to accommodate its thirty to thirty-five children.[3] The facilities are spread out on spacious grounds. Hallways are open to the air but are covered by awnings extending from the buildings; these corridors are decorated with planters and hanging plants. The school is flanked on the back and sides by parking lots, playgrounds, and fields: several full-size basketball courts, a soccer field, a baseball field, multiple tetherball and four-square courts, several volleyball courts, and two different play structures.

During the time of my study, the physical environs at Foresthills got regular upgrades, most often through the efforts of parents. The PTA often funded or executed various beautification efforts (e.g., hanging plants in the corridors, decorating classroom doors) as well as raising money for new school structures and upgrading facilities (e.g., building the lower-grade play structure and purchasing new audio and video equipment for the school). Through its efforts, the parent group had historically raised upward of $80,000 a year for the school. Though parents often were active in deciding how that money was spent (with some disagreement from the staff), these funds did allow the school staff to spend their allotted state and district moneys much more creatively than they otherwise might have. The PTA also regularly gave teachers at the school extra money to purchase special supplies, update classroom libraries, take field trips, and organize special school assemblies. Extra PTA funds also enabled the school to supplement the regular staff with part-time school psychologists, extra librarian time, and additional classroom aides.

In addition to the classroom teachers, the regular, certified school staff consisted of the principal, a resource specialist, three special education teachers—all full-time—and a librarian, a nurse, a psychologist, and a speech therapist, who worked at the school part-time. In addition the school had a number of instructional assistants and clerical/custodial staff. Parent volunteers were also at the school daily in large numbers monitoring the yard; assisting in the computer lab, office, and lunchroom; and helping in classrooms. With the exception of one African American, one Asian American, and one Latina, the certified staff was entirely white (and almost entirely female). Staff had primarily professional relationships; only small clusters spent free time together outside of school. Relationships between adults in the school tended toward the formal. People were generally friendly but task-oriented, coming together to plan or work on a project but otherwise spending most of their time at school inside their classrooms. Teachers whose classes shared a lunch hour most often ate together in the lunchroom and engaged in friendly banter about current events (both local and national). School events, troublesome parents, and particular students were also periodically the subject of lunchroom conversation but more in the context of information sharing than of problem solving. This was break time.

Beginning just before nine o'clock every morning, a steady stream of adults and children on foot, on bicycles, and in cars flowed along surrounding streets toward the school. Parents in minivans, luxury sedans, and midsize Japanese cars circulated through the parking lot, pausing to release their children by the front entrance. Groups of students and parents approached from sidewalks on foot and bicycle. Some parents moved on quickly, while others paused to chat with other parents or children. Although I am using the general term *parent* here, in over 90 percent of the cases the parent who was involved in and around the school was the mother. Most students in fact lived with both biological (or adoptive) parents or one biological parent and a stepparent. I knew of only one or two students who lived with other relatives (grandparents or an aunt and uncle). In almost all cases, nevertheless, female guardians were the ones primarily involved in school life.

Students were not officially allowed on school grounds until nine o'clock. When they arrived early, they stood around in clusters waiting for the gate in front of the main corridor to open so they could get into the yard for ten minutes of preschool play time. Children waited in largely grade- and gender-segregated groupings, often shivering slightly in the morning cool. Except for a few rainy periods in the winter, the school received an inordinate amount of sunshine and warm temperatures; students often arrived at school in shorts and t-shirts, unprepared for the early-morning chill.

The school was run on a complicated and strictly enforced schedule of bells, which marked the beginning and ending of recess, lunch, and the school day itself. When out in the yard, students lined up in classroom-designated spaces after the bell rang and waited for their teacher to come and walk them down the appropriate corridor to their classroom. The lines were never perfectly straight or even mostly silent for the short outdoor walk to class.

As in the other two schools, the principal selected the classroom where I would be located. In directing me to Mrs. Moch, the principal explained that Mrs. Moch had a fourth-fifth combination class and that she, the principal, thought Mrs. Moch dealt with "these issues" (diversity and multiculturalism) well and would be interested in the project.

Mrs. Moch's class was somewhat more diverse than others: the thirty-four students included one biracial African American child, two Korean students, one Filipino student, two Latino students, and five other biracial/bicultural (white-Asian or white-Latino) students, though at least several of these biracial white-Asian, white-Latino students identified themselves as white. Although all students interacted in the classroom, in the schoolyard the few nonwhite or biracial students hung out together. So, for instance, among the fourth-grade boys, the nonwhite or biracial students (even those biracial students who identified as white) almost always played together in the yard.

Mrs. Moch herself had a great deal of experience teaching in a variety of settings. She was known as a center of power in the school and was one of two teachers in charge when the principal was absent. Not afraid to yell when necessary, Mrs. Moch generally ruled through a complicated set of behavior-management strategies including verbal admonitions, yellow warning cards for minor transgressions, and notes home when the yellow cards turned to red. Although friendly to most people, Mrs. Moch tended toward gruff rather than warm and did not tolerate much nonsense. Generous with her students, she preferred to have less rather than more contact with their parents and complained with some regularity about parents who, as she put it, "want to go through fourth grade all over again." Like most teachers at Foresthills, she took parents' constant presence for granted, glad to have their assistance but also somewhat exasperated with their questions and requests.

Every school day was organized by a detailed schedule that Mrs. Moch wrote out by hand and posted each morning at the front of the room just before school began. For example, a typical day in April had the following schedule: 9:15—attendance, pledge; 9:20—spelling pretests; 10:05—social studies; 11:00—recess; 11:25—snack; 11:30—writing; 12:30—math; 1:05—story; 1:20—lunch; 2:05—silent reading; 2:30—play practice; 3:45—clean the room, chairs up; 3:50—dismissal. Mrs. Moch never seemed more than mildly interested in my research project, inviting me in as much because it was useful to have someone to cover the room occasionally as because she was interested in the work.

Multiculturalism

When asked about examples of multicultural curricula at Foresthills, the principal listed the state-mandated textbooks, which had themselves been the subject of some controversy for being multicultural in often superficial ways,[4] and activities like black history month and the practice of counting to ten in different languages during physical education class. As at many other schools in the United States, the little multiculturalism that existed at Foresthills took traditional forms. When asked how she dealt with issues of race and multiculturalism in her classroom, one teacher immediately started talking about demographics rather than curriculum. "Haven't had a whole lot of it, uh uh um . . . other than Asian/Caucasian, uh . . . Have—sometimes have one black child, in a year like we did this year. [coughs] Um, my own attitude is, people are people, and . . . we treat people with respect, and that's what you get back." When pressed about multicultural classroom activities, she explained that the district mandated they do some. Her class had performed a skit. Mrs. Moch's class constructed posters about famous African Americans. Even for these somewhat limited activities, however, the school did not have the proper materials available. As Mrs. Moch reported, "[The one black staff member] was wonderful because she knew my kids were researching and were having a hard time finding books at the school. She went to this black bookstore. She went there, she came in one day and she had bought . . . must have been over a hundred dollars' worth of books—brought them into my classroom, for my kids to use." For their participation in the activity, students drew on their available knowledge of African Americans and reported on those they were familiar with—athletes and, in one case, Oprah. Even so, the posters they produced (along with the teacher's store-bought posters about famous African Americans) all came down March 1st, as soon as black history month was over.

During my time at the school, I saw Mrs. Moch make some attempt to offer a multicultural history of the state. She explained her efforts this way:

> Well, let's see, we start off with things like California Native Americans, and I do not have a high opinion of Junípero Serra. . . . You know. I talk about genocide, I talk about whether it was deliberate genocide, or it was because the Spanish knew that they had a higher moral . . . sense. And therefore were going to use force, but that it still was wrong. But it was right in their eyes historically, and therefore, you know you have to look at it, um, that way. I do look for and purchase as many books as I can that have representations of color, in California. Particularly in California, but in general. And have them available for kids, so that they see it was, was not a state or country that was ever

really white. It never was. It never will be. And it shouldn't be. And so, I try to tie those things in.

Though she did more than other teachers in the school, even these lessons were somewhat ambivalent (e.g., she asked students to empathize with Spanish motivations as well as with Native American subjugation), and they were not used by students to inform their understanding of the present. For example, when I interviewed children from her class and asked why some people were rich and others poor, most talked about hard work and laziness.[5]

As with Wills's (1996) findings in his study of high school social studies classes, if the goal of the curriculum was to sensitize students to others' experiences, then the curriculum was at least partially successful. But if the goal was to have students use history to inform their understanding of events today, then the curriculum fell far short. Students saw the injustices they learned about as specific to an earlier point in time, as problems that were solved rather than being linked to contemporary forms of racial exclusion (Wills 1996). For example, the students did not appear to use anything they had learned about the settling of California, the genocide of Native Americans, or the subjugation of the Chinese to understand or interpret present-day racial realities (e.g., wage inequality, wealth inequality, Native Americans' socioeconomic status).

Ironically, the little multiculturalism that was introduced at the school was not always received well by parents. Several parents I spoke to were, in the end, quite cynical if not outright hostile about explicit efforts to inject multiculturalism into their children's classes. When asked about multiculturalism in the school, most immediately referred to black history week (or day, or month as they described it). Though they would initially say they thought it was okay, once probed, most expressed a number of reservations or objections: "we should all be Americans" or "talking about race is divisive." One mother exclaimed, "I'm so tired of Martin Luther King!" For the most part they did not object to the history curriculum because they viewed it (just as their children did) as just that, history, not lessons about the present. In regard to current race relations, most white parents believed (or hoped) that their kids were just taught that everyone is the same, that they should be color-blind.

Color Consciousness

When I raised the subject of race at Foresthills, its salience was downplayed, trivialized, or challenged. From the beginning, people made it clear that they were not certain why I wanted to conduct my research there, and they also wanted to make sure I did not misread anything I saw. When I first contacted the school, the principal clarified the situation for me: "You understand that this is a pretty homogeneous school. We don't have much diversity here." She was not the only suburban principal I spoke to who felt that the absence of students of color (or the presence of only white children) in their school would make it a less-than-interesting place to conduct research on race.

On my first day in the classroom, Mrs. Moch pulled me aside before the children arrived and said, "You should know one thing: we have one mixed-race child whose father is black and mother is white. She's dealing with a lot of fourth-grade girl stuff, but she tends to play the race card a lot." Even as Mrs. Moch explained to me that Sylvie was misreading the significance of race in her daily experience at the school, she explained that she had asked the one black staff member in the school to explain this issue to Sylvie.

These were early signs of a pattern that was clear throughout my time at Foresthills: members of the school community had complicated and conflicting understandings of the relevance of race. When they did talk about race, it was primarily in relation to "others"—people of color, primarily blacks. For example, during an interview, I asked a mother what the school did to teach about issues of diversity and multiculturalism. She responded, "Well, I think that a certain part of that they don't have to deal with because the school's not extremely multicultural. You know. It's not . . . uh there's not a . . . a lot, a lot, a lot of black people that go there. So I think maybe they don't have to address it too much."

Was it true, as many adults claimed, that race did not matter at Foresthills? Were community members truly color-blind, treating everyone the same? Was, for example, Mrs. Moch right about Sylvie (the one black student in her class) playing the race card? Was Sylvie misreading (or misrepresenting) her school experiences? In her conversation with me, Sylvie's mother talked about Sylvie's early time at the school:

Mrs. Cooper: I mean it started from the very beginning, you know . . . an incident happened where somebody used the "N" word with her. And she waits until she's going to bed to tell me these things, so of course I run to the phone and leave this scathing message to the principal, who avoids me . . . and then when I talk to her she says she'll talk to Sylvie. Well, I keep asking Sylvie, "no, I haven't talked to her, haven't talked to her," so I'm just getting angrier and angrier. And then it turns out that she's trying to get Sylvie to confront this boy, and deal with this. And I'm thinking to myself, why does Sylvie have to deal with this? This is the teacher's responsibility . . . or the principal's. Sylvie shouldn't have to deal with this. This is, you know, she has to be protected. And then I find out that . . . she keeps . . . she won't discuss it. Her grades are getting worse, and everything and . . . and then finally we have a sit-down, with the teacher and the principal and find out that the teacher dealt with it. Sylvie had been avoiding the meetings with the principal, with understandable valid reasons, you know. But nobody was communicating with *me*. So, I—I'm not very happy with the way things are handled like that. It just—I shouldn't have to bug the principal, force a meeting, to get . . . to get some answers. And, just this week she had two other incidences.

Amanda: Oh really? What kind of thing?

Mrs. Cooper: Uh, middle-school boys out on the playground during the after-school care, calling her "Blackie"—which they said they couldn't do anything about 'cause it wasn't one of the schoolkids. And then a little kindergartner [used a racial epithet] . . . and, you know, I tried to explain to her, the kindergartner's like trying out a cuss word, you know, but it's—and I told her, I said that the sad thing is that he heard it somewhere . . . but it's just the idea that she knows that this is gonna come up over and over and over again.

Sylvie's mom then described how Sylvie, after making one good friend, began to rebound. Clearly Sylvie was dealing with a stressful situation. I got independent confirmation of Sylvie's reading of the world in interviews with students. In response to generic questions about why some kids do not like to play with other kids, over half of them acknowledged that kids did not want to play with Sylvie at first because she was "different."

In fact, blackness was not the only color that carried negative connotations, and Sylvie was not the only student to confront racial hostility in school. One day I was standing in the schoolyard checking on the kids, and, as was not unusual, the three biracial fourth-grade boys (Angus, Cedric, and Michael—each of whom had either a Latino or an Asian parent) were playing together. After a few minutes, Angus ran over to me and asked, "Is it illegal to call someone something because of their race. I mean can you sue them?" I asked him what he meant, and he told me that Ricky, a white fifth-grader, had just called Cedric a "black boy." When I asked Cedric what had happened, he told me that Ricky called him and Michael "you brown boy." I looked around the yard but could not find Ricky. Mrs. Moch told me where to look for him, and then we got them all together. After giving each side a chance to tell its version, she told Ricky not to use "derogatory names" and headed back to the classroom. Interestingly there was some confusion about whom exactly Ricky was directing his comments to. Angus assumed it was not him, Michael assumed it was only Cedric, and Cedric assumed it was both him and Michael. Michael and Cedric both have brown complexions whereas Angus is light-skinned. Cedric and Michael were especially hurt, while Angus was just angry and wanted to talk more about the legalities of such a comment. Later, trying to understand what he thought he was doing, I talked to Ricky and asked him why he had said it.

Ricky: Just because . . .
Amanda: Is it okay to say that to people?
Ricky: [Looking down at the ground and speaking slowly] Nooo.
Amanda: Why?
Ricky: Because of racism.

Unfortunately our conversation was cut off by the bell, but the exchange made it clear that Ricky was quite purposefully using a designation of color, of racial otherness, as a put-down. In truth, Cedric, a fairly dark-skinned Filipino, is a "brown boy." But it is telling that in this setting the mere allusion to color substituted for a racial epithet. These kids and their teacher seemed to understand that, in this case, in this context, to "see" or to acknowledge race (particularly to identify one as black or brown) was negative or, as Mrs. Moch put it, "derogatory."

In her interview with me another mother related how upset her Latina daughter had recently been after school.

Mrs. Carter: The other day, it was this year, she was—I guess having lunch at the cafeteria. And somebody says, "Oh, Catherine . . . since you're Mexican you can have free lunches." You know. And then, and then this other kid said to her, "Where's your sombrero?" But, um, I said to her, "If you don't feel comfortable, then talk to a teacher because she shouldn't be doing that." And she did.
Amanda: And how did the teacher respond?
Mrs. Carter: Well, [the other student] . . . she got benched [lost her recess], and that was it.

Mrs. Carter was also especially upset by the incident because they are Colombian, not Mexican.

As these examples of racial logic in operation at Foresthills show, school personnel's limited interventions in or downplaying of such incidents did little to address the anxiety and upset of those who were the victims of the hurtful behavior. Nor did it go far to address the ignorance or hurtful behavior of the white students. Moreover, it demonstrated that rather than being benign, the trivialization of racial incidents had a pernicious effect. In fact, there was some evidence that teachers were at least moderately aware of these kinds of incidents, but they understood them to be relatively unimportant and, to some extent, deracialized them: Mrs. Moch said to me, "I don't see a lot of racism in the class, I mean occasionally a remark's made . . . but frequently what I find with the remarks is that they aren't as clearly defined as racist as they are . . . kid put-downs. And that they kind of—sometimes just can get lumped into everybody else's put-down kinds of things. So I haven't seen much here."

Here racist put-downs were glossed over as not really being racial—as being just the regular things kids say to one another. As Essed (1997) has discussed, this strategy of deracializing incidents where racist slurs are used implies that they are like regular, everyday conflicts in which both parties should be held equally responsible; such ways of addressing racist events make it seem as if the victims rather than the perpetrators are the ones with the problem, as if they are making a big deal out of nothing. Implying that racist slurs are like other put-downs and just happen to be racial functions as tolerance for the slurs. As Essed (1997: 140) argues, these kinds of microevents crystallize "the structural and experiential differences between the two parties; one party enjoys the safety of dominant group protection, whereas the other experiences the unsafe conditions of his 'race,' a group subjected to violence and discrimination." Such events, though sometimes seemingly minor, can reinforce the victims' sense of outsiderness.

Color-Blind Talk

In addition to their tendency to deracialize racial incidents, Foresthills community members denied the cogency of race in a variety of other ways.[6] For example, when asked what role she thought race had played in her life, Mrs. Moch stated, "Not a whole lot." When pushed further she offered a nonracial, individualized characterization of herself:

Amanda: When you think—are there ever times now that you think of it or it comes up or you think about your own racial identity?

Mrs. Moch: Not to any great extent, I just think of myself as . . . me. I'm just that kooky lady at the school.

However, as discussed earlier, she did seem to recognize the importance of race in others, as in her decision to have the one black teacher in the school explain to the one black student in her class that the student was blowing incidents out of proportion.

Although we might generally assume it is good that adults in the community asserted that race did not matter, these adults' color-blind ideals were expressed along with color-conscious, group-level racial understandings. For example, a white mother, Mrs. Morning, stated, "I really don't think these kids see black or white . . . which is good." Moments later when asked how she would explain racism to her kids, she offered a quasicultural explanation of racial-group difference and why she would not want to live in a black neighborhood.

Amanda: If, if um, one of the kids asked what racism was, how would you define it for them?

Mrs. Morning: Um . . . I guess I would define it that, there's different cultures, and, with different races—um, like Chinese—they have their own culture and their own churches that they go to, and their own food that they eat, and the same way with black people. I mean they . . . like certain things, and when they go to their place of God or whatever, um, it seems to be more . . . when I drive around or whatever, you know you see all these blacks coming out of a church, well that's where they go—I don't know what goes on in there and stuff, but it seems that certain . . . people seem to gravitate, and, and live in certain areas. I don't know why, but that's the way it, it seems. I mean personally, I don't think that we'd go looking in a neighborhood that was black.

Another Foresthills parent, Mrs. Carter, a high school teacher in a multiracial school in another district, told me, "Well I try to tell 'em that people are who they are, and you have to not make a judgment on what they look like or anything like that." She explained that she wouldn't even be able to tell me how many African American, Latino, or Asian students she had in her classes because she just didn't "notice" such things. Later in the conversation, however, she talked about her displeasure with some groups' behavior and performance in class and explained how she understood the differential success of the kids in her school: "Do I think of those groups differently? . . . yeah. I do. I think that the backgrounds, that a lot of the—the attitudes that those people have towards . . . how to be successful, are different. And I think that, um, the Asian attitude, from parents who aren't far from being, you know, born in, in some place in Asia. That their attitudes towards success are that you work hard, and you keep working hard, and you keep working hard, that's how you're successful. I don't find that attitude among Latinos or blacks."

She was not the only one who had quite different assessments of different racial minorities. Mrs. Karpinsky was one of the few parents I spoke to who admitted to being "a little prejudiced." She was emphatic, however, that she did not pass these ideas on to her kids. She regularly affirmed for them that everyone was equal. Later she provided an indication of exactly how equal.

Amanda: Um hm. Do you think it would be a problem for you or your husband if your daughter or your son married someone from a different race?

Mrs. Karpinsky: It depends what race . . . I do, to me, Asians aren't—to me it is, I hate to say this, it sounds so prejudiced, but to me it's more like blacks are, African Americans would be the only . . . to me Asians are just like—white. And I guess I just am realizing I am saying that [laughs]. . . . But I wouldn't feel um, uncomfortable at all if my daughter, you know, married a, an Asian person or I wouldn't have felt strange dating an Asian person in college, but I would have felt a little bit—I would have felt uncomfortable dating a black man.

Within each of these parents' comments was a clear understanding of race and social phenomena—that is, individuals live segregated lives because they choose to, because of racial/cultural differences; different groups succeed or fail because of cultural differences; certain groups would be okay for interracial contact but not others. As some authors have discussed, these sorts of cultural explanations of achievement and segregation ignore the role of institutional racism in producing these racial realities (Bonilla-Silva 1997; Bobo, Kluegel, and Smith 1997).

In a slightly different example, when asked how she talked to her kids about race, Mrs. Harry, another parent, explained that she would tell her kids, "Well, it's just like, I say, 'Well, you know, everybody's . . . try to be like everybody's the same.'" She soon after related events she had witnessed in which race clearly mattered

Mrs. Harry: Well, I feel . . . it's terrible when a black . . . I mean uh, in [the nearby suburb where I grew up] I remember a black family moved in, and they were forced out. They went to the church, and they were just like . . . my mother said, "Well they're just gonna have to move—it's horrible."

Amanda: Oh. That's when you were a kid?

Mrs. Harry: It wasn't that long ago.

Yet, events like these were understood as being the result largely of the unfortunate racism of a few, other, "bad whites."

In fact, many of these parents contended that racism was not the issue; it was the attitude of racial minorities and blacks in particular that kept them down. One mother stated that the problem was racial minorities' "chip-on-the-shoulder" attitude: "There is a certain amount of that racism that I feel like is brought on by the groups themselves and not by the outside group. Because, there's a certain amount of, um . . . kind of chip-on-their-shoulder attitude, that they kinda carry around with them, whomever they meet. And it, it is apparent to whomever they meet, and it turns you off. And that doesn't help the black

image.... [laughs] It doesn't help ... it doesn't help their case, if they're try ...
if, if you know, we're all trying to work together... it doesn't help a race's case,
for them to always be sayin', 'Well you're givin' me an F because I'm black, and
you are ... keeping me out of being homecoming king 'cause I'm black,' you
know. Always using that as an excuse constantly."

In another interview, when I asked whether she ever talked to her kids
about race-related current events, Mrs. Karpinsky stated, "I mean maybe Rodney King, because he was kind of playing the black card, you know, 'It's because
I'm black.'" Even in extreme cases such as this (the severe beating of a black
man at the hands of white police officers), this parent doubted minority claims
of harm.

In another example, a parent expressed frustration at what she perceived to
be the "whininess" of blacks on television:

Amanda: Anything recently that caused you to think about [your own racial iden-
tity] or any interactions you had, or ...

Mrs. Miller: [pause] N-no—not recently, no. I do get annoyed when I see all of these
black family TV shows on TV. I have to say that. There's one of these
stations that has a lot of those. And I do get annoyed, I don't like to
watch them. That's why I know I might be a little more unaccepting.
Because it bugs me. It just—it just bothers me the, the portrayal I
guess, of it.

Amanda: Which part of it?

Mrs. Miller: Maybe that, maybe the hints they might make against the white people.
Or ... I don't like the corny attitude. I just—that kind of stuff. I'm very
strongly into "we're in America, now be an American."

In this case, the identification of race as a problem in African Americans lives,
even as expressed in sitcoms, was understood as un-American, divisive, and possibly itself racist against whites (see Hochshield 1995 for a related argument).

We can see both from the experiences of the few students of color and from
the racial logic of the adults in the community (school personnel and parents)
that race mattered at Foresthills. Yet, in almost every way, whites there denied
that it mattered locally or nationally—with a few exceptions. The three parents
interviewed with biracial children (one Latino mother, one Asian American
mother, and one white mother of a biracial black/white child) had different out-
looks. All affirmed that race mattered both in their lives and in the lives of their
children. Although they varied in the extent to which they thought race shaped
their children's day-to-day school experiences, they all talked about it as a community issue. They worried about the lack of diversity and were careful about
whom they let their kids play with or whom they themselves socialized with—

avoiding those who were "close-minded" or "backward." All had grown up in and moved from much more diverse surroundings and expressed some ambivalence about Sunny Valley. In many ways the experiences of these families—for example, having to be strategic about which of their supposedly color-blind neighbors they spent time with—highlight the contradictions in how race is thought about and lived in the community.

The Social Geography of Race and the Creation of White Suburbs

The denial of the salience of race at Foresthills obscures the large role race has played in establishing the school as an almost entirely white community and in keeping it that way. Suburbs like Sunny Valley are part of a long history of racial policy and practice in the United States (Logan and Molotch 1987; Massey and Denton 1993; Oliver and Shapiro 1995). A number of authors have written about post–World War II suburbanization, outlining how a series of private and governmental practices together led to the formation and maintenance of all-white suburban neighborhoods (Abrams 1955; Jackson 1985; Lipsitz 1998; Logan and Molotch 1987; Massey and Denton 1993; Oliver and Shapiro 1995; Quadagno 1994). Not only were blacks prevented from moving into these neighborhoods, but many middle-class blacks were blocked from moving out of the urban black belts (Massey and Denton 1993; Oliver and Shapiro 1995). Government transportation, housing, and taxation policies encouraged both white homeowners and white businesses to move to the suburbs. Massey and Denton (1993: 44) note, "The suburbanization of America proceeded at a rapid pace and the white middle class deserted inner cities in massive numbers." Taxation policies rewarded relocation to the suburbs. Specifically, tax and housing policies encouraged the building and purchasing of single-family, detached dwellings (Logan and Molotch 1987). Transportation policies resulted in heavy investment in highway programs and left mass-transit systems to flounder. The Federal Housing Authority (FHA), responsible for much of the financing of suburban growth, engaged in numerous racialized practices. Lipsitz (1998: 6) points out, "By channeling loans away from older inner-city neighborhoods and toward white home buyers moving into segregated suburbs, the FHA and private lenders after W.W. II aided and abetted segregation in U.S. residential neighborhoods." Reports published in the 1990s confirm that many of these discriminatory banking, mortgage, and realty practices are still in effect (Bonilla-Silva and Lewis 1999; Oliver and Shapiro 1995; Yinger 1995).

Moreover, although black suburbanization has increased, black suburbanites are still relatively disadvantaged. As David Harris (1999) and others have noted,

_____ *Table 2.3.* _____

Whites' exposure to racial minorities in selected social settings

	All/mostly own race	Half and half	All/mostly other race	Base *N*
Adults (1975)				
Neighborhood	95.5%	3.1%	1.1%	1,632
Workplace	89.0	10.3	0.2	870
Shopping center	79.9	18.3	1.0	1,627
When they were in high school[a]	66.2	12.1	3.8	1,631
When they were in grade school[b]	71.1	9.0	3.5	1,633
Clubs/organizations	94.9	4.6	0.3	901
Adolescents (1997)				
Friends	87.1	9.7	3.2	1,685
Neighborhood	90.0	6.4	3.6	1,688
When they were in grade school	81.5	13.4	5.2	1,693
High school	73.6	17.9	8.6	1,691
Workplace	82.1	13.0	4.8	1,495

Sources: Adult data from the Survey Research Center Study: Jackman 1994. Adolescent data from the Monitoring the Future Project, Institute for Social Research, University of Michigan, Ann Arbor.
Note: Totals may not equal 100 percent because of rounding.
[a]17.8 percent of respondents replied "don't know."
[b]16.3 percent of respondents replied "don't know."

black suburbanites remain concentrated in suburbs with low socioeconomic status (SES) and are vastly underrepresented in middle- and high-SES suburbs.

Whereas several authors have documented the isolation that many African Americans confront as a result of discriminatory policies and practices (Massey and Denton 1993; Wilson 1987, 1996), few have given much attention to the flip side of the problem—the persistent racial isolation of suburban whites. Lipsitz (1998: 7) reports that, in 1993, 86 percent of suburban whites lived in places with black populations below 1 percent. Moreover, as Orfield and others have documented, most white students in the United States continue to attend schools that are almost all white (Orfield and Eaton 1996; Orfield 1993; Orfield and Monfort 1992). In national surveys conducted in 1975 and 1997, we see surprisingly consistent self-reports from whites about their exposure to racial minorities in various social settings (see Table 2.3). In both years, at least 90 percent of whites self-report living in almost-all-white or all-white neighborhoods. And Orfield and others (Orfield and Gordon 2001; Orfield and Yun 1999) have documented that school segregation is increasing: "Statistics from the 1998–99 school year show that racial and ethnic segregation continued to intensify throughout the 1990s" (Orfield and Gordon 2001: 1). Unlike African Americans, who prefer integrated neighborhoods, who have historically been isolated as a result of others' attitudes and behaviors, and who are penalized in multiple ways because of segregation, most whites choose their racial isolation (Krysan and Farley 2002). Moreover, as a number of sociologists have documented, this vast residential segregation has large implications socially, economically, politically, and beyond (Drake and Cayton 1962; Kinder and Mendelberg 1995; Oliver and Shapiro 1995).[7]

White suburbs then are a creation of the racial order in the United States. They are not the result of an accidental process but of a deliberate operation fueled by private and public policies that sought to create "safe" (white) communities separate from the urban "terror zone." The current invisibility of this history—the pervasive sense that neighborhoods just happen to be all white—is closely connected to general amnesia about even relatively recent racial history, along with pervasive denials of persistent racial discrimination. This residential segregation has proven social and economic costs.

Race was clearly at play in parents' decisions to move to Sunny Valley. A view has emerged over time of suburbs as distinct (both separate and independent) from the central city, which has its own interests. In Sunny Valley people talked about living in the city as exotic and dangerous. Several mothers spoke of not even wanting to drive in the city. At one point during the school year, a woman in an even wealthier community nearby was killed in her home. This event led to weeks of discussions in the teachers' lunchroom about whether they were "safe" enough, "far" enough, whether they would have to move to gated communities with walls. The narrative at the time explained the killing as a result of the mass-transit stop less than a mile from the victim's home. The community was thus understood to be too accessible to outsiders from that most dangerous of places, the city.

Many related their move to the suburbs to having children who were nearing school age. As Harris (1997) found, having children ages two to six (soon to enter or entering elementary school) was an important predictor of white flight. In this way Sunny Valley was more the norm than the exception. As one teacher stated in describing her neighborhood and justifying her and her husband's decision to move from an urban area to Bloominghills, a wealthy suburb near Foresthills, "My subdivision [is not very diverse], it has two blacks. And one of them's even gay. You get two points there. Uh . . . that's what he tells us. 'You get two points for having me in your neighborhood.' It's very much a lily-white suburb. When we moved out here, it was a concern of ours. And we looked at our kids—we had two at the time—and we looked at the schools, and we looked at the schools in [Urban Area 1], we looked at the schools in [Urban Area 2]. And we said 'no way.' And uh, if we had to . . . penny-pinch so we could afford a house in Bloominghills, so that . . . we moved strictly for the schools. Knowing that there wouldn't be the diversity—that we'd have to provide it. But we wanted good schools. They were the best schools around."

Generally white parents in Sunny Valley offered a standard narrative of having moved to the suburbs "when we had kids" or "for the schools." As they explained it, the urban or semiurban communities they had lived in before were fine for them but other considerations surfaced when it came to their children. For example, Mrs. Fulton had lived in Sunny Valley for five years. Before moving to the suburbs, she had lived in a small city, Townside, on the edge of an urban center within the metropolitan area.

Amanda: Why did you move back out here?

Mrs. Fulton: When I started to have kids I came back out. For the schools and stuff. For the schools.

Amanda: They're better out here?

Mrs. Fulton: Yeah. Better . . . I hate to say it, but better neighborhoods. Not so rough, you know, I mean there's probably drugs, but not as much.[8]

Mrs. Fulton had herself grown up in Townside and reported it being fine then, if just a bit "rougher" than she would like. She and her husband had thought about staying there but never considered sending their children to the Townside public schools.

Mrs. Fulton: When we lived in Townside. We thought about, it was either live in Townside and send them to private school, but then I'm thinkin' well I probably wouldn't let 'em hang out with the kids in Townside. So, do we move out and send 'em to *public* school and then at least he has a community. So what's more important, the private school or the community? So we thought, *I* would feel more comfortable with having more of a community. Because it would be kind of sad to send him to private school, then he'd come home and be alone.

Amanda: Was Townside pretty diverse?

Mrs. Fulton: Oh yeah. It was mostly I think, I would say, it was mostly black. And then there was the white, and then a few Asian. You know. I mean that's kind of the way that I remember it.

When I asked about the racial composition of Mrs. Fulton's former neighborhood in Townside (as opposed to the city as a whole), she reported the following: "Um, on our block, there really, I hate to say it, but there really wasn't any black folks around, on our block. We maybe had one that moved in one time, but we just didn't hang out with them. There . . . we had our own friends or I mean, we had cousins around the corner, we'd say . . . you know you just had all the friends that you kind of did stuff with. Um, but our block was basically, um, white." Thus, though the Fultons had moved to the suburbs so their son could have neighborhood friends, their neighborhood in Townside was not all that different from their current all-white neighborhood in Sunny Valley. The public schools in Townside, however, would have looked somewhat different: Townside is more diverse than Sunny Valley. However, her description of the town as "mostly black" was not quite accurate. In 1990, just before she moved away, Townside was only 23 percent black. As Gallagher (2000) and others have argued, whites often overestimate minority populations nationally, and some evidence indicates that they do so in their neighborhoods also. Mrs. Fulton used frequent euphemisms in her explanations (e.g., "rougher"), but race was clearly at issue in her decisions about where to live and send her child to school.

A few parents had never lived in a city and would never have considered it. Mrs. Harry and her husband had moved from one suburb to another. She explained that they would rather have stayed in Bloominghills, the fancier town nearby where she had grown up, but they could not afford it (the median housing price there in 1998 was over $500,000—more than twice that in Sunny Valley).

Amanda: What did you like about Sunny Valley?

Mrs. Harry: I heard the school system was good. And, uh . . . [chuckles] I don't know, it's not too far from Hillside . . . my husband works there.

Amanda: Oh, he does. Did you guys ever think about living in the city?

Mrs. Harry: [chuckle] No! [laughs]

Amanda: No? [laughs]

Mrs. Harry: No . . . that wouldn't be good. [laughs] No I'm from Bloominghills. So the city . . . noooo. [laughs] No . . . [laughs] I don't like to go there even. I don't drive in Hillside. I'll never drive in Hillside. [laughs]

All Sunny Valley neighborhoods were all white or almost all white. Most parents described having one black neighbor if any. Mrs. Cooper, Sylvie's mother, lived in one of the few large moderate-income apartment complexes in Sunny Valley, and even there she had only one black, one Asian, and one Latino neighbor. This minimal neighborhood diversity was often the only contact people had with other groups. As Mrs. Grant explained when I asked her about her daily contact with racial minorities, these relations were not hostile, but neither were they very friendly. "Our neighbors that live up on the hill are black. And they um, I mean, we have some contact with them. But that's not any, at least there's no, you know, friction or no . . . they come to parties, so they associate. Um, we have, my husband works with a bunch of people who are Asian who we, you know, see and do stuff with. Which I don't really think too much about until they cook. [laughs] And that's not what I would cook . . . I don't really think too much about it, but um . . . you know my, our community right here, everybody that lives right here is white, you know, except the people that uh, that live just up the street. And we go to a church that is about 90 percent white, so, we don't really have much contact [with people who aren't white]." As Mrs. Grant described an existence of distant but not hostile contact with the one black family in the neighborhood, she also described the only other substantial contact she had with people of color—also not hostile, also distant. Her family's social network was, for all intents and purposes, white. Though most seemed happy with the status quo, a few parents objected to Sunny Valley's lack of diversity. Sylvie's mother, Mrs. Cooper, had moved out of the city with her biracial daughters two years before only because of problems with her ex-husband, and she had worried about the choice ever since. . Though she wanted to move back, she could not afford it.

> *Amanda:* Do you miss living in the city, or . . . ?
>
> *Mrs. Cooper:* Yes. [laughs] Very much. Living in the suburbs is *so* different.
>
> *Amanda:* Are you—did you consider moving back to the city?
>
> *Mrs. Cooper:* [laughs] It's been talked about, yeah. But uh, since I just bought this place, and it's so expensive there now . . .
>
> *Amanda:* What do you like about it here?
>
> *Mrs. Cooper:* Convenience of everything, you know—shopping and, everything is right there. And the—being five minutes away from their school, is really good.
>
> *Amanda:* What don't you like about living out here?
>
> *Mrs. Cooper:* Uh, the lack of diversity. And the, the uh . . . um, narrow mindedness. [both laugh] Yeah, that's a big—big frustration.

In general, parents and children at Foresthills reported little contact with people of color in their daily lives. Children could list by name the two or three black people they had known in their lives. Their parents were not much different. Some talked about having some limited contact with blacks or Asians at work or of having one black neighbor. Otherwise, none had any regular contact with other racial groups, especially not with blacks. People's daily lives were typified by direct contact almost entirely with people "like them" with only intermittent or occasional vicarious (mostly through the media) contact with others, whom they were glad to have remain at a distance.

Ideology and Color Blindness

While I was at Foresthills, many of the most explicit expressions of racial understanding at the school presented a benign if not idealized picture in which members of the community understood all to be equal members of the human race. A fourth-grade student said, "We're all human." "Everybody's the same," remarked a fourth-grade parent. "People are people," said an upper-grade teacher. Although these three quotes represented the racial discourse and overt/explicit racial logic operating in the Foresthills Elementary School community, throughout my time at Foresthills it became clear that this explicit color-blind discourse masked an underlying reality of racialized practice and color-conscious understanding. As many others have documented, this kind of color-blind ideology has various detrimental effects (Peshkin 1991; Schofield 1982; Wells and Crain 1997). Although all members of the Foresthills community in various ways denied the cogency of race in their locale, it was clear in multiple ways that race did matter there—in relation to history, current practices, and everyday beliefs, attitudes, and understandings.[9] Community members were not trying to fool me in their denials of the local salience of race. Nor were they just naïve. Why then did they fail to see race as important even as they talked about the exclusion of racial groups? In many ways, this apparent contradiction can be explained as part of the operation of racial ideologies that are gaining preponderant influence in the United States today.

Ideologies tell particular kinds of stories about the way the world works. As Hall (1990: 8) states, ideology refers to "those images, concepts and premises which provide the frameworks through which we represent, interpret, understand and 'make sense' of some aspect of social existence." They are not individually generated but are part of a larger set of stories told over and over again in political speeches, on situation comedies, by neighbors, and in newspapers. Ideologies emerge out of social struggles, what Gramsci (1971) called "wars of position." The power of ideologies lies in their ability to facilitate collective domination in a way such that they often make vast inequalities understandable and acceptable to those at both the top and the bottom of the social order.

For example, in schools, ideologies of meritocracy based on the belief that individuals succeed or fail according to their own merit help both students and professionals "understand" why some excel and others flounder (Apple 1990; MacLeod 1995). In that way schools are seen merely as transmitters of useful knowledge, as neutral instructional sites rather than as cultural and political sites in which the existing social order is reproduced (Giroux 1983). Although individual merit and effort do matter for school success (in this way ideologies are built on kernels of truth—in this case, merit matters for success), significant bodies of research have demonstrated that merit and effort are quite differentially rewarded, supported, encouraged, funded, and framed depending on whose talents and efforts are being evaluated. The ideology of meritocracy, however, manages to successfully naturalize the resulting large gaps in school achievement.

When people deploy ideological narratives, they are most often not being duplicitous. As Jackman (1994) argues, these kind of ideologies are interpretations of social reality that are consistent with the dominant group's experience. They are collective property, permeating the main institutions and communication networks and propagated with what Jackman (1994: 8) calls "an easy vehemence that can come only from uncontrived sincerity." Ideologies then are not fabricated justifications but are the widely available chains of meaning, stories, or narratives we have to draw on in explaining social existence. They work most effectively when we are least aware of them, when, as Hall (1990: 10) states, "our formulations seem to be simple descriptive statements about how things are, or of what we can 'take-for granted.'" In this way, socially constructed premises appear instead to be natural—for example, black people can dance, boys like to play rough, those who work hard succeed.

These narratives are not static—in order to make sense they must change with the times. As new racial formations emerge, so too do new racial ideologies—new ways of understanding relations between racial groups. For example, during slavery it was widely understood that races were biologically separate species; it was all right to enslave Africans because they were not human. During the Jim Crow period, in which segregation was strictly enforced, the one-drop rule still reigned supreme, and biological understandings of race abounded, though they were not the same as during slavery (Davis 1991). Following the Civil Rights Movement it was no longer acceptable to assert genetic difference as the explanation for racial gaps. Even then, however, racial inequalities persisted (Bobo, Kluegel, and Smith 1997; Bonilla-Silva and Lewis 1999; Lipsitz 1998). Trying to explain how gaps in wealth, health, and life chances have persisted in the absence of organized, legal segregation has led to the emergence of new racial narratives; these new accounts utilize a different set of rhetorical strategies along with variations on old themes. In fact, the disjuncture between Sunny Valley residents' assertions of color blindness and the reality of their color consciousness must be understood as part of the dominant racial ideology functioning locally and in the nation today (Bobo, Kluegel, and Smith 1997; Bonilla-Silva 2001; Crenshaw 1997; Smith 1995).

This ideological form of color blindness has several dimensions, all of which are reflected in the data from Foresthills. Color-blind ideology presumes or asserts a race-neutral social context (i.e., race does not matter here). It stigmatizes attempts to raise questions about redressing racial inequality in daily life through accusations such as "playing the race card" or "identity politics," which imply that someone is trying to bring race in where it does not belong

(Bonilla-Silva 2001; Crenshaw 1997; Gitlin 1995; Tomasky 1996). Color-blind ideology substitutes cultural for genetic or biological explanations of racial disparities (e.g., Foresthills parents' cultural explanations of housing segregation and gaps in school achievement). It also involves nonrecognition, the process of noticing but not considering race (Crenshaw 1997).[10] Under these new terms, equality is reframed to mean not equality of life chances but "the formal removal of race categories across society" such that "race is precluded as a source of identification or analysis" (Crenshaw 1997: 103). In this vein, explicit and traditional Jim Crow–style racial discrimination is stigmatized, but so are efforts at challenging institutionalized racism.

As Crenshaw (1997) argues, in its assertion that race does not matter, color-blind ideology attempts to mask the power of race as it simultaneously demonstrates precisely the difference race does make (that is, when one asserts that one does not pay attention to race, the implication is that to notice it would have deleterious outcomes). In many ways color blindness is powerful precisely because it espouses the ideal Martin Luther King Jr. expressed in his "I Have a Dream" speech. Yet it is particularly troublesome because it operates in a context, as in Sunny Valley, in which color consciousness remains pervasive and pernicious, just more covert than during Jim Crow.[11] In this way, color-blind ideology serves to explain and thus protect the status quo—the current racial formation. As was echoed in the discourse of Foresthills adults, it suggests that "the problem" is not a historical or a present-day pattern of racism but instead is a result of bad attitudes, and if we just let things be, it is only a matter of time before racial gaps fade away naturally. As Bobo, Kluegel, and Smith (1997: 16) describe it, "Institutionalized racial inequalities created by the long era of slavery followed by Jim Crow racism are popularly accepted and condoned under a modern . . . racist ideology." Such color-blind ideological assertions fly in the face of "substantial and widening racial economic inequalities, high levels of racial residential segregation, and persistent discrimination experienced across class lines in the black community" (Bobo, Kluegel, and Smith 1997: 40).

In many of the ways described above, color-blind racial commonsense shaped how people in the Foresthills community understood their context and their place in the world, and it thus also shaped their practices. Rather than being a benign phenomenon, it in many ways helped to enable the reproduction of racial inequality. Color blindness enabled all members of the community to avoid confronting the racial realities that surrounded them, to avoid facing their own racist presumptions and understandings, and to avoid dealing with racist events (by deracializing them). Moreover, at the same time it enabled people to feel as if they were on righteous racial terrain, following in the footsteps of Martin Luther King Jr. Persisting racist ideas about group difference along with continuing evidence of racism in interpersonal interactions, life opportunities, and neighborhood housing patterns all were ably diminished if not erased with the simple declaration that race no longer mattered and was thus not important. As the stories above demonstrate, this was not a benign outcome either for the children of color growing up in such a context or for a society that aspires to function in truly color-blind ways rather than merely being blind to the effects of color (Fish 1993).

What Can Schools Do?

Arguing that the color blindness witnessed at Foresthills extends far beyond the school's bounds is not an argument for neglecting it in school. On the contrary, schools may be one of few places where such racial understandings can be successfully challenged. As discussed, racial inequity in schools is talked about today most often in the context of multicultural education. Clearly this is not an uncontested concept: multiculturalism has always meant different things to different people and, in practice, has taken many different forms (McCarthy 1995; Rezai-Rashti 1995; Sleeter and Grant 1988). Traditionally directed at improving the school experiences of students of color, multiculturalism has typically focused on either teaching the culturally different in order to assimilate them into the mainstream or increasing the sensitivity of dominant-group children in order to help all children get along (Rezai-Rashti 1995; Sleeter and Grant 1988).[12]

A number of authors have criticized this kind of traditional multiculturalism for its emphasis on culture rather than on social stratification, which tends to leave social inequality unchallenged. As Olneck (1990: 166, as quoted in Rezai-Rashti 1995) notes, "Dominant versions of multicultural education delimit a sanitized cultural sphere divorced from sociopolitical interests, in which culture is reified, fragmented, and homogenized, and they depict ethnic conflict as predominately the consequence of negative attitudes and ignorance about manifestations of difference, which they seek to remedy by cultivating empathy, appreciation, and understanding."

Multiculturalism as currently manifested not only does little to challenge students' understanding of culture, difference, and race but in fact serves to defend the status quo. As Crichlow et al. (1990: 103) argue, traditional multiculturalism has little impact on the "grip of Eurocentrism on the construction of knowledge." Particular kinds of ways of knowing, ways of telling stories about the world, are left at the center, as the way things are, while only surface-level representations or manifestations of cultural pluralism, in the form of what some have called the tourist curriculum, are added as a thin layer on top of existing structures (Derman-Sparks 1989, 1993–1994). This approach, as Crichlow et al.

(1990: 103) state, "masks itself as social justice in the curriculum, while it actually accepts and thereby legitimizes monocultural curricular dominance."

We should understand this way of doing business in schools not as normal or inevitable but as the product of a social organization that favors some groups over others. The fact that schools operate as social and political sites rather than as neutral arbiters of knowledge was never raised at Foresthills, a community peopled almost entirely by members of the dominant social group. This was no accident. The structure of the community, of the school, of its practices and curricular policies helped to reproduce the status quo. Both directly and indirectly it reproduced social inequality through fostering or enabling color-blind ideology to operate unchallenged and by allowing whites therefore to continue to see themselves as racially neutral, outside the racial hierarchy, deserving of their own success, and not responsible for the exclusion of others.

To address the shortcoming in traditional multiculturalism, many have turned to another tradition of educational reform, critical multicultural, or antiracist, education.[13] As Rezai-Rashti describes this approach (1995: 6), "While the central assumption of multicultural education is that sensitization and celebration of difference can counteract biased and prejudiced attitudes . . . antiracist education concentrates on examining the histories and the practices that prejudice supports. Anti-racist education insists on closely studying and revealing the sites, institutions, and ways in which racism originates."

For example, critical multicultural education locates the origins of student failure differently than the traditional view does. Although traditional multicultural education may acknowledge that the system is partly to blame, the focus remains primarily on the home and culture. Antiracist, or critical multicultural, education says that though we cannot ignore social, cultural, and home factors, much of the blame must be assigned to institutionalized racism in the classroom, school, and society. Differences in performance are understood as being produced not solely by differences in ability or motivation but by the "organization, conduct and content of pedagogy, curriculum, and assessment" (Olneck 1993: 243). This type of approach would in many ways serve as a direct challenge to the color-blind ideology dominant in settings such as Foresthills, forcing those in schools to see the "racialness" not only of their own existence but also of their institutions, neighborhoods, and communities.

Critical multiculturalism then involves the examination not only of school practices but of school outcomes. In this way the goal is not merely, or primarily, about fostering an appreciation of diversity but about ensuring equal access to the kind of education that translates into access to real opportunities. Given parental resistance to even the limited multicultural curriculum currently offered in Foresthills, it is difficult to imagine such a critical multicultural curriculum being put into place immediately, but we cannot give up arguing that it should be. A more honest, critical educational experience will help students better understand their place in the world and what it would mean to operate in a truly color-blind context.[14]

I am arguing here that it is essential to talk about how race operates even in settings where people say it is not important. As we will see in the next chapters, race mattered as much in an (almost) all-white setting like Foresthills as it did in multiracial inner-city schools—perhaps even more. In particular, if we continue to have an investment in a future of greater racial equity, we must confront the way race operates in white settings as much as we do in other settings. As Giroux (1998b: 132) states, "Education works best when those experiences that shape and penetrate one's lived reality are jolted, unsettled, and made the object of critical analysis." Yet in many ways the stakeholders in Foresthills seem unlikely to open their arms to such jolting and unsettling changes. It is no accident that traditional multiculturalism remains focused primarily on minority students and that more radical forms remain at the level of theory, rarely put to work in schools and even more rarely considered in white settings.

Still, if we recognize schools to be institutions responsible for challenging the status quo, for initiating new, more critical, and more honest understandings of the world, then we must continue to try to imagine what more critical educational experiences might look like, even in white settings. This process involves both interrogating injustices and, as Giroux (1998a: 1994) points out, investigating possible "contributions for humanity." It does not suggest laying blame on students, families, and schools but rather working to imagine a different kind of public sphere in which schools can begin fulfilling the role they have long been cast in—that of the great equalizers.

In short, education that is critical, multicultural, and focused on racial justice cannot be reserved only for students of color. On multiple levels it is clear that the children in almost-all-white schools like Foresthills Elementary need critical multicultural education. Most immediately, the experiences of the one black child in the class show that lack of discussion about race is neither benevolent nor even neutral. As Carter (1997: 205) points out, although students of color can learn how to cope and achieve within a racist context, they cannot end their victimization by themselves: "Victims of oppression cannot stop their victimization. They can fight against it, protect themselves from its effects, learn to achieve in spite of it, but they cannot stop something they are not creating. Whites invented race and maintain racial oppression in all its forms: individual, institutional, and cultural. The white person who comes to feel this reality and is able to communicate it no longer looks to the victims for solutions to their oppression."

Whites need to learn more not only about the reality of racial inequality but also about their own role in its reproduction. As the experiences and beliefs of those I interviewed demonstrate, whites who grow up in racially homogenous settings often have no idea of how race works or how their lives too are racialized.[15] As Wills (1996: 385) suggests, without counternarratives available, white students will become dependent on stereotypes and other racist assumptions: "A multicultural history curriculum is extremely useful for white, suburban students, who often have little contact with people of color in their everyday lives and are, therefore, much more dependent upon cultural stereotypes and assumptions when trying to imagine the situations of others in American society. These efforts are sure to be met with resistance and anger from parents, teachers and students, as we have already seen in the debate over multicultural curriculum reform throughout the United States. These efforts are necessary, however, if we are going to prepare all our students to live together amidst the diversity of American society."

A more critical multicultural education must not only seek to produce students who can think critically about their world but also endeavor to serve the larger goal of changing that world. As Carby (1992: 197) puts it, "In this social, political, and economic context . . . it is appropriate and important to question the disparity between the vigor of debates about the inclusion of black subjects on a syllabus and the almost total silence about and utter disregard for the material conditions of most black people." These are political issues, directly involving who does and who does not have power and likely to be engaged with only after some struggle. We must ask ourselves, can much change if the educational experiences of white middle-class children do not undergo some transformations? Ironically, any movement toward a real and substantial color-blind world, one in which all children have truly equal opportunities to realize their dreams and to live dignified lives, is limited if not halted in its tracks by the dominance of color-blind ideology within a context in which race still shapes access to resources and opportunities. In this way, color blindness, in the way it functions both in Foresthills and far beyond, serves as a defense of the unequal status quo. Ironically, until we are able to recognize the "racial" in our life experiences, we will not make progress toward undoing the effects of race in our lives. Sunny Valley isn't an idiosyncratically "racist" town—it is probably better than many, worse than some. This story then is not of some "bad white folks" who are in denial but of our collective inability to confront racial realities in their everyday manifestations. Particularly in schools, where there is a suggestion of, an expressed effort toward, providing all children with the ability to assess their worlds honestly and accurately, perpetuating color-blind myths is ultimately a disservice.

Three

Struggling with Dangerous Subjects

Race at West City Elementary

W̶est City is a fairly small elementary school within an urban school district. It was neither one of the best nor one of the worst schools in the city, though few students from the surrounding white, middle-class neighborhood attended. It was at times a warm, tense, lively, disorganized, sad, and joyful place. As one teacher put it, "It is as fine as a dysfunctional family can be . . . but isn't that the only kind of family?" Like most families, it had within it an abundance of genuine love and care.

However, despite the best intentions of many, it did not serve all its students equitably and well. If it was a family, it was one that some felt more a part of than others. Large numbers of low-income Latino and African American students entered as eager five-year-olds and left as sometimes engaged, often disenchanted, and generally underperforming and undereducated ten- and eleven-year olds. How this happened was not a story that began and ended at the school door; however, school culture and school practices played a key part.

As I will describe, at West City the physical and social geography was racially coded, racial tensions were present, and racial understandings played a role in daily life. Yet it was also a place where race was seldom discussed. Whether people did not recognize race as an issue, did not know how to talk about it, or did not want to talk about it are questions I address below.

The Setting

West City was in many ways a traditional urban school community. Almost 90 percent of its almost 250 students were children of color. Latino and African Americans students made up almost 75 percent of the school, with white, Chinese, and "other nonwhite" far behind.[1] The school had recently been renamed and undergone a partial personnel change. Even with the turnover in personnel, the school's teachers and administrators remained over 80 percent white. The classified staff—including the secretary, custodian, student advisors, and classroom aides—was more diverse. However both race and status interacted to produce tension, particularly between the mostly white teaching staff and the three high-profile people on the lower-status classified staff who had daily contact with the students (Ruby Fellows, the secretary, who was African American, and Jennifer Guzman and Marcus Jordan, the student advisors, who were Latina and African American, respectively).

The school was located in an almost-all-white neighborhood within a diverse metropolis (it was one of a few neighborhoods in the city that were over 80 percent white). The neighborhood was becoming more and more financially exclusive (e.g., a two-bedroom house purchased for $75,000 in the late 1970s sold in the late 1990s for close to half a million dollars; rents also skyrocketed, with two-bedroom units costing well over $1,500 a month). Despite these figures, the neighborhood was not fancy; aside from the high cost of housing (in a city where the general vacancy rate was very low), it had few signs of wealth (e.g., fancy cars, expensive restaurants).

Few West City students lived in the surrounding neighborhood, and nearly all those who did were white. Almost without exception, students of color were conveyed to and from school on the yellow buses that traversed the city every morning and afternoon. The buses themselves were racially distinct—African American and Latino students arrived from different neighborhoods and therefore rode on different buses. Almost all African American students were bused in from either the Barnsworth public-housing development across town or from the large Lancaster Valley area in the far corner of the city, which contained a number of public-housing developments and other low-cost housing. Citywide, African Americans were concentrated primarily within a few neighborhoods. For example, in a city that had a black population of less than 10 percent, Lancaster Valley was over 70 percent black. It was also the only area of the city where census tracts contained 40 percent or more of the families living in poverty. Barnsworth was also primarily African American and had high poverty levels. However, the area adjacent to Barnsworth was undergoing major gentrification, and housing prices had risen exponentially over the previous decade.

Though Latinos were more widely dispersed throughout the city, the neighborhood West City drew on had the highest concentration of them—over 80 percent. Almost all the Latino students were bused in from this area, which was several miles from the school. Though made up of groups from all parts of the Americas (Mexico, Guatemala, Nicaragua, El Salvador, Colombia), this neighborhood had some cohesion, at least in relation to the rest of the city. In interviews, many parents who were recent immigrants and who lived in the neighborhood reported having little to no contact with people other than Latinos. Despite some important internal divisions (e.g., at least two teenage gangs struggled regularly over territory; the gangs split along ethnic lines—one group was Mexican, the other was Central American), these immigrant families had a sense that they could operate well in the vicinity and would not be harassed for their limited proficiency with English.

The few West City students who did not come on the bus were dropped off and picked up by their parents, often on their way to or from work. At the end of every school day, the bused students ran out the back of the school building to the yard, where they lined up and waited, while the students walking or waiting for parents to pick them up headed out the front door. This split was often the first sign of racial division—a local manifestation of the city's segregated racial geography.

As indicated, though these students shared classrooms, they did not share home neighborhoods. Particularly in the upper grades (third grade through fifth grade), white students who attended the school often did so by default. They had recently moved to the city, had been unable to continue attending private school, or had undergone some other transition and were assigned to the school. At least half of these white students regularly talked about moving to another school and were filing appeals with the district, figuring out a way to afford private school, or making plans to leave the city. The white students for whom this narrative does not apply were among the few low-socioeconomic-status white students in the school.

The exceptions to this pattern were in the kindergarten and first-grade classes. The year I was there, the school had just been designated an alternative school. As part of this transformation, the district office encouraged parents who had not been able to get their kids into one of the established alternative schools to select West City. The principal had a good reputation in the district, and many parents decided to give the school a try. As the kindergarten teacher explained to me, many of these parents were willing to send their child to the school for kindergarten and first grade, the logic being that it would not be too costly to their children's future educational success to be in an unproven school for these early grades.

At approximately 8:15 on any particular school day, buses started arriving, and students (the same children who ate free or reduced-price lunches) trailed in from the yard to the cafeteria to have free breakfast (cereal, milk, and juice). They sat together at one table in the corner. While third-, fourth-, and fifth-graders tended to rush in to eat and then rush back out to the yard to play before the bell, kindergartners had to be cajoled into finishing and moving along.

During lunch the room was a cacophony of sound, with children flowing in and out steadily from 11:20 until 12:15. Each age level had fifteen to twenty minutes to eat lunch before they were shooed into the yard for recess. There was no seating chart, and most students sat with friends from their class. These friendship clusters were almost entirely self-segregated by both gender and race. The student advisors and occasionally a classroom aide or teacher circulated through the room keeping students to the business of eating. When the noise level got too high, Mr. Jordan, one of the student advisors, would yell, capture attention by loudly dropping folding metal chairs from the raised stage, or otherwise engage in dramatic means to silence the crowd. On particularly rowdy days, the third-, fourth-, and fifth-graders sometimes spent their entire lunch-period recess "learning how to sit quietly." On these occasions, teachers who had stayed with their classes for a few minutes would come to the teachers' lounge and report in hushed tones that Mr. Jordan had "them all sitting in there silent as church mice." Other teachers would go to watch this dramatic performance on Mr. Jordan's part (once he lost his voice from all the yelling). The silent time would last anywhere from five minutes to the entire lunch period and would involve anywhere from the entire upper grades to only those tables that had been rowdy. This was one manifestation of the school's focus on order. Authority and control were regularly asserted in dramatic fashion. Yelling and threats in the hallways were not uncommon. Some teachers were known as particularly "successful" because their rooms were "orderly."

The school's hallways were clean and intermittently decorated with posters. Some posters were child-created announcements for that week's food sale; some were staff-made banners dealing with the curricular focus of the month, espousing a particular school rule or value, or recording the daily success of a particular fund-raising drive; and others were glossy store-purchased posters acquired from the school district or from some member of the school community. With the exception of class artwork regularly displayed by two teachers, relatively little student work was seen on hallway bulletin boards.

Just inside the main office sat Mrs. Fellows, the school secretary. She operated as gatekeeper to the connecting rooms—a staff lounge (complete with copiers, refrigerator, paper cutters, laminator, tables for sitting/eating, phone, and restroom) and the principal's office. Though most of these extending rooms also had entrances to the hallway, these doors were usually closed and locked. People moved in and out of Mrs. Fellows's space all day: children who were sick, sent to the office for behavior problems, or wanting to visit with Mrs. Fellows; parents picking up their children, wanting to ask questions about the school, or trying to talk to the principal; visitors; and staff. Generally all members of the school moved in and out of the room freely. It had no high counters or other barriers typical of many other school offices. Fifth-grade students could often be found sitting behind the desk answering the phone when Mrs. Fellows was out or at lunch. Mrs. Fellows greeted most parents by name; having worked at the school as long as or longer than other members of the staff, she was likely to know more about the students and families than anyone else. When teachers wanted to find out what was going on in the life of one of their students, they often turned to Mrs. Fellows. From moment to moment, she was just as likely to be giving a crying student a hug as chewing out a third-grader for giving her "attitude." Teachers treaded lightly around her, recognizing her as a power hub in the school. Although she was quite warm, she could also be moody and had a short fuse.

The door leading to the teachers' lounge/lunchroom was always open, except during the lunch hour, when it was usually closed so teachers could get some "peace and calm." During lunchtime, the room could be either loud and raucous or silent and empty. On loud days teachers chided, teased, and joked with one another while passing food or making copies. Although several teachers spent their lunchtime sitting on a stoop in the neighborhood smoking and reading, most used the time to pass a few social moments with adults. The conversation rarely stayed on school matters long and only occasionally strayed into pedagogical issues (e.g., "When are you doing the science unit?" "What are you giving for homework tonight?"). When the bell marked the end of lunch, few rushed into the yard to pick up their classes. In fact, several times the student advisors had to remind upper-grade teachers that lunch was over at 12:30, "not 12:35," because they were so slow to head out to the yard.

The principal's office was reachable through a small storage room. Ms. Grant, or Pat, as she was known to the staff, was one of a small cadre of well-known and especially highly regarded principals throughout the city.[2] She was rarely in her office or at her desk for any extended period during the day as she was constantly moving around the building, filling in for someone, answering the phones, visiting a class, dealing with an injury, handling a conflict, talking to a parent or teacher or volunteer, observing a lesson, or out of the school at a district-level principals' meeting. Though I never saw her in any particular classroom for long, in conversations she always seemed aware of the ongoing intricacies of her school. She knew every child's name and often singled one or more of them out during an assembly or a morning circle for not paying attention. A white woman in her early forties, Ms. Grant dressed neither formally nor casually; though not substantial physically, she had a large presence.

Every school day began at 8:40 with all members of the school (teachers, stu-

dents, and staff) forming a circle in the yard. Though some days it was a struggle to get kids lined up, holding hands, and paying attention, they usually moved
into the circle as part of the daily routine. Each day of the week involved a different ritual—singing, saying the pledge of allegiance, or reciting the school
rules. Ms. Grant stood at the center of the circle, making that day's announcements and leading the daily rituals. Occasionally she brought students into the
circle to help her. She often ended with an African folk song the whole school
had learned, and classes walked off the yard singing. Ms. Grant's key role was
made especially clear on the days that she was absent and a teacher was
assigned to take her place. Sometimes the teachers would just decide to skip the
ritual altogether, though usually it was performed, if with much less energy and
enthusiasm. In any case, by 8:55 the hallways were jammed with students on
their way to classrooms.

Because of the school's relatively small size, many activities were conducted
as whole-school events (e.g., performances, assemblies). Most of the school
building functioned as "community" space in which ownership was not as important as membership. In fact, Ms. Grant had put a lot of effort into building
strong connections with the surrounding community. These were reciprocal
relationships: rooms in the school were rented cheaply to local organizations
needing meeting space on nights or weekends, or these organizations donated
goods or time to the school in exchange. West City had a particularly close connection with a local church that had "adopted" the school and was providing volunteers and tutors along with other resources. Thus, although both internal and
external boundaries existed, they were permeable and flexible: teachers moved
in and out of each other's rooms, children regularly visited other classrooms,
student advisors popped in and out of classrooms for short visits, and volunteers
and visitors regularly moved up and down hallways and in and out of rooms.

The Classroom

When I approached the principal about doing research in the school,
she was immediately open to the idea. I had explained that I wanted to be situated primarily in one fourth-/fifth-grade room, though I would also visit other
classes and spend time in schoolwide spaces and at school events. Ms. Grant
immediately suggested I work with Mr. Ortiz. As in the other schools, the
principal recommended the teacher she thought was "best" on "race issues."
Though Mr. Ortiz was a newer teacher than the other fourth-/fifth-grade
instructor, as a youngish Puerto Rican ex-Air Force officer, he was understood
to be more savvy with regard to racial issues than some others in the school. As
I did at the other schools, I accepted the principal's nomination in that it seemed
to assure that I would see the best the school had to offer.

After talking to me for a few more minutes, Ms. Grant heard Mr. Ortiz's voice in the main office and called him in and introduced us. Mr. Ortiz was open to working with me though he cautioned me that he was relatively new to the school and that some of his methods were unorthodox. For example, as we walked up to his room, he explained that he repeated himself often because he believed students absorbed something only after they'd heard it for the hundredth time. (This was an apt assessment, as I soon found out. Two of his favorite expressions were "You're either part of the solution or part of the problem" and "Get on the bus or get off the bus.") He expressed enthusiasm about having help in the class and seemed ready to utilize me, explaining that he thought it would be good for the girls in the class to have a "female presence."

Mr. Ortiz was an eccentric figure. He was quite energetic, almost always talking and moving. If anyone in the building needed help moving, fixing, building, or lifting anything, they would turn to him. Around the edge of his classroom, room B2, were piles of books, boxes, folders, maps, papers, and miscellaneous items he had collected. Throughout the year, Mr. Ortiz would spend entire weekends rearranging and organizing the room with little apparent effect. Clearly he struggled to keep the room and all his paperwork orderly. His classroom, like the other two upper-grade classrooms (another fourth/fifth and one third/fourth), had incomplete materials. None of them had complete sets of textbooks, and they had to share math and science kits. Until the teachers got a grant to purchase books during the spring semester, none had literature books for their classes.

In addition to the schoolwide morning ritual, room B2 had its own routine. The classroom's thirty-two students, who mirrored the larger school demographics, entered from the yard every day, pushed the desks back, and carried their chairs to form the morning "circle." Initially this was a process of students shoving desks loudly and not far enough back, dragging chairs across the floor, bickering about who would sit next to whom, and whispering about schoolyard gossip, and of Mr. Ortiz yelling about making enough space in the circle for everyone and struggling to get students to listen to one another. Eventually students learned to pick their chairs up and move more quickly (though many of the other problems continued throughout the year). Circle usually began with attendance and ended with "compliments," with various forms of student or teacher sharing in between. These sessions often went on for up to forty-five minutes and, as the following excerpt from my fieldnotes shows, covered a wide range of topics and generally reflected the broad array of student experiences and concerns:

Mr. Ortiz decides to go around the circle this morning for sharing. Starts with Priscilla, "On Saturday I might see [a movie]. It's coming out on Friday." Mr.

Ortiz asks her if she's moving but she has no new information, it may not happen until the end of the year. Luis is next and he reports "On Saturday they killed one of my cousins. Some guys, they tried to steal his truck and [my cousin and his friends] said no so they shot him. [One of his friends] is injured and in the hospital. He was twenty-one years old." Mr. Ortiz reminds several students to move their chairs away from the hamster table and then asks Luis about the funeral. It is going to take place in Mexico next week. Luis may go. Lucia is next: "Yesterday my mom had lost her keys and um, we had to walk all the way to her job and get the lady's keys and open the back door." Mr. Ortiz asks why she told the story. She said she doesn't know. He tells her in the future to figure out why she is telling a story and how she feels about it. Sally: "My mom's friend and her kid got run over by a car. Her two-month-old baby and her daughter and her got run over. They're dead." Mr. Ortiz asks how the car is. She doesn't know. Thompson: "On Saturday went to a city park and Sunday went to a mountain." Lisa: Yesterday, her big dog ran out the door and bit a small puppy and the little dog was bleeding on its back. Mike—nothing. Catherine—nothing. Rebecca—nothing. Mr. Ortiz asks about her book in Spanish but she forgot it again. He's going to call her aunt. Vanessa—nothing . . .

During the first few weeks, Mr. Ortiz's "unorthodox" strategies became both more apparent and more puzzling. As the sharing time above shows, he often offered seemingly callous responses to students' reports of personal or family injury. When I asked Mr. Ortiz about it, he explained that he was trying to get them "to care about each other." Though vague, this explanation seemed to tap into the earnestness and vehemence with which he took on what he seemed to understand as his calling—to (by coercion or persuasion) get the students in his classroom to control themselves and treat each other well. Potentially troubling, however, was the amount of time spent each morning on nonacademic issues. For example, in comparison, the first hour of the day at the other two schools was usually spent covering one if not two academic lessons (see Mrs. Moch's morning schedule in Chapter 2).

Moreover, though community building in classrooms seems like a good idea, the time spent in circle and on "compliments" each morning was in fact often rancorous and was typically overtaken by other objectives. For example, for a period of time Mr. Ortiz forced the students all to compliment the same body part (e.g., eyes, ears, feet) but to use different adjectives to do so (e.g., "you have outstanding eyes," "interesting eyes," "pretty eyes," "nice eyes"). The procedure took the form of a vocabulary lesson; students cared little about whom their compliment was directed toward and focused instead on trying to think of an adjective that had not already been used, yelling or groaning in frustration when someone else used the one they had thought of. Later, when Mr. Ortiz had become frustrated with all the bickering in the room, he had the students give insults instead of compliments—to, as he put it, "get it out of their system." Throughout this exercise thick-skinned students would giggle and dish out venom, and others would be on the verge of tears, waiting for the ball to drop as the circle moved around to them. For example, one day began with the following series of exchanges:

Mr. Ortiz starts put-downs with Julio. Julio begins by telling Robin she's fat and ugly. Robin tells Thompson he's ugly. He tells Nicole she's stupid who tells Laura her shirt is ugly. She tells Mario he has ugly hair. Mr. Ortiz asks him why he doesn't use gel like the suave brothers Mike and Julio. Mario shrugs in response and then tells Maria her hair is ugly. She tells Catherine she has ugly shoes. Catherine tells Rebecca she doesn't like her earrings. She has to tell Darnell—Mr. Ortiz gives her several suggestions, melon head, etc. She told Darnell that he is ugly. He tells Gloria that she's dumb. She tells Jessica that she stinks. She tells Loquita that she's stupid. Mr. Ortiz sarcastically tells them that he loves how they smile when they give put-downs. Loquita tells Lynette that she has a big head. Mr. Ortiz says, "That's it? You could tell her that her hair [newly braided] looks like spaghetti." Lynette tells Rodney that he's dirty. Rodney tells Christina she's ugly. Mr. Ortiz gives Rodney a hard time, teasing him about his coat (Mr. Ortiz had confiscated it on Friday as punishment for a transgression). Christina tells Mark he's small and stupid. Mark tells Sally she smells like doodoo. Sally tells Mike that he needs a new watch. They tell her that's a pitiful put-down, "What, do you like him?" Mr. Ortiz asks. So she tells him that he needs to study. They think that is extra pitiful and tell her to do another one, "Come on Sally." She tells him that he's retarded. They all laugh. Mike tells Priscilla that she needs to change her everyday clothes. Mr. Ortiz tells her its because he wants to wear her frilly clothes. Priscilla tells Luis that his shoes are ugly. Mr. Ortiz tells her that those are new shoes and she has to do a new one so she says that his pants are ugly. [Luis] tells Lisa that she stinks. She tells Daniel that he dresses like a rag. He tells Rose that she farts too much. Rose tells Joshua that he's a boogerhead.

Many of these comments were directed at sensitive areas. For example, girls who were particularly sensitive about their appearance were told they were ugly. In fact, Mr. Ortiz did make small efforts near the end of these sessions to deflect comments about clothing and hygiene made to two children in the class (Priscilla and Luis) who were particularly struggling at home financially. However, when students tried to say something mild or even neutral to a child they knew to be extra sensitive, Mr. Ortiz made them go again, saying, "Come on . . . that didn't count" or accusing them of "liking" the other child. On days when they exchanged compliments, he often expressed a great deal of cynicism about the genuineness of the compliments; this cynicism took the form of messages to hurry up "because I know you don't mean it anyway." All these various tactics he explained to me again as his way of trying to get the students "to care." Drawing on military metaphors, he talked about "securing the perimeter" and about "breaking the students down" as necessary for creating a safe environment in which students cared about themselves and each other.

The morning circle evolved and changed during the year. The activities were shifted to different times during the day; sometimes they were eliminated for periods, sometimes extended. Yet that time became symbolic of the way the class functioned. In many ways, this or similar kinds of unstructured "social-learning" time took over the class. The class would sometimes go days without any formal science, social studies, or math. In fact, I did not witness a math lesson or see any evidence of a math curriculum until the beginning of October. I was not the only one who noticed these gaps in the curriculum. Mike, a precocious Latino fifth-grader, would periodically ask me to show him how to do something (e.g., long division). Regularly he would ask, "What grade were you in when you learned this?" Other children sensed that they were behind, but Mike was the most confident in his abilities and most clear that if he did not know something it was not his fault—he just had not been taught it yet. Less enamored of authority, he was more likely to question what was going on than were most of his peers.

Just after one of these conversations with Mike, I interviewed the principal for the first time. I took these concerns to her, asking in general and vague ways what she knew about the classroom's curriculum.

I think I'm pretty aware. On occasion I go in and mess with it. On a lot I don't. Mainly because I really feel like, when teachers are supported, and have the materials, and get the staff development they need, my sitting in the classroom saying "You've gotta do this, you've gotta do that" doesn't always work. And you know, for example, I pick on [Mr. Ortiz]. I mean you've been in his classroom, and he's somebody who's, say, [relatively] new to teaching. In a fourth-/fifth-grade classroom, where there's a lot of high academic needs. I know that there's a lot of subject matters that are missed. I know that he's not—that, for example, science is not really happening in his classroom. I know that he's spending a lot more time on community building, per se, than on academic stuff. More than I would—but it's not going to hurt the kids. If anything, when they get to middle school they're going to know how to function as human beings. And if that's what they get out of fifth grade, then that's what they get out of fifth grade. And it's going to help them in the long run, so much more than getting in the ninetieth percentile on the math. I mean that may not be a philosophy that everybody would agree with, but I feel like he knows how to build community, and knows how to build rapport. You know, like I said, [he] is going to plug the curriculum in as they go along. I feel like the fourth- and fifth-graders he got had so little of that. When he got them. The third- and second-grade experiences here [weren't] a help. I mean James was the third-grade teacher of Malik, and he couldn't teach him. Malik was out of control. And I feel like Malik is very much in control now, and going to middle school. You know, if he doesn't get kicked out of middle school by seventh grade, that's 'cause of what [Mr. Ortiz] did.[3]

Having witnessed the careful parental and administrative monitoring of classroom curricula at Foresthills and Metro2, I thought that Ms. Grant's ability to make these claims was likely associated with the low social status of most of the children and families at West City.

Much of Ms. Grant's justification for the lack of an academic curriculum centered on students' inadequate early education, particularly their inadequate early social training. In fact, West City did have high turnover among teachers in the early grades during much of the time Mr. Ortiz's students were in the lower grades. Educational practices that left students unprepared academically for middle school were justified because of their poor social and academic training in kindergarten through third grade. It was not hard to imagine middle school and high school teachers offering the same, and possibly quite accurate, explanations for modifying expectations (and thus the curriculum) to address students' unpreparedness. Unfortunately, the result was that these West City children already, through no fault of their own, were not receiving the kind of academic training necessary for future success. Thus, though standardized tests in later years may rate these children as having low "abilities" (or learned skills/knowledge), these scores will have little to do with their capabilities (potential for development).

Though in many ways these students were being set up for failure, this was accomplished through practices their teachers understood to be in the students' best interest. Payne makes a similar point when he discusses the role of urban schools in larger processes of producing the structurally unemployed:

Were we to look more closely at some particular black child, we might find that some first-grade teacher in a slum school decided he had little chance to learn much because children who looked like him, dressed like him, and talked like him seldom did well in school and so the teacher, having many other responsibilities, made only the most minimal attempts to teach him. Accordingly, some sixth-grade teacher found him so far beneath the skill level at which she had been trained to teach that she taught him nothing at all; and therefore some high school counselor later took one look at the child's record and suggested that he might do well in shop courses; and so some personnel officer four years later looks at the youngster's performance on an employment test (which is likely to be quite unrelated to the ability to do the job in any case) and suggests that the young man maybe look elsewhere and come back when he has some experience. . . . You can call the process racist, but there need be no racists in it. At nearly every step in the process, people can act in accord with established norms of fair play, perhaps even with the best interest of the young man at heart. (Payne 1984: 38–39)

In regard to maintaining discipline, it was not just Ms. Grant who assessed Mr. Ortiz's strengths in this area as good for his students. Mr. Ortiz was known throughout the school as one of the few who was able to "help" students get control of themselves. At least one advantage of his strategy was that, relative to students in other West City classrooms, his students were rarely kicked out of the room. Ms. Guzman and Mr. Jordan talked about Mr. Ortiz as an exception to the rule of teachers' constantly sending students out of their rooms for misbehavior. As Mr. Jordan put it, curriculum did not go on in Mr. Ortiz's classroom until problems were cleared up. "Whether it was in the yard or on the bus or with homework, whatever the issue was, everything's stopped until that's addressed." Mr. Jordan and Ms. Guzman both described his classroom as similar to a family in that most families cannot afford to send away a child who is not behaving. Mr. Jordan said, "You can't just kick the kid out because they're not cleaning their room or whatever the case is. You have company and they're acting up, you can't just send them away to another room. It's not realistic. So, you deal with it. You work on it. You teach, they learn, you go on."

As Mr. Jordan noted, nothing went on in Mr. Ortiz's classroom until students' behavior had been addressed and until it was addressed for the whole group. But some days little else went on. Long periods were filled with Mr. Ortiz yelling at the class or working out schoolyard disagreements. As punishment, students sometimes spent large chunks of class time "writing lines" (e.g., writing ten pages of "I will respect myself and my class") or doing what Mr. Ortiz called "dictionary work." At the beginning of the year this work involved writing words and their definitions from the dictionary, but after several weeks the assignment was changed to writing just the words themselves. Students would be told to start at the beginning of a randomly selected letter of the alphabet and write from three to thirty pages of words (e.g., dab, dabble, dabbler, dace, dacha). Whatever the success or failure of these "social" lessons, it was hard to imagine students' long-term interests being served well when they were getting so few academic lessons. Even if Ms. Grant was correct—that if Malik made it to eighth grade, it was because of Mr. Ortiz—Malik's ability to sit quietly and compliantly in a classroom did not mean he would know how to read, write, or multiply well. This tension between competing demands was exemplified in Mike's regular queries about what he should know "by now." It is not hard to imagine how long room B2's classroom-management strategies and curricular limitations would have lasted in either of the other schools where I spent time. In fact, more than one West City parent I spoke to voiced reservations about both classroom management and the curriculum. Yet, as I outline below, the school often deflected blame for shortcomings in these areas onto the children themselves.

On a largely white teaching staff, Mr. Ortiz's self-described Hispanic heritage gave him "expert" status with the predominantly minority student body, and so other staff seemed reluctant to question his educational practices. Moreover, many admired his ability to handle even the toughest students. As in urban schools nationally, a great deal of emphasis at West City was put on the ability to maintain order (Ayers, Dohrn, and Ayers 2001; Ferguson 2000); this was a skill Mr. Ortiz had mastered. Though his specific pedagogical choices were often questionable, he was often one of few staff members at the school who were willing to take on students whom others perceived as unreachable. His commitment to such students was, as he described it, a direct result of his status as a man of color committed to fostering the school success of children of color. This did mean that he was in practice especially committed to students; however it also meant that many of his questionable strategies went largely unchallenged. Race was thus at play not only in school practices and behaviors but also in people's explanations for and understandings of what transpired.

Racial Geography, Rules, and Practices

The racial geography of West City was multilayered. The school operated within a larger, highly segregated metropolis. Some of the most profound aspects of that segregation were manifested locally. Although the neighborhood was primarily white, the school was not. Students bused in from other parts of the city recognized that they were on someone else's turf. For example three African American boys, walking with me in the neighborhood one day, looked around curiously and asked me whether any blacks lived there. Some parents had, in fact, picked West City because of its neighborhood. Some, in hopes of having their children attend school in a safe place, went so far as threatening to sue the district in order to get their children into West City. Tanesha Clive, the mother of Ivy, an African American fifth-grader, lived in the Barnsworth projects. Ivy was originally assigned to Eureka, the school next to the projects. At the time Eureka was ranked in the lowest 10 percent of schools in the state. As Mrs. Clive put it, "They were trying to send her to Eureka and *that was just out*." With a great deal of organization and effort she was eventually able to get Ivy into West City and to arrange for the public school bus to service the corridor between Barnsworth and West City.

Although housing segregation patterns affected both school assignment and the demographics of West City's student body, a clear social geography of race also existed within the school. Defined by Frankenberg (1993) in her book on white women, the social geography of race refers not only to how physical space is divided and inhabited but also to how that space is understood and to what kind of relations take place within it (e.g., close or distant, equal or unequal). As discussed earlier, the school's student body was overwhelmingly black and Latino, and the certified staff was overwhelmingly white. At the time I began work there, the school had just hired a second black teacher, and though Mr. Ortiz's racial identification was ambiguous, he identified ethnically as Hispanic. The lower-status classified staff was much more diverse. Of the three classified staff members with the highest visibility and the largest roles in the school, two were black and one was Latina. Thus, those with the most status and power in the school were primarily white, while those on the lower end of the hierarchy were not.

At different points throughout the year, tension erupted between the lower-status staff of color and various white teachers. There were several large blow-ups and several strains of animosity. These disagreements involved status, power, and process. Though not all the conflicts were explicitly about race, all reverberated with racial tones. For example, Ms. Shafer (a white third-grade teacher) and Mr. Jordan, the African American student advisor, got into a loud and heated argument in front of students one day. It was ostensibly about her bringing her class down too early for lunch. As she relayed the incident to me later, Mr. Jordan rudely told her to go back upstairs. She refused, telling him never to talk to her like that in front of her class. Mr. Jordan explained later how tired he was of teachers' not abiding by established times for lunch and recess: "I'm sick of them not listening to [Ms. Guzman and me]." Ms. Shafer, in turn, was exasperated with Mr. Jordan's disrespect, saying that she sometimes felt as if he was "prejudiced" against white teachers. Eventually they just did their best to avoid one another.

When I asked whether there had ever been any racial issues between staff members, Ms. Sullivan, the other third-grade teacher, mentioned one between

Ms. Harrison (an African American teacher) and a white upper-grade teacher; this was one of several feuds I knew to exist. In fact Ms. Harrison had tense relations with several staff members. Mr. Jordan, the black student advisor, also had had minor confrontations, if not outright blow-ups, with several teachers. Mrs. Fellows, the African American secretary, similarly had strained (and sometimes hostile) relationships with some of the white staff. It did not seem only coincidental that the major tensions among the adults in the building existed between African Americans and whites on staff. The tensions between these staff members were tied up with issues of status and differing understandings of who was and was not good at their jobs, who was and was not committed to the children in the school, who did and did not belong. All these dynamics were racially inflected. Over time I discovered that many of the tensions involved disagreements over the treatment of specific students, over questions of respect (e.g., Mr. Jordan's struggles with Ms. Shafer), or over cultural differences in communication style.

Among the students themselves, there was also much racial separation on the playground, in the lunchroom, and in friendship networks.[4] Though some teachers thought that students at West City crossed racial boundaries in games more than at many of the city's larger elementary schools, as Mr. Ortiz and others reported, racial animosity still existed between groups, and this animosity manifested itself in various ways throughout the year. When I asked Mr. Ortiz whether a conflict he had mentioned between Latinos and African Americans in the classroom was frequent or rare, he commented, "That's pretty constant."

Racially coded ideas and assumptions were a regular part of the school space, both implicitly and explicitly. For example, in mid-March Ms. Harrison, one of the two black teachers, stopped me in the hallway to describe an incident in her class the day before. She had overheard one of her first-graders, a Latino boy, call an African American girl a "black monkey." She asked him why he had said it, and he explained that he did not like black people. Ms. Harrison immediately called a class meeting and asked every child in the class one by one what each thought of black people. Almost all Latinos affirmed that they, too, did not like them: "They stink." "They're loud." "They swear too much." "They're mean." She related feeling stunned as she listened to their assessments: "I just kept nodding and saying, 'Hmmm, okay. And you?'" She was, she said, overcome with "wanting to laugh and cry" when Leon and Rashaad, the two black boys in the class, chimed in from the back, "But what about Ms. Harrison? What about Ms. Harrison?" as they tried to figure out how their peers could say they did not like black people in the presence of a black teacher they all loved. Did not they see Ms. Harrison sitting right in front of them as always? Why did her warm, caring, and well-loved presence not disprove their general dislike for blacks? The rest of the children seemed not to understand the significance of the boys' repeated question, and their pleas were not acknowledged. Ms. Harrison struggled for the rest of the year with what to do about these attitudes.

Latinos were not the only students to have distinct understandings about the nature of blackness. One day in the yard I witnessed a conversation between Rodney, an African American fourth-grader, and two of his former teachers, Ms. Sullivan and Ms. Hill. Ms. Sullivan had been explaining to me her efforts to get her students to think about their futures and what they wanted to do with their lives. She stopped Rodney, a student in her class the previous year, and asked him what he wanted to do. He said he wanted to go to college but first he had to go to prison. When Ms. Sullivan looked horrified and asked him what he was talking about, he spelled it out for her: "All black men go to prison." He thought it would be more efficient to get his prison term out of the way before he went to college rather than having to do it afterward. He was impervious to both teachers' efforts to convince him that it was not true, leaning back and seeming skeptical of their naïveté.

White children also had distinct perceptions of blackness. One example surfaced during an exchange I witnessed in room B2. Mr. Ortiz was talking to the class about "wasting time." He was threatening to reorganize the table groups and wanted to talk to the class about why they were getting out of hand. As I wrote in my fieldnotes:

> Mr. Ortiz tells the class that he doesn't understand "why you choose to be called bad or a problem when you could be not." Alex (one of two white boys in the class) says, "Well maybe it's cause they're called bad at home." Mr. Ortiz concurs that maybe that is true. He tells the class that there are six students who regularly take time away from the rest of the class. Rodney offers that he knows he is one of them. Mr. Ortiz asks him if he can name the others and Rodney, with some help from another boy at his table, correctly names the other five. In total there were three black boys, two black girls and one Latina on the list. Mr. Ortiz then asks them why they "do it." Ivy and Darnell say that it isn't because their parents tell them they're bad because they don't tell them they are bad at home. Mr. Ortiz again asks them why they act out. Ivy said maybe she does it for the attention. Mr. Ortiz prods Darnell repeatedly and he just keeps repeating that he "doesn't know." Mr. Ortiz says he thinks Darnell really doesn't get it. Mr. Ortiz eventually threatened to put the six students in the one table group and then has them write about why they should be put into one group.

Several things are going on here. Alex, a white fourth-grader, clearly understood that he was not part of the group being reprimanded—even though at that moment Mr. Ortiz was speaking to the entire class. Alex suggested that maybe "they" were called bad at home. Underlying his hypothesis was some understanding about pathology or bad parenting at home. I was not surprised to hear this comment from Alex. Though his parents were "liberal" and supportive of the school, his dad, Mr. Hargrove, had explained that he worried about his son's picking up some of the "city stuff" or "macho stuff" at a public school. As Mr. Hargrove put it, the "macho stuff" came from the "project kids," who, he guessed, "have to be tough to survive." Alex's family lived in the middle of the Latino neighborhood where most of West City's Latino students came from. Alex, however, did not have any friends from that neighborhood. In many ways the family was "in" rather than "of" the neighborhood. When I asked Mr. Hargrove why Alex did not have friends from nearby (I had seen kids playing outside when I arrived for the interview), Mr. Hargrove hesitated, stating haltingly, "Um, I think there's, I guess I should be honest, whatever, I think there's just the difference, you now, um the kids are different here, you know, its um, and a lot of his friends are from, go to his old school and um people that we can *more relate to* and stuff." He was referring here to friends of Alex's from the private school he attended before (which was 80 percent white). Alex transferred out of the school when the family could no longer afford it.

In many ways Alex received messages that he was different from those whom he lived near and with whom he spent many hours at school. Thus it was not surprising that when the entire class was reprimanded, Alex understood himself to be outside of the "bad" group to which the teacher referred. Alex's dad indirectly explained that this sense of sympathy with but separation from his peers was one of the lessons he hoped his son was learning in school. For example, Mr. Hargrove explained that he was initially quite upset about some of the (rather minor) diversity and "get-along" programs the school was doing. However, he had come to see that they were important for "inner-city" kids:

> That was something that really kind of bothered me about the school when it was changing the name and they did the whole thing. I thought, "Oh god, this is so politically correct." I came out of this meeting and they were changing the name and they said it's gonna be this, this school for diversity, and I said, "Oh god I thought I came here to learn about how they were going to educate the kids and this was, you know, this is the day club [social club]." . . . And then I heard about this little thing, "get-along sessions" or whatever they do on Friday, and I thought, "Oh god, what is this?" But then I think that maybe for a lot of kids it really is an issue and that it's a good thing to do with a lot of the kids. I thought the most important thing was to *educate* them, which I still do, but maybe for inner-city school kids you've gotta do that.

Whereas for Alex you gotta teach him that there is, that they need help, they need to know how to do conflict management, and they need to know how to, how to work something out without their fists or whatever. At first I thought, "I don't want him educated in that, it's just ridiculous," but now I'm starting to see the sense in it.

Implicit in all Mr. Hargrove's comments was a clear sense that the black and Latino students at West City were different from him and his son. He could not relate to them, though he did sympathize. Alex's comment in class was quite similar. It was in some ways a sympathetic comment, but it also implied distance and difference from those whom he spoke of (and sat next to).

Ascriptions of characteristics to other racial groups did not flow in only one direction. Representations and understandings about whiteness were as rampant as those about blackness, if harder to pin down. One day while driving three African American boys (Darnell, Malik, and Thompson) to a school to watch a basketball game, I explained to them that I had never been to that school but my understanding was that it was at a pretty "fancy" place. Malik assured me that it wouldn't be a problem: "Don't worry, Ms. Lewis, Darnell knows how to talk white." Darnell proceeded through a series of impersonations that the other boys practiced imitating in between their fits of giggles. Darnell's impersonations included among others, a haughty, refined accent ("Get me my slippers, Geoffrey"), a hillbilly voice ("Whaddya say, Billy?"), a sort of military tone ("All right, son"), and a repressed sounding teacher ("Okay, class"). This particular incident provided a glimpse of two clear understandings about whiteness. Not only was my signal about class status ("fancy") immediately read as a racial signifier, but the boys' impersonations were almost all voices of authority giving instructions to subordinates. In interviews, these and other boys talked about whites as people who were sometimes racist, often mysterious, and definitely powerful.

The fusion of ideas about race and class, or the imagined link between whiteness and access to resources, proliferated. Ivy's mother, Mrs. Clive, told me a story about Ivy's coming home from school asking why white people all had money and new cars. Ivy explained that all the white people she knew from school (teachers and students) seemed to have a lot more than blacks did. This perception did not by any means imply that Ivy (or any of the other students of color) had any desire to be white. In several incidents black and Latino light-skinned students got angry when they either mistakenly or in jest were called white. Malik wrote a story for Martin Luther King Jr. Day saying that he was grateful for King because his efforts allowed him to have white friends like Julio. On hearing the story read out loud, Julio exploded out of his seat yelling,

"I know you ain't talkin' about me. I ain't white." Julio viewed whites as those who had treated his Mexican family poorly when they first immigrated to the Northwest three years earlier. The hostility of students of color toward whites was sometimes directed toward the few whites in the school; the label "white boy" was used disparagingly in the yard.

In adult discourse, whiteness remained more obtuse as an unspoken referent to the "cultural" behavior of the minority students. As Perry (2001) discusses, whiteness is often understood as a "post-cultural" position within current discourse, which often uses "multicultural" as a code word for racial minorities and thus tacitly labels only people of color as "cultural." To many adults in the West City community, then, whiteness involved those normal or neutral folks to whom Alex's father could easily relate, those whose families spoke in more normal tones, and those who helped their children with homework and sent them to school clean and well fed. Conversely, to many folks of color, "white" referred to those whose behavior Mrs. Fellows had to watch carefully, to whom Ms. Harrison had trouble talking, and to those who regularly directed disrespect toward Mr. Jordan. They were never unaware of the whiteness of the space in which they worked. On more than one occasion one of them referred to West City as a "white" school.

The children and the adults at West City thus had complex understandings of the racial landscape, all of which were at play implicitly or explicitly in their interracial relationships in the school. It is unlikely that the children's understandings—like Ms. Harrison's first-graders' negative perceptions of African Americans and Rodney's ideas about the necessity of prison terms—were generated solely during the students' time in school, but schools are not off the hook. Those in schools need to confront students' understandings of race and difference, to talk about the issue as students already talk about it between and among themselves. For example, in the incident with Rodney described above, after Rodney ran off to play, the teachers talked about the incident as resulting from his individual, distorted (and sad) understanding. They did not see it as a possible window into a more general set of issues that needed to be confronted collectively. Such larger discussions about race rarely took place at West City.

Shared Space but Unshared Understandings and Experiences

My interview with Alex's father illuminates the multiple dimensions of the social geography of race—in this case, the way in which the diverse citizens of Hillside (including West City teachers and parents) have distinct life experiences and distinct understandings of the world, despite sharing a small geographical space. For example, though both Alex's father, Mr. Hargrove, and Thompson's grandmother and guardian, Sadie Davis, talked about being "tired" when I asked about race, they did so for diametrically opposite reasons. Mr. Hargrove just did not want to hear any more about what he believed to be an overplayed subject. As he said to me once, "It's just one of those things I'm just tired of hearing about."

For Mrs. Davis, the African American grandmother of a fourth-grader, it was racism itself that she was tired of and that made her tired. After growing up in the 1950s and 1960s in segregated East Texas, she expected experiences with discrimination just as she expected heat in July. She related a long story of growing up in segregated schools with hand-me-down, broken-down books, of her uncles teaching her how to "yes ma'am" and "no sir" the white folks in town. She spoke of the security guards in the projects where she now lived with her nine grandchildren (a project reported to be the worst in the city on a number of measures). She described how the guards let Samoans get away with everything and always harassed the blacks (even though a group of Samoans sold drugs outside her bedroom window). When I responded by asking Mrs. Davis what impact being black had had on her life, she said, "Ain't played no role." But it became clear that she meant she was not going to let anyone get in her way.

Mrs. Davis had been working at a large discount store for almost a year and had confronted discrimination on a number of levels in that short time. As she explained, "White girls and some nationalities, they come in there and in less than two weeks' worth, they got Level 1. Then to Level 2, Level 3. While the blacks been there almost two years and they still doin' the same thing." Although a white young woman who had started with her had a store shirt within two weeks, Mrs. Davis had to stay there three months before she got hers. "My probation had to be up, I had to be interviewed again, then I could get the shirt. But she didn't, see. See I notice all these things. But like I told them, it doesn't make a difference with me. I said, 'I don't care how you deal with it, I'm not gonna walk away.'"

Recently Mrs. Davis had had a run-in with another white worker. "She look at me and she thought, 'Well this person's black, that's all she used to, just work, work, work.'" When Mrs. Davis arrived at work that day she had three carts full of merchandise to organize and return to the shelves. As she began to work on them, the white woman went and got three more full carts for Mrs. Davis to take care of. As Mrs. Davis put it, "That made six. So I figure let me finish this, then bring some more." Instead the woman took Mrs. Davis to the warehouse and showed her fifteen more full carts, "and she tell me, 'You gonna have to do this before you leave work.'" After the woman left, a co-worker told Mrs. Davis that the woman was just passing her work on to Mrs. Davis, as a supervisor had already told the woman that she was going to have to take care of the carts before she could go home. "And that pissed me off. And see when you like to make me upset, my mind gets real bad, and I don't think right. I went and got in my car and said, 'Send my check in the mail. I don't have to take nobody's shit.' But there's a black lady down in receiving. And she said, 'Sadie,' she said, 'You need to wait and talk to your team leader.' So when he come, he was admirin' how good I work. And I called him over an' I told him about it. And he really got on her case about it."

Not only did Mrs. Davis have to deal with racism at work, but she was sure her grandchildren were going to face plenty of it in their lives. She just wanted to make sure they did not use it as an excuse not to work hard and get a good education. As she said, she was tired not of hearing about race but of having to deal with racism day in and day out.

This pattern was generally true with the parents I interviewed. Whites either did not think race was very important or at least did not perceive it to have played a role for them. They seemed perplexed when I asked what role race had had in their daily lives. At the other end of the continuum, black parents tended to respond by asking rhetorically, "How hasn't it?" Most Latino parents believed race mattered. As one mother, Mrs. Jiminez, stated, "You know that, in a way, there's a lot of racism, and the doors are kind of shut for Latinos." However, many who lived in the large Latino district reported little to no contact with anyone other than other Latino immigrants, and thus they encountered little racism in their daily interactions with other mostly Mexican or Central American Latinos. Even these parents, though, voiced concern about the growing anti-Latino sentiments they saw expressed in the anti-immigrant and antibilingual movements. Importantly, these parents talked about interactions at work or in public institutions (e.g., hospitals) where they felt discarded, ignored, overlooked, and just poorly treated.

Although black and Latino adults both talked about confronting racism, the tenor and the nature of the discrimination they had experienced varied. For example, though both blacks and Latinos felt attacked in public discourse for supposedly "using resources they didn't deserve" (i.e., public assistance), blacks perceived they were labeled as lazy while Latinos felt characterized as interloping foreigners. Blacks were never targeted as noncitizens sneaking across the border to steal jobs from hardworking Americans. They were, however, targeted as a burden to hardworking Americans, as people who would rather accept welfare than work. In parallel fashion, both Latino and black students had some problematic experiences in school, but Latino students received different treatment than did their black peers. As I discuss below, black males were particular targets of negative attention at school, while some Latino children received little attention at all.

"Silence" on Race

In their studies of school desegregation, both Schofield (1982) and Wells and Crain (1997) talk about race being a taboo subject in desegregated schools. They found that, despite significant resegregation within schools through tracking, despite the cultural confrontations and struggles that inevitably accompany the busing in of students of color from far-away neighborhoods, school personnel acted as if race did not matter, and they did not talk about it with the kids.

Similarly at West City, conversations about race seemed to be understood as dangerous talk and as such were generally avoided. Though I identified, or staff identified for me, multiple racial patterns in school practices along with the various racial tensions discussed above and though coded race talk was rampant, explicit discussion of anything racial was avoided by all but a few adults in the school. It was not clear that adults at West City really thought that race did not matter. But they did believe it mattered in ways they could not do anything about (e.g., assumptions about widespread group cultural deficits), in ways they did not understand (e.g., why some children did not respond to their curriculum), or in ways that they felt distinctly uncomfortable about (e.g., large numbers of students of color scoring low on state exams). Teachers at West City, like many others working in underfunded urban public schools, believed they were there to help even though they could be making more money working fewer hours somewhere else. Day to day they were doing what felt like their best.

Under these conditions, talk about race was dangerous: they could be judged as failing, could be accused of racism, could be forced to confront realities that contradicted the racially liberal narrative that framed their professional identities. For all these reasons and more, racial talk was generally avoided and often met with defensiveness when it did occur. For example, after I had been at the school for five months, I had a conversation with the principal about racialized discipline patterns I had observed and asked whether the staff was aware of them. She frankly stated that the staff might acknowledge the patterns but would be quick to explain them as having nothing to do with race. "I think they'd be defensive. But I think they'd know it's true. There are some people here who are very liberal, and would react very defensively like, 'I don't do that,' and 'Of course that's not true.' But when you say, 'Who are the ones you send out?' they would know. 'Well it's [African American boys], but there's a reason, [laughs] they're disrupting my class.'"

As the principal reported, staff were defensive about the racial reality of which they were a part. They believed their hearts and intentions to be in the right place—the fact that their outcomes did not fulfill their objectives was either deflected (as the fault of disruptive students or dysfunctional families) or avoided. When I asked whether they ever talked about any racial issues as a staff, the principal stated that they had not yet but that they were "working on developing that."

In reality, the issue of race did get raised in certain situations, but as Ms. Sullivan, a white third-grade teacher, explained, that happened only when the one or two people of color on staff raised what were perceived to be "their" issues. In fact, Ms. Sullivan was one of the few teachers I spoke to who wanted more of this kind of discussion, who recognized that the school needed more talk about race. But even she could imagine such discussions taking place only if a black person was hired to fill an open slot for the upcoming year. At the moment, she explained, race was raised only when Mr. Ortiz "comes up with 'the Hispanic' stuff." These discussions seemed to be understood as not the white teachers' responsibility, not their area of expertise, or just too sensitive to touch.

When I asked in various ways whether race ever was talked about in relation to children, achievement, or curriculum, Ms. Sullivan replied:

Well only like, you know, like Martin Luther King Day and then African American month is next month. I don't understand why it's not with Martin Luther King month—Mrs. Fellows [the secretary] did that, I think. And then we have the Lunar New Year next week so we'll have to, you hear me, "gotta make sure that we get the Chinese thing touched upon." I don't like it isolated so much. I don't know, I think sometimes if we make it too much an issue, heritage, you know, like foods, customs, on holidays and stuff, to hear all of that is really cool but to make it like an isolated, "gotta make sure I get in the Chinese book next week," you know, that's not right.

Affirming Ms. Sullivan's statement about who brings up racial issues, Ms. Harrison stated that throughout her career, including her time at West City, she had had to be the one who raised issues of race and equity. And this role was never easy. As she said, "I'm pretty outspoken about certain things and in all the public schools I've been in, but the issue of race is always a difficult issue to talk about in predominantly white settings."

Ms. Sullivan was not the only white teacher I spoke to who said the subject of race did not come up unless a person of color on staff raised it. Though Ms. Sullivan was happy to have it raised, others felt somewhat differently. As one teacher stated angrily as she described one of the few meetings where lack of diversity on the staff was raised, "It's okay to criticize white people all the time and I'm sick of it." In fact there had been no direct criticism of anyone at the meeting, but she had taken the emphasis on diversifying the staff to be indirect criticism of the (white) folks presently there. When I asked Ms. Harrison about the meeting, she offered a different analysis:

The thing is, is that teachers in general feel like no one really appreciates us and if you put on top of that, that white missionary-type vibe like—"I'm trying to help these poor kids! I spend [so many] hours here!"—and then there's issues of power of like "What, me give up mine?" I mean the bottom line is, when you talk about diversity of staff it's like "What, me give up my shit? *That ain't gonna happen!*" And it's not going to happen you know. I mean it was an interesting discussion. Yeah when Ms. Sullivan leaves, we might get a person of color, but no one else is going to leave here nor is anyone going to step up and say, "I feel committed to [diversity], it should be a diverse staff and I'm willing to give up [my spot]," *no one's* gonna do that, and that makes all the difference in the world.

Though she was disappointed that the discussion of hiring even one more person of color caused a fuss, Ms. Harrison, as she put it, "was not surprised." As she said at other times in other ways, she understood part of the problem to be that white teachers could not figure out why folks were not more grateful for their presence and sacrifice. The "missionary vibe" that Ms. Harrison found so infuriating in its condescension was exacerbated by her sense that no teachers were going to give up their "mission" for principles of diversity. Thus although teachers took a posture of sacrificing themselves for the good of the children and in the interest of equity, they would not sacrifice their power or position for these same causes. Moreover, this progressive (or "missionary") narrative may well have contributed to teachers' inability to discuss the racial reality surrounding them. Being there "for the good of the children" did not mesh well with the reality of mediocre student outcomes. Thus it became difficult if not impossible to confront a reality that both practically and visibly challenged teacher narratives of helping, sacrificing, and saving. Moreover, resentment quickly arose when teachers perceived themselves to be underappreciated for their sacrifices or (even indirectly) criticized for their lack of success. Similar to the findings of Wellman (1993), Blumer (1958), and others, Ms. Harrison's experience of her white colleagues was of people who were, in important ways, unwilling to yield their power. As she put it, "That ain't going to happen!"

Contrary to Ms. Grant's and Ms. Sullivan's characterizations, however, Ms. Harrison reported that staff talked about race all the time; they just did not do it explicitly. She noted that race was part of many everyday conversations in that (white) staff constantly projected cultural-deficit models onto their students and their families. As she explained, staff might not have "known" they were talking about race, but the code words were clear.[5]

Amanda: When issues of race come up like in the lunchroom or in meetings and staff meetings, how do they usually come up? What usually brings them up?

Ms. Harrison: I think that they come up in an informal way. And I think it's because some of those people are very unconscious that they're talking about race. But I hear discussions and comments. . . . When we're talking about in particular, African Americans, this kind of automatic assumption comes up that these kids live in a dysfunctional family. I think that all teachers don't want to feel that they can't do something for children. So I think that the blaming the children happens quite a bit. Or blaming their family or blaming that they came to us in this broken condition and we just don't have enough resources to fix it.

The kind of language Ms. Harrison describes is not uncommon in current racial discourse. As Essed (1991) and others (Bonilla-Silva 1997; Bonilla-Silva and Lewis 1999; Edsall and Edsall 1991; Omi and Winant 1994) have pointed out, there has been a shift in ways of talking about race in the United States. Although "the traditional idea of genetic inferiority is still important in the fabric of racism, the discourse of black inferiority is increasingly reformulated as cultural deficiency, social inadequacy, and technological underdevelopment" (Essed 1991: 4). Racial ideologies that perpetuate commonsense understandings of racial groups as different (and inferior/superior) have not entirely fallen by the wayside, but they are expressed less in terms of innate characteristics and more in terms of "cultural" attributes, manifested often through the use of code words such as "urban," "inner-city," "welfare," and "crime."

On numerous occasions staff used these and other local variations of code language to talk mostly about black students and their families. Comments about the "project kids," "Barnsworth" folks, or some other variant were usually shorthand references to children or families who were perceived to be missing something, taking up too much energy, or causing problems. Many of the staff would deny that they were talking about race in their diatribes about various families, but their assumptions about families and children were focused specifically on African Americans and drew on common racialized narratives (e.g., families were dysfunctional, chaotic, did not value education, were disorganized).

There were, in fact, often quite distinct characterizations of Latino and black families. For example, one teacher explained differences in achievement this way: "I think Hispanic families are pretty concerned about their kids and really have this deep respect for teachers, and it's not that the teachers will like cater to their kids, it's that the family are checking up on it more and making sure that their kids are doing their homework. And I think [in] a lot of other kids' families it's kind of such a chaos. You don't know if the kids are doing their homework, you don't know when to check up on them, and sometimes there are more kids there, a bunch of kids are living with their grandmother. Like in

Thompson's [an African American fourth-grader's] family." In this case it appears that how parents interact with teachers (deferential, respectful, confrontational) determines whether they are understood to be supportive and functional families. More confrontational African American families or those who were not able to come to school were understood as unsupportive no matter what they were actually doing at home with their children.[6]

This disparaging view of some students and the families and neighborhoods they came from was not unique to the West City staff. In a study of another urban middle school, Noguera (1996: 11) reported teachers' talking about their students' communities as "'unsafe,' using terms such as *dangerous, violent,* and *drug-infested. . . .* One simply stated, 'It's not the type of place where I would want to live or raise children.'" In fact, Mrs. Fellows raised her own children in just such a community. Mr. Jordan grew up and still lived in the Lancaster Valley neighborhood. These black staff members understood these children and their families to be "one of them" and took them on as part of their responsibility.

As Ms. Harrison suggested, some of the remarks of white teachers were intended to deflect blame for school failure from teachers and the school onto children and families. Although teachers were perhaps correct that they and their schools could not do everything, it did not necessarily then follow that children and families were to blame.[7] Moreover, not only did having this particular excuse ready and available make failure easy to explain and thus lighten the pressure to initiate change and improvement, but the excuse itself could be seen as one cause of failure, as it inhibited the potential for families and schools to work together.[8]

Ms. Guzman and Mr. Jordan, the student advisors and two of the uncertificated staff of color in the school, reported similar patterns in the white staff's inability or unwillingness to talk about race even though, as Ms. Guzman and Mr. Jordan asserted, it was a constant issue in school practices. As Mr. Jordan stated, "They don't deal with it, no racial issues are brought up." Like Ms. Harrison though, he quickly corrected himself and explained that race did come up but in more "subliminal" ways: "It comes up all the time but it's not conscious." It was not that teachers simply did not want to talk about these patterns, often they did not even notice them. As Mr. Jordan explained, "I don't think that teachers even understand or see the pattern that the only children being sent out to Ms. Guzman and myself are African American boys." He and Ms. Guzman laughed when I asked whether the staff ever talked about this pattern as a group. Mr. Jordan said:

> I think that there should be some awareness, but when you say that there has to be a boss [school leader], that says, "This overall has to happen," and the

first thing you can do, well the only real thing I've seen is, "Well okay, we'll have a workshop." "We'll have staff development day." "We'll have a training." "We'll have somebody come out here and talk about that." And that's not, that's not how you deal with diversity. That's not how you deal with it, you know, strategies, trainings, and workshops. Don't get me wrong, they're great. They're good, depending on who facilitates them and all, but it's almost like a test or the SATs or something where that's really not what you're going to be doing in the real world. When you're in the classroom it's not a workshop situation.

Mrs. Fellows, the secretary, also raised race as a school issue . She explained to me that one of the reasons she stayed at West City, despite a long commute, was the need to have someone there who would point out racism and protect the African American kids. "If there's some racism, I must say I'm the first to confront it. The teacher or whoever, to let 'em know how I feel. 'Cause I think it just needs to be done. You know, that's all. That's one of the main reasons why I'm staying here, is because of my African American children. I just want to make sure that, you know, they're treated [right]—and I'm in a position right now where I know what's going on. So if I feel there's some injustice goin' on, then that's my job."

Importantly, Mrs. Fellows talked about these students as "my African American children." Just as Delpit (1988), Ladson-Billings (1994), and Foster (1997) have described other school personnel, Mrs. Fellows's perception of the students as her responsibility rather than as "other people's children" is key. She felt a duty to stay in the school precisely because her outlook was different than that of other (white) staff—these were not folks she felt she could trust with her (black) children's well-being. Mrs. Fellows's sense of responsibility for these children was partly about her identification with them—they looked like her. She specifically talked about her criterion for evaluating the school: whether she would send her own children there, whether she would entrust her children to the teaching staff.

The burden of constantly having to raise issues and defend these children could be a heavy one for minority staff members. As Ms. Harrison said, "Sometimes I just want to feel that people on the staff are not my enemies and that we all have the same goals as far as, you know, participating in this environment for children." But she had doubts. She was willing to assume the role of educating her peers because, as she said, "That's what my interests and my studies have been for, for years," but that responsibility could be exhausting. If she needed only to raise issues and educate her peers that would be one thing, but constantly having to edit the expression of her emotions so that people were able to hear what she had to say had left her feeling alienated. "There's this poem by this woman, Cherrie Moraga, 'This Bridge Called My Back,' and I have it in my house, because you know, sometimes I get tired of initiating or explaining this or that. And how I deal with it tends to be through cynicism and humor, which [are] just [ways of expressing] my anger that are more socially acceptable. They are not particularly healthy for me personally, but more socially acceptable. But [it's been a struggle], trying to, as an educator in this district, trying to find a home."[9] The various roles Ms. Harrison took on not only accentuated the differences between staff of color and their white colleagues but highlighted the gulf of understanding that sometimes divided them.

In a different conversation, Ms. Harrison talked about one of the few moments in her career in which a white peer brought race to the surface:

> I was so fascinated when I first came here that Instructor Andrews came up to me, it was after a meeting, [and] said, "How do you feel being like one of the, one of the only black people you know, here at this school," you know. We had some kind of discussion that race came up and I was just really surprised because I've never had a white person come up and ask me how do you feel about being in this situation. And I mean I was so taken aback, I didn't know how to respond. I said, "Wow this is really cool that you think of that," you know, "that I might feel you know slightly uncomfortable or concerned or whatever."

Moments such as this were, as Ms. Harrison said, sometimes initially shocking because of their rarity, but they were met with relief and joy by staff of color because these expressions recognized and made visible what for them was a daily experience of "outsiderness." They acknowledged that though these white and minority staff existed in a shared geographic space, their lived daily reality was often quite different.

The subtle, "subliminal," or inferential ways race surfaced in conversations and practices in the school made the general silence on race particularly disturbing. These silences imposed a high burden on staff of color, who had to negotiate spaces that only occasionally recognized realities they saw and experienced daily. They were even more disturbing when viewed in the light of the racial patterns of discipline and achievement that permeated the school and that had clear long-term ramifications for student success and identity. As I discuss in the next section, the silences around race allowed racial inequality to be reproduced almost without question.

Racialized Discipline and the Exclusion of African American Boys

As alluded to earlier, silence on racial issues did not occur just around staff tension but also in regard to the children. One pattern that became clear during my time in the school was racial patterns in discipline. For example, when a child was being "disruptive," the regular practice was to send that child out of the classroom. This practice had been so overutilized the year before that the student advisors, to whom most students were traditionally sent, were working with the principal to initiate a system whereby teachers would have to demonstrate that they had tried other strategies before calling them. The goal was to make sure that sending children out was a last resort rather a first strategy. Ms. Guzman said:

> I mean we tried to change our discipline policy this year a little bit, and we really tried to put that responsibility on the teacher. "What are you doing before it gets to this point, before you call us?" And there's a little thing they can check, "Okay, I moved his chair." "Okay, put him on time out." "Okay, wrote three checks on the board." "Okay, warned him with a phone call." Then come down and talk to us, because before it was just like for any little thing, any little thing, huh? [to Mr. Jordan; he nods]. "Blah, blah, blah was tying his shoe and wasn't listening to me." "Blah, blah, blah talked back to me or he was talking after I was talking, and he wouldn't be quiet." Put the responsibility on yourself. Take care of it. But that comes along with knowing each child and, like [Mr. Jordan] said, everybody learns differently. You have to sometimes use different strategies to show each child how you want them to behave in the classroom.

Though many teachers continued to call the student advisors regularly, many would, as a second option, send students to Mr. Ortiz's room. When I asked why, he explained, "The truth? Because, it's the reputation that's built up. 'Oh, Mr. Ortiz's mean. Oh, he's gonna yell at you, he'll—he'll get in your face,' basically. So, it gives teachers another—I want to say it's another tool." On most days I was in the school, one or two children would come to Mr. Ortiz's for one to two hours at a time. After several months I realized that almost all the students sent were African American boys (a few were African American girls, and there were one or two Latino boys and one Samoan boy). Though each incident had its own narrative and details, in a school where fewer than 35 percent of the children were African American and slightly less than half of those were boys, it was alarming that upward of 90 percent of students sent to Mr. Ortiz were African American males. When I first asked Mr. Ortiz about these statistics, he hedged for a moment and then confirmed that there were some patterns.

Amanda: Right. But how come it's mostly African American males that are sent here? I mean, they're not even a majority of the school, right? I mean there's more Latino kids in the school than there are black kids, right?

Mr. Ortiz: Yes, exactly. But you're right, I mean overall, if you took, if you took a number, definitely it is [mostly African American boys] sent here. But it does happen occasionally [that other kids are sent]. From Ms. Shafer's room, Jesse, he's Samoan, he's sent up here enough. But, otherwise, you're absolutely correct, you're right, it's more African Americans, it's more males.

I asked the students advisors whether this pattern held for the students they were sent. Both of them responded with a vehement "yes!" They offered their reading of the reasons:

Mr. Jordan: I think that out of all of the groups, [black males] are the most notorious. They have a reputation and [are] probably the most misunderstood. I really think that a lot of people don't understand men on the one hand . . .

Ms. Guzman: [interrupting] . . . or the culture of where they're coming from . . . another thing too to add to that is if the [teachers are] willing to educate themselves about other cultures and not just that superficial, "Okay, Cinco de Mayo, let's have a taco, put up the Mexican flag," you know, right? "Let's do our little Mexican hat dance." It's deeper than that. There's . . . Spanish people at home, we're loud, we're expressive, we use our hands, we talk. Some teachers in the classroom, they think that that's a disturbance, but that's the way that we express ourselves. Now, I've been in African American homes and I know that there's a certain tone in the house but that's a comfortable tone for them, all right? And for me, that doesn't affect me because that's just the way it is in my house, there's a tone. But some people could come from a different culture or background and it's like [leaning back with hands up in front as if to ward off a blow], "Oooh, it's kinda loud." We've been told to be quiet in certain restaurants because we're all talking and, we're not even arguing, we're just talking. I think it's important for people to do home visits. Don't just know that I come to school every day. If you really want to know me, know that I have these many siblings, know that I'm living with my mom or this is my foster parent . . . yeah, my dad is in jail or my dad is on [the street] going like this [with thumb out] to get a ride to go to work. It helps to understand the child; if some of these teachers could take that extra step it might, *might* help. It would be more beneficial to them and for the student to feel more of a connection.

Mr. Jordan: There's sort of like a saying, you know, there's a rule that just says that all children can learn and I think that helps teachers as much as it hurts teachers. They think, "Oh this child can learn so let me just teach." Well, all children can learn but all children can't learn the same way.

These two staff members were speaking to a problem a number of researchers have documented in different settings (Au and Jordan 1981; Cazden 1988; Cazden, John, and Hymes 1972; Erickson and Shultz 1982; Heath 1983; Ladson-Billings 1994; Philips 1972). These authors have long talked about the cultural clashes that take place in the everyday life of schooling and that regularly put nonmajority students at a disadvantage. Language patterns and assessments of communicative competence affect whether children are heard and understood, whether they are read as cooperative and articulate, and also (because of the impact of how it is delivered) what counts as knowledge in the classroom (Cazden 1988). When white, middle-class styles of interaction are considered *the* acceptable mode of school interaction, many students lose out. As Gould (1999: 172) suggests, "When the major institutions in a society are constructed within the culture of and in the interests of one group instead of another . . . [those] organizations may systematically favor the culturally constituted performances of one group over the developmentally equivalent, substantively different, performances of another group." Thus, whether or not students are performing at equivalent levels, the substance of their presentation may lead their performance to be differently evaluated and rewarded. Ms. Shafer, who often sent students out of her room, talked about these kinds of cultural clashes when she explained some of the "behavior problems": "Well, I think part of it is about the inability to teach in a classroom when kids are loud and rowdy. And I think that every African American family that I've called to talk to the parent . . . it's like, Jesse gets on the phone, and there's tons of people, tons of noise, tons of noise stimulation. That's kind of a norm. And that gets brought into the classroom, and it's like, it's not a normal thing for them, for a lot of kids to contain that or to remember to contain it. But in my impatience and intolerance for it . . . [shrugs]."

Although, in part, she understood the clash between what she was comfortable with and what her students were comfortable with, the students were inevitably on the losing end of the exchange. It was their job to contain themselves. Mrs. Fellows talked about this outcome as a deficit in teacher knowledge and skills—a problem of teachers' communicative competence.

A lot of these teachers here at West City, they really want to help but . . . you need to have some training with how to deal with African Americans. Not only African Americans, but even Latins [sic]. My thing is, it's not enough to go to college and get all the kind of degrees you want. It takes commonsense and street smarts to educate children. Okay? And a lot of the teachers here, they don't know how to relate to children of different ethnicities. You know certain kids, they take care of things differently. You know their families take care of things differently, and some people have no understanding.

As Lareau and Horvat (1999) point out, these kinds of clashes are at least in part about social and cultural capital. When students' social and cultural resources are not held as valuable within a social setting, when their learned styles clash with the reigning rules of the institution, when their learned modes of interaction are read as inappropriate or illegitimate, they are systematically disadvantaged (Delpit 1988).

Conflicts in class are not always simply cultural clashes or misunderstandings, however, but often are miscommunications. As Ladson-Billings (1994), Butchart and McEwan (1998), and others discuss, a great deal of child behavior that teachers read as disruptive and in need of elimination can instead be understood not as a sign of disinterest or as an effort to create disorder but rather as clues or information to teachers about a child's needs. In this way behavior can and often should be understood as communication.

Without other avenues available for expressing feelings of frustration, alienation, confusion, or discouragement, students may resort to nonparticipation, calling out, disrupting peers with questions or jokes, or other forms of acting out. In this way student acting out can be as much a product of teacher practices, gaps in instruction, or classroom organization as a manifestation of student deviance. In these cases, "disruptive" behavior represents a need for help, explanation, or motivation. Often, however, rather than understanding noncompliance as being rooted in the class organization, in a lack of instruction, or in a history of poor treatment in school, teachers construct students as the source of the problem, as "disturbances." Moreover, as Ferguson (1998b: 281) discusses, the same behavior can be interpreted differently depending on the race of the students involved. He quotes a study that found white student inattention was read as "an indication of teacher need to arouse student interest," while black student inattention was seen as "boredom due to a limited attention span." Corsaro (1996) found similar patterns in his work on transitions to formal schooling. Zena, an African American girl he had seen as "slightly above average" academically and socially in her African American preschool, had a number of problems in her early years of formal schooling in a predominantly white setting. She had trouble relating to her peers. Her white teacher described her as an "outsider" and as having "attitudinal problems," an outcome, Corsaro argues, of differences in interactive and communicative styles.

Generally, when a teacher responds to "disruption" by removing a student from the class, as was often the case at West City, an important message is conveyed—specifically, a lack of commitment to having that child participate as an equally important learner or member of the class. As the student advisors noted, underlying issues are avoided when teachers call someone else to handle the "disturbance" so they can get on with their job—teaching—and "the issue of race or any other issues aren't addressed." Again, rather than responding to the situation as a pedagogical or curricular issue, the teachers understood the problem to reside within the student; thus the solution was to remove the student. As Mr. Jordan related, teacher behavior suggests that the business of teaching can continue only when the "disrupter" has been neutralized or silenced. The disrupters are then effectively excluded.

Ms. Guzman related an illustrative incident involving a second-grader. Briana Jones was an African American widely recognized in the school as an intelligent child. There was some discussion about having her skip third grade and placing her directly into fourth grade the following year. As was not unusual among low-income urban families, Briana had also experienced a lot of personal tragedy in her life. Not long after learning that Briana's mother had just passed away, Ms. Guzman was called to Briana's classroom by the teacher, Ms. Hill. Ms. Guzman said:

> Briana Jones, now her momma just died, okay. I've known Abby since back in the days, when I was thirteen I met her when she used to work in my mom's job. Nice lady, real nice lady. So, she passes away and I just found out, and things seemed okay. And I hurt for these kids. Okay, in these last couple of weeks [Briana's] flipped out in the classroom, but before she gets to that point of flipping out, it begins with [banging head on the desk in rhythm]. Now you, you can still catch that child doing that before it [claps hands loudly] explodes in your face. Now I walked up there, in fact, *yesterday*. Mrs. Fellows calls me up, says go up to Ms. Hill's room. I went up there. Now everybody is doing literature circle or writing. The only person standing by the bookshelf is Briana, and the only thing she's doing is going like this [imitates her with arms crossed in front of chest pouting]. I'm thinking, "Why can't [Ms. Hill] take care of it. Why doesn't [she] take an interest and find out, 'So your mom died. I understand. Let's talk about some issues. I'm here for you.' Let her know. Take the time out. Sit with her at recess. Loose a *fucking* lunch just to have her come and *sit* with *you* so that she knows that you care." How hard is that? Fifteen minutes? One day out of your week? And believe me, then it's easier because then you bring that child back in and you don't lose her and you don't lose that child in the cracks because she's down here spending time with me. So, when I go to get Briana, [Ms. Hill] had everybody in there doing

their stuff and they were sitting down by themselves and Briana was just
going like this [again imitates her standing pouting]. She was just standing
there refusing to do her work. But, she was getting agitated and it was heading toward that, "I'm going to explode" kind of a thing. So, I took her down
here. And what did we do? It was cooler down here. We brought her work. We
sat down. She didn't want to talk, so that's fine. So we did her work, she did
it while I was sitting next to her, like this close [gestures sitting right next to
her at the lunch-table bench], and I was like, "You okay? Okay. I'm right here.
All right." And she just [imitates child wiping her nose and writing away] and
did her work. She finished it in ten minutes! Like [clapping hands together
once] *this,* man!!!

Briana's nonparticipation or "acting out" was directly related to her life outside of school. Her behavior was most likely not a deliberate attempt to subvert
the teacher's authority but involved her emotional vulnerability. Ms. Guzman
explained that all Briana needed was someone to recognize that she was going
through a hard time. Ms. Guzman described her own success with children as
being a combination of knowing them well, listening to what they were telling
her, and then integrating that information into her practice. In this case she was
upset that Ms. Hill could not make a few small adjustments for a child who was
having a hard time but who was generally trying.

Though it might on the surface be factually accurate to describe some of the
behavior of students who were banished as "disrupting the class" or "interrupting the learning process," this could be true only if one assumed that learning includes only the academic or intellectual curriculum and that all students
should be learning material in identical ways. If one understands learning to
extend beyond intellectual issues, to include social and relational issues as well,
it is clear that once a student has been excluded from a class, the opportunity
to teach that student other ways of getting his or her needs met is lost. For
example, Ms. Guzman spent a few minutes with Briana after she had finished
her work, finding out what had happened and helping her to strategize other
ways of dealing with her frustrations.

[I brought up] the child's name that Ms. Hill gave [as part of the reason for
Briana's] refusing to work. I said, "What about Benny Flint?" And she said, "I
don't want to work with him." I said, "why?" "Because he don't know nothin."
I said, "But you know what, do you think Ms. Hill sat you with him because
she believes you're like this intelligent person and you know how to spell, you
know how to read, and you could go like this [slaps hands together], but he
needs help?" "Yeah, he needs help." "I know he needs help. You know he
needs help." And she said, she thought about it and she said, "Yeah." I mean,

I said, "Next time, if she sits you with him or someone else, you could always ask her, 'I don't feel like helping him today.' You, you can tell her that. Or you could say, 'Could you ask somebody else to help him today? I don't feel like it. You need to let her know with 'I' messages, too. She'll understand."

Mr. Jordan and Ms. Guzman, like Ms. Grant, talked about Mr. Ortiz as one of the only other people on the staff who dealt with similar issues in his class. As I have discussed, Mr. Ortiz's classroom-management strategies had some drawbacks, but it was quite true that he, like Mrs. Fellows and the student advisors, considered the students in his class to be his responsibility and the business of teaching to include explicit lessons about how to function in a classroom. This inclusive conception of learning is, as Delpit (1988) and others have discussed, essential for those students whose cultural resources are not valued in school. The rules of what Delpit calls the "culture of power" should be made explicit and taught, rather than assumed and put to use implicitly without explication. Only in this way will disenfranchised students who come from racial, class, and cultural groups not represented in the hierarchies of schools have any chance of succeeding under a set of rules they otherwise do not know or understand (Delpit 1988). Only in this way will white students come to recognize their own understandings of norms and values as specific rather than normal or universal.

Ms. Sullivan expressed a similar sentiment when we talked about these patterns. She said that it did not occur to her to send a child out of the classroom because once she had, she could no longer have any impact. Although she was disturbed about racial patterns in discipline in the school, trying to confront what she perceived to be, at the least, faulty educational practice would have violated her interpersonal style (because it would mean making people uncomfortable). It would also violate the well-established norm in school that one does not comment on a peer's pedagogical choices—classrooms are individual fiefdoms. Consequently, though she was outraged by what she perceived to be misconceived and unjust practice and though she considered herself an advocate for disfranchised children, she did nothing beyond the confines of her room. The only change in behavior I did notice over the course of my stay there was that she pulled further and further away from collective planning with the other teachers, organized more single-class activities for her students, and generally retreated into her room—at least with regard to school activities and issues.

While Ms. Sullivan's strategy was to retreat, Ms. Harrison utilized different tactics. As discussed earlier, she raised racial issues periodically, though with some cynicism. She also spent a lot of time talking with friends and peers outside of school. As she revealed, her own blackness did not make her immune;

racist presumptions and their pervasive messages about black deviance had also invaded her psyche. These were issues she constantly struggled with and talked about because she knew it was her problem, not the children's. She struggled because she recognized that the power she had as a teacher could have a deleterious impact on her students if not wielded with care, that it could enable her to turn her problem into their problem:

> I think teachers have limited resources, abilities, and probably desires for dealing with African American children in general and boys in particular. Sometimes I think if you look at African American boys as a cultural group, I think that this environment is more alien to them than other situations. In elementary school, structurally and everything, it's from a very Eurocentric viewpoint, even just looking at the environments. But I think it's also very female. I mean even looking at my experiences, the children who tend to get to me the most are African American boys. I always have to go back and think about what it is in their behavior, about what they're doing, and what is it in *my* behavior that is contributing to it. I also have to look to find situations where I can talk about that—which are very limited. I'll go to conferences and I do have African American teachers that I talk to and friends and stuff in general, but that's something that's always an issue.

She talked about going outside of West City to find assistance. In the context of our conversation, it became clear that she did so both because at West City she was cast as a racial expert (which made it difficult to give voice to her own confusion and struggles) and because she did not trust her peers there in regard to these issues.

Some of these patterns are clearly gendered. Some of the pervasive ideas about blackness did not apply to black girls. For example, teacher struggles with African American males were an issue not only of culture and linguistic style but also of what Mr. Jordan captured when he said black boys were the most "notorious." This is not to say, however, that being black did not affect African American girls' school experiences. For example, Lynette, an African American fifth-grader who had regular conflicts with Mr. Ortiz, clearly understood his ability to get away with certain kinds of treatment as being about the students' minority status. On several occasions when she witnessed me taking notes during one of Mr. Ortiz's diatribes, she leaned over and, whispering, asked whether I was going to show my notes to the school board. Loquita, Ivy, and other African American girls had particularly close relationships with Mrs. Fellows, the secretary, and regularly went to her with claims of discriminatory treatment by teachers or staff. Black girls' blackness did affect their schooling experiences but not in the same way as it affected black boys.[10]

Racist notions about African Americans generally and black males in particular pervade our social context; teachers are not impervious to their impact (Hopkins 1997). For example, I was startled one day in the lounge when the teachers, trying to get me to apply for an opening at the school, quite seriously commented to one another that I would be great because I "wasn't afraid of the kids." Later, when I joked with Mr. Ortiz about the idea of being afraid of eight-year-olds, he offered this interpretation of the comment:

> Well—it's like—I'll give you an example. You put on a news program—CNN, ABC, NBC, CBS. Look at the news. And you'll see increasing numbers of aggravated assaults by youngsters. I think it gets translated back, saying, "I heard in the news last night that a twelve-year-old was arrested for aggravated assault with a weapon. And I have eight-year-olds but one of those eight-year-olds is a little larger than the rest . . . " So I believe that that adds to the apprehension. And then I think that again we're going to come back to race because I think that some teachers, they hear, "Oh, African Americans. I'm not gonna get involved with their families." "Latinos, I'm not gonna get involved with their families." Why? Because they hear in the news about gang shootings, drive-bys, car jackings, again—I mean I may be way off, but—I really feel more and more that what individuals see and hear then gets translated and it gets convoluted. Because I agree with you—it's a thirty-year-old [whose talking about being afraid of an] eight-year-old.

Every staff person of color I spoke to about African American students in the school at one point or another suggested that fear was at play. In a conversation in the hall, Ms. Harrison told me she had "even seen teachers who, even on the kindergarten level, you know, are very fearful of African American boys."

Some black parents I spoke to were worried about the treatment of their children in school. They were struggling, however, with the powerful school narrative alluded to earlier that suggested they or their children were to blame. Ms. Jones-Washington, whose son Darnell, a fifth-grader, was quite bright but had only recently been recognized as such, had struggled with these issues for years.

Amanda: Have you been happy with the school overall?

Mrs. Jones-Washington: Its been okay, but I feel like it can be better. We've struggled so long with the behavioral thing. This is the first year that he was actually a "good student" and all of that.

Amanda: What do you think the behavioral stuff was about?

Mrs. Jones-Washington: Two things, I think partly I worked at night for three years, and I had to break his sleep every night so he was tired, and the other thing is he had a lot of anger issues about his father [who was largely unavailable], and he would take out his anger in the classroom. That's what I guessed because outside school people would always say what a "good kid" he was, you know like at church or anybody else that was around us, and he became a "demon" at school.

Amanda: Have you worried about racism at all at West City since you've been there?

Mrs. Jones-Washington: Well, actually it was an issue. I have wondered about it a lot. Because I really feel that everybody speaks to cultural diversity and how we're all equal and all this and they pay lip service to all these things but I think really they . . . you have to respect the cultural differences. There's differences in the way African American males behave. I noticed the first couple of years at West City, like the kids that they label as the problem kids, the behavioral problem kids, were always the African American males, not the girls but the boys, so I went through all the hoops like, you know, I did all their recommendations just to make sure it wasn't any of the things that they said it was, but then none of it seemed to help and I was always concerned about [racism].

Mrs. Jones-Washington had for years been concerned about what her son was not learning academically. As she stated, "I get worried about him though because, he's really bright, but he doesn't know as much as he should as far as like cursive writing or like he should be further along in his math now, and I don't see a lot of math homework." Yet, in most interactions with teachers she found herself on the defensive, having instead to talk about or explain her child's behavior. Thus the focus remained on what he was doing rather than on what he was not learning. Though she wondered about racism, she still felt obliged to try all the school's recommendations to make sure it was not her fault or some inherent problem in her child (after all, the teachers were the experts). Mrs. Jones-Washington herself had a long history of poor treatment and low expectations in school. As she explained, in both high school and college she and her African American peers had been made to feel inferior. It had taken her years to rebuild her self-esteem. In fact, because of her own school experiences and Darnell's at West City, Mrs. Jones-Washington decided to pull him from the top academic middle school to which he had first been assigned for the next year (one that was predominantly white and Asian) and to enroll him instead in a black-focused and black-run alternative public middle school near where they lived. She felt the social costs of going to the high-performing white school were such that it was worth the risk academically to send him to the new black school. She believed that he was more likely to succeed in a place where he felt less alienated, even if the resources were not as good. "I don't want him to have to, I mean speaking of race relations, I don't want him to have to be pressured by racism right now, having that as a problem, as an obstacle, and it was a hard decision to make, but just based on my own experiences, I just decided it might be better for him." She was already struggling with how to talk to him about the racism he would confront in the world and did not want him to have to face it in his classes everyday at school.

Early in the year I was amazed to learn that Darnell, the charming young man I had been so impressed with and whom I had casually assessed to be one of the smartest children in the class on almost every measure, had for most of his elementary years been on the verge of referral to special education. By his fifth-grade year, Darnell was almost unanimously recognized as the student leader in the school: kindergartners raced to hold hands with him in morning circle; students fought to be on his basketball team; teachers joked with him at recess; upper-grade girls pined after him. Rodney, an African American fourth-grader, once called Darnell his hero. Yet, for years teachers had been calling Mrs. Jones-Washington up almost weekly, if not daily, to complain about him. She had been at her wit's end before he got into room B2 and Mr. Ortiz got "control." By the time I met him at the beginning of fifth grade, Darnell already had a tenuous relationship to school. He was quite aware of his contradictory location there. Though he was quite popular, he also knew, as he explained to me, that he used to be one of the "bad" kids. In many ways he seemed confused about whether the labels of a "bad" and possibly "slow" student described who he was or whether these were just mislabels applied while he had been cutting up with his friends and getting in trouble. Darnell was struggling with one of the central quandaries of identity—how to grapple with external ascriptions that differ from one's inner sense of self.

One result of these various contradictory inputs was Darnell's ambivalence about his own intellectual abilities. Though at moments Darnell came off as confident, what some teachers regarded as "arrogant, " he was also deeply insecure about his own abilities. Though he was further ahead than most of his peers, he understood that he did not know many things fifth-graders were supposed to know. As I explained Roman numerals to him one day, he grew frustrated and said, "I should already know this, shouldn't I?" This ambivalence also manifested itself during standardized testing. In every formal testing situation during the year, Darnell would inevitably throw a minor tantrum. At the beginning of the timed period, he would go right to work and plow through early answers, seeming confident and capable. Within minutes, however, as he came across answers he was unsure about, he would just stop, refuse to go on, throw the papers, break his pencil in half, push the papers aside, put his head down, or just space out and play with whatever he had in his pocket. Darnell had found a strategy to save face when confronted with a set of exams that had every year led to the report to his mother that he was an underperformer or, less positively, not capable academically—he just did not participate. Then, no matter what the outcome, he would know he had not even tried. He rendered the results meaningless. Darnell was not the only student who altogether rejected these exercises. Malik (another African American fifth-grade boy) would either copy from whoever was next to him, even if that student was doing a different test, or take the first few minutes of the exam to fill in all the bubbles on the answer sheet before even looking at the questions. Although Malik was below grade level academically, Darnell was not. He just lacked confidence in his ability to perform well on these imposed tests. So he opted out, subverting the process altogether.[11]

Claude Steele and his colleagues have developed a set of theories to explain not only African Americans' underperformance in schools and on exams but these kinds of responses to the testing situation itself. As Steele (1999: 46) writes, "stereotype threat" involves the "threat of being viewed through the lens of a negative stereotype, or the fear of doing something [e.g., performing badly on a standardized test] that would inadvertently confirm that stereotype." Multiple experimental situations confirmed that when stereotype threat arose, testers performed worse than would be predicted based on their ability. One solution for those experiencing the stress of this kind of threat is to, as Steele (1999: 46) puts it, "disidentify" with the arena in which the pain arises. This "disidentification" can take the form of rejection of whole arenas, like school; it may also take the form of merely learning to care less about situations or activities (e.g., testing) in which stress arises.

Darnell had high aspirations. For him, maintaining these aspirations did not involve the traditional track of excelling on tests but rather disengaging with those parts of school that told him he was incapable and unlikely to succeed. However, as Steele (1999: 46) states, "This withdrawal of psychic investment . . . can have real costs." Those reviewing Darnell's standardized test scores will not likely interpret them as psychic withdrawal or disidentification but as a sign of his aptitude.

The various school practices that demonize, ostracize, label, or otherwise exclude African American boys have a negative impact on those targeted. And those who sit in class with them everyday, who see them disciplined, kicked out, and excluded, are not immune to these impacts. When I was talking to Ms. Guzman, the student advisor, about my early surprise at Darnell's history in school, she related the story, recounted earlier, about Briana's being sent out of class. In this case, a child's emotional turmoil was translated into deviance or misbehavior and then punished. Briana's classmates, rather than learning empathy for a grieving peer and how to provide comfort and accommodation during such a time, learned to see her as a troublemaker who would not do her work. Moreover, not only were they learning about her but she was learning about them. As Briana talked to Ms. Guzman about her behavior, Briana easily placed her peers along a continuum of "smart, not smart." Ms. Guzman said, "And then we were talking about, we were looking at her class list and I said, 'Briana you're so smart! Who else is pretty smart like you?' I said, 'Let's look it over.' We talked about the class list and I said, 'How about Jeremy Wilson?' And she was like, 'um . . . half.' 'How about blah-blah-blah?' 'No, he needs help with his spelling.' She knows, right?" This was one example of the clear lessons children were learning about their peers' dispositions and abilities.

One day, while standing in the park helping to supervise three classes out enjoying a beautiful spring day, I noticed a row of six African American boys of different ages, sizes, and hues sitting on a bench, lined up, in trouble, watching as their peers played in the park. As their legs dangled over the edge of the bench, they occasionally yelled to their friends who were playing a game nearby, leaned forward to try to see the game, or called to their teacher to see how much more time they had. When I asked Ms. Shafer, with whom I was standing, how she thought other students interpreted discipline patterns captured at that moment by the benching, she said, "I think other kids probably do think black boys are more unruly, but I don't think they have like any deep thoughts on why. They probably just know it as a fact."

That the children probably did not have any deep theories was precisely what was so powerful, though—they just knew "as a fact" that black boys are unruly. Rather than having any understanding of a social or cultural institutional context that constructs that supposed "unruliness," they understood it as a problem located within the minds, hearts, and bodies of those boys. Not only were students understood to be deviant, but their rightful place in classrooms was undermined every time they were sent from the room. As Ms. Harrison put it, "[It sends the message to the other kids that] there is something wrong with them. You know, that they don't belong here. Yeah, that they really don't belong here." At the center was an issue of membership: Who were "real" members of the school or class community? Who belonged?

Latinas: Forgotten, Overlooked, or Just Ignored
The flip side to the kind of racialization or demonization that African Americans, and black boys in particular, faced at West City was the absence of

attention given to Latinas. Latinas expressed their alienation from school as silently as African American boys did loudly. In many ways their silence was just as potent and destructive as the negative attention black boys got: these girls' needs still were not recognized or addressed. As much literature has discussed generally, girls' silence in school fits well with the desired mode and is interpreted as understanding or cooperation (or both) (Sadker and Sadker 1994). However the Latinas' silence went beyond good behavior to a particular kind of nonparticipation, a pattern that did not receive much attention because the girls were not interrupting or getting in anyone's way. Latinas, as I will discuss, often felt confused or disengaged, but they acted out their problems by retreating rather than by making noise or asking for assistance.

Several months into the study I was looking through my fieldnotes and noticed that though Latinas constituted the largest group at two of the schools where I was working, they rarely showed up in my fieldnotes. Not only were they not getting attention from teachers, they were not getting much of my attention. Though I had noted the patterns in their interactions with peers (they almost always spent their free time with other Latinas), my only other minor notations were comments like "Catherine sits quietly in the corner doing her work," "Lucia is spacing out," "Gloria is drawing rainbows on her binder." As I shifted the focus of my observations, I began to notice all the ways they ducked attention, avoided being called on, or gave quick responses and then retreated. There were a few exceptions: a middle-class biracial (Latino/white) child who hung out with other white students and was quite vocal in class; and the daughter of politically active parents (one of whom had been a PTA officer for several years), who was quiet but often raised her hand to answer questions. Otherwise this sizable group of students remained mostly silent and often invisible in the classroom. With few exceptions, they neither demanded nor received much attention.

Gloria, Jessica, Laura, and other Latinas would sit quietly, doodling, staring, and waiting during all the various confrontations between Mr. Ortiz and one or another student in the class. They shared occasionally during sharing time, giggled or blushed during compliments, lined up quietly when the recess bell rang, and worked patiently, cooperatively, and anonymously. However, with the exception of Catherine, they were often among the last to finish assignments or were among the "nonfinishing" group. They toiled away at their desks, confused, asking help only of each other if they were sitting close enough. Often when I circulated while the class was completing a worksheet, I would discover one of them doodling on the corner of the sheet or doing the assignment incorrectly. Yet, unlike their white, African American, or male peers, they rarely asked questions or requested help. As a result, their questions went unanswered, and they rarely got assistance. Because the class had plenty of squeakier wheels, their needs often went unmet. As the following examples show, this was not a benign neglect.

Gloria, a fourth-grader, was often on the lowest priority list. Not only was she quiet during class, but her skill levels were neither so high nor so low as to draw attention her way. She got by. She got along well with the other children but spent almost all her time with two other Latinas in class. Though Mr. Ortiz would speak highly of her if asked, in many ways she was losing out in the class. For example, when early in the first semester Mr. Ortiz was organizing reading groups, he did so based on observations he had made over the first month of school. No systematic assessment was done. There were two high groups, two middle groups, and two low groups. Gloria was bumped around several times—not because of her reading level but because he was not sure where she fit and because she got along well with other children. Almost as an afterthought, she was finally put in a low reading group because she was likely to help the children in it stay on task. Gloria went from the second highest to the second lowest reading group in a matter of minutes. In fact, Gloria's mother was concerned about Gloria's academic progression since their arrival from Mexico. She explained that when she brought Gloria to the United States from Mexico, Gloria already knew her multiplication tables and how to do division, and she was a good reader. "Here she has gone down. She was in second grade there, she's now in fourth grade, and she doesn't know how to multiply. . . . And she already knew all that, so she has gone down a lot."

Catherine was a fifth-grader who, like Gloria, was neither excelling in school nor falling far behind. She came to school everyday, hung up her book bag, grabbed her completed homework or her signed field-trip slip, and sat at her desk waiting. Though Catherine was not as far behind as some other students, her mother, like Gloria's, was unhappy with the class: "Well I'm a little unhappy because, for example, she's already in fifth grade, and until now they have just started teaching her math; *until now* they have started . . . when she was in third grade she didn't know anything yet, she didn't know the numbers very well, she didn't know how to read. . . . I don't know if it was our fault or what, that we didn't pay as much attention in her learning how to write, or read, or I don't know, maybe it was more our fault because we didn't make her write more often." Like other parents, Mrs. Padilla worried about Catherine's education but was not sure whom to blame—herself, her daughter, or the school. Here we can see the power of popular narratives that say minority families are to blame for their children's academic shortcomings. In this case, even when her daughter was not being taught any math in school, Mrs. Padilla wondered "if it was our fault." This construction not only leads low-status parents like Mrs. Padilla to question themselves but leads them to less often do what other parents (e.g., white, middle-class parents) readily do—blame the school, demand more, and hold the school accountable for their children's learning.

Rebecca, a fourth-grade Latina, showed up at West City in early September, recently arrived from Mexico. Because she had little to no knowledge of English, it was unclear why she was placed in Mr. Ortiz's class. Though he was bilingual, the class was not designated bilingual. Mr. Ortiz talked about getting Rebecca into a bilingual class in another school, but the move never happened. She struggled along, spacing out a lot of the time. Occasionally a student nearby would translate for her, but the general technique was sink or swim. For example, I recorded this series of exchanges in the early part of the year: "Mr. Ortiz started the day with compliments, asking them to compliment each other's eyes. They begin with Mike who goes to his right and tells Daniel he likes his eyes. Daniel thanks him and then turns to his right. . . . When the circle gets around to Rebecca, who has been staring at the wall, she is startled. Six kids simultaneously lean forward and translate for her what is going on." As this example shows, even if Mr. Ortiz did not want to do a lot of translating for Rebecca, others in the class could have helped. He rarely asked them to and sometimes chided them for doing so.

In the first two hours of school one morning, I captured some of the many mixed messages about language that students got. During the morning assembly, I was standing next to Julio. We had been chatting before the whistle blew for whole-school circle time. The students began reciting the pledge of allegiance in English and then in Spanish. When we got to the pledge in Spanish, Julio suddenly fell silent. I leaned over and told him he needed to participate. Julio replied that he was not going to say the pledge in Spanish. When I asked him why not, he responded that he did not know it. "Don't you know how to speak Spanish?" I asked. "Yes." "Well then translate as we go along," I said. Julio looked at me and stated defiantly, "I don't want to. I hate Spanish; it's a stupid language." Startled I responded, "Spanish is a beautiful language; I wish I could speak it." Angrily he replied, "Then come to my house and my mom can talk to you." He stood still, daring me to try and make him do something. I put my arm around his shoulders and finished doing the pledge with the rest of the school. Later that morning I filled Mr. Ortiz in on my exchange with Julio. Mr. Ortiz was upset, saying it was "a tragedy" but clarifying for me that probably a lot of others in Julio's generation feel that way. "It's way too common." Yet, later that day during math time, I witnessed the following in his class: "Rebecca is called on to give the answer to 32/8 and she says *quatro* and then corrects herself and says four. Mr. Ortiz says, 'Look, Becky, you're in America now, let's use English, not that Spanish stuff.'" Although sometimes other students remarked admiringly about the ability to speak two languages, there were also lots of disparaging remarks. One day Laura was explaining something to Rebecca, and Darnell snapped, "You all need to speak in English, damn!" Laura told him to shut up and then finished what she was saying, but Rebecca seemed taken aback and was particularly quiet for the rest of the morning.

The categories I have used to talk about racial practices in the school reflect general patterns and are not exhaustive. For example, one Latina was often in trouble—usually for "whining" about not understanding what was going on. Yet, because she would usually listen after being told once to be quiet, her confusion was rarely addressed. Patterns with Latino boys and African American girls were less clear than with the Latinas and black boys. Some were near the top of the class and some were at the very bottom. They were loud, quiet, and in between. They were not ignored, nor did they receive an inordinate amount of positive or negative attention. As I discuss further in Chapter 5, though, much of what went on in school clearly affected their understandings of their own and others' racial/ethnic identities. Similarly, although the few white students in the class were neither particularly silent nor particularly vocal, they were in a confusing and sometimes difficult position as a small but visible minority. Their situation was rarely discussed. It is not difficult to understand why these white students felt separate from much of what went on. Though the school served many of their needs, it did not help them understand the racial realities of which they were a part. There were exceptions. Ms. Shafer was particularly concerned about the only white student in her class, Josh, who was bright but "nerdy" and was often a target of other students' teasing. He reminded her of herself as a child, and when he was called "white boy" in the yard, she called a class meeting to talk about experiences they all had had with prejudice. Ironically it was the first time it occurred to her to discuss issues of race and prejudice.

Recognizing and Confronting Racial Realities

In many ways, teachers at West City did not talk about group-level patterns in achievement or discipline because naming or identifying such patterns flies in the face of the individualistic, meritocratic ideology that dominates in schools (Apple 1982, 1990; MacLeod 1995; McQuillan 1998). Discussing the patterns also seemed especially difficult because the teachers appeared not to know what to do about them. Moreover, acknowledging, for example, that black students were failing felt racist if doing so somehow implied that something was systematically wrong with the students, but it also had the potential of labeling the staff members themselves as inadequate if the situation was constructed as the school's fault. Busy, underfunded schools have few if any procedures in place to confront the institutional and social mechanisms that set teachers and their students up to fail.

Teachers' denial about or avoidance of racial issues may also have been somewhat functional to the extent that it allowed the school system to continue to work "smoothly." Though it was not "functional" with regard to equity issues, it did keep conflict muted. Schools necessarily juggle competing priorities on a daily basis; the many demands of keeping a school working sometimes make discussions about difficult issues seem like minefields—best avoided. As long as school personnel were able to limit racial conversations to those that could take place within existing routines, they not only avoided potential conflicts but also forestalled having to develop new mechanisms to deal with racial issues. Without confronting these realities, however, staff members in schools allow them to be reproduced with little interference. As a result, teachers participate, even if unwittingly, in the production of another generation of underprepared and disenchanted students of color. With students for whom excelling in school is one of few roads to future success, this outcome is especially troubling.

Malik, one of the fifth-graders in Mr. Ortiz's class, never had much going for him. He had seen much violence in his ten years. He had lost both parents to drugs and violence. His current guardians were overstressed, and rumors suggested they were involved in drug dealing. Yet he came to school every day and usually started out with a smile. He skipped lunches to work with me on math. But, by the end of the year, when he missed graduation because of a suspension, it was hard to imagine a positive outcome for him. Here he was, ten years old, and though his fate was not sealed, it potentially had been stunted. When he entered school as a kindergartner he was, his teachers informed me, as excited as any child, ready to learn. Something transpired during the next years that led him to be a skeptical fifth-grader, one whom the principal felt was unlikely to make it through seventh grade. Because the social pressures, challenges, and distractions increase in middle school, along with class size and student anonymity, it was hard to imagine how he could sustain his optimism. In January, Malik and his brother were kicked off the bus and missed school for a week. There was no transportation at home. Their guardians threatened to pull them out of school when it looked as if they would not be allowed back on the bus for over a month. Malik's tutor and social worker worked with the principal and the bus company to get them back on. But efforts like that were not likely to continue when he arrived at his middle school of more than a thousand students. Teachers at West City might protest that there was never much they could have done for Malik. Some I spoke to claimed students like him were "doomed" from the start. Yet Malik did not begin his school years disenchanted and disengaged. Even when I knew him, he still firmly believed that school was his chance. He was, as Ferguson (1998a, 1998b), Conley (1999), and Mickelson (1990) discuss, like most African Americans, who believe strongly in education in the abstract but also have somewhat cynical views of their own concrete chances of gaining access to a good education.

Rather than accepting the failure of large numbers of students of color as part of the normal outcome of schooling, we must recognize that these students enter school with hope and momentum. What energy interfered, what action occurred to reverse the momentum and to dampen their hope? The teachers I knew at West City cared about those children, labored for them, and persisted for them. They were underpaid and worked under difficult and challenging conditions. Why did their good intentions too often not translate into good outcomes?

First and foremost, people cannot fix a problem that they do not see. If personnel cannot see or recognize the ways the school is systematically underserving certain children, then little will be done about it. Second, teachers have not found the means, the courage, or the understanding to confront, to recognize, and then to do something about the way race shapes much of what transpires in their school community. Ms. Harrison once called West City a "white school," despite its preponderantly minority student body. I asked her to explain:

> Systematically being in a public school institution—for instance the schedule. I mean everything, from the most minor thing of how the bell rings to the way we line up, to our emphases academically—how we do language arts, math. Not to say that I would do away with all of it, you know. The kids supposedly go to school to take orders and go to school to get a job and do something, but I'm not clear what exactly we want them to do. That's always been kind of confusing, I'm not as sure as I used to be when I was younger. The administration also, I mean you know, it's primarily a white teaching staff. Even the events we have, I think it's a very Eurocentric view of like these holidays and assemblies and history months, you know.

Until white teachers at West City can recognize and confront their own whiteness, the limits of their understanding of others, their fears of being called racist, and the racist notions that inevitably pervade their understandings, students like Malik, Julio, Catherine, and Darnell will not be well served. It is true that teachers cannot feed and clothe students, provide jobs for their parents, or make sure their homes are clean and their neighborhoods safe, but they can help students understand the world they actually live in. Rather than reproducing meritocratic myths about individual success and failure, they can help students understand that they live in a society where some have more opportunities than others—a world created by and transformable by everyday people—thus moving closer to the vision Giroux (1988: xxxii) suggests of schools as "public places where students learn the knowledge and skills necessary to live in an authentic democracy." In this way, teachers can address the reality of racial inequality that pervades the larger context and help students to question and challenge the racial messages that pervade the culture and that they bring to school with them. African American and Latino children understand that they will face discrimination. Avoiding talking about race does not reduce its impact. Nor is failing to talk about race and racism a neutral act; it enables the reproduction of the status quo—a status quo that is deeply and broadly unequal.

Other researchers have documented the way race becomes a taboo subject in schools (Schofield 1982; Wells and Crain 1997). Whites resolutely avoid the subject. Others (primarily people of color) regularly talk about race or racism, but when they do so publicly, they pay for their expressions or "transgressions" in feeling alienated, expending a lot of energy, being labeled, and having to contain their anger and frustration. So race becomes an issue constantly at play but only rarely named. Though it is the covert subject of many conversations and though racial code words proliferate ("ghetto kids," "project kids," "Barnsworth kids," "macho kids," "inner-city kids"), the subject itself seldom breaks the surface. Race shapes understandings, attitudes, and behavior; race affects where students live, whom they play with, and where they go to school; and race shapes how kids understand their life chances. Ironically, though it is often at play in children's conversations with each other, the adults in their lives are often afraid to step in and engage them on the subject.

In the next chapter I talk about a school where racial realities were at least confronted if not always transformed, where racism and power were talked about and struggled with. Though the outcomes weren't necessarily all that different, this next setting does provide some idea of what it would mean to try to initiate change—perhaps giving students like Malik the chances they deserve.

Four

Breaking the Silence

*Race, Culture, Language,
and Power at Metro2*

In demographic composition (including student body and staff), curricular focus, location, and language policy, Metro2 had a complex racial and cultural landscape that many would define as a Latino space. Yet during my time at the school, more than one staff member referred to it as a "white school." Why? What did they mean by "white"? This paradox lies at the heart of much of what went on at the school. Metro2 was distinguished by its efforts to create a new kind of school and initiate new results, yet in many ways its outcomes were not always that different from those of other schools. At its center the school was full of lived contradictions. At some moments it seemed a multicultural institution. At others, it seemed to be just a slightly different version of other high-functioning, highly-sought-after alternative urban schools dominated by white, middle-class families and students. As I discuss, much of the power to shape and influence the school remained in the hands of high-status (mostly white) parents. Thus though the school operated in many culturally progressive ways, the personnel's collective efforts to subvert traditional racial hierarchies still faced many challenges.

Like West City and Foresthills, Metro2 struggled with issues of racial equity. However, many of Metro2's struggles, unlike those at the other schools, occurred in the open. Racial discourse in the school was more explicit than implicit; issues of equity and access were talked about openly and often. As I describe below, Metro2 was not an alternative school merely in its academic focus; it presented an "alternative" racial space in which current racial hierarchies and meanings were acknowledged and contested rather than ignored. However, Metro2 also demonstrated even more powerfully than the previous

87

two schools just how deeply the current racial formation is entrenched. The progressive racial discourse, the committed staff, and the multicultural curriculum—all of which recognized and attempted to address inequities locally and beyond—were moving the school in a different direction. Yet, for important reasons, these forces were not enough to fully mitigate the powerful racial realities that schools like Metro2 confront.

The Setting

Metro2 was an alternative school organized around a Spanish-language immersion program. Spanish was the primary language in the school both for instruction and for almost all informal teacher-student and staff interactions.[1] Though ideal enrollment for this kind of language program is one-third Spanish-dominant students, one-third bilingual students, and one-third English-dominant students, the Metro2 student body was two-thirds English-dominant and one-third bilingual/Spanish-dominant. Moreover, few of those entering kindergartners listed as "bilingual" were truly bilingual. In my conversations with them, several teachers reported that even children whose parents listed them as bilingual and who came from bilingual households often came in English-dominant and speaking only a little Spanish. This gap between ideal and real enrollment resulted from the ways students were assigned to schools in the district as a whole. Because Metro2 was an alternative school, students were admitted through a separate enrollment process in which parents had to fill out a set of forms requesting the school. (Otherwise the children were automatically assigned to their neighborhood school. See Chapter 6 for more details about this process.) The paperwork had been simplified somewhat recently, but the process was still complicated. As a result, savvy middle-class families took the best advantage of this optional enrollment process and were thus overrepresented in the city's cadre of "highly acclaimed" alternative schools.

The alternative schools in the city were sought after for several reasons. Unlike enrollment at the few strong neighborhood schools, enrollment at the alternative schools was not geographically bound. Thus, they functioned almost as magnet schools; most had higher test scores than the nonalternative schools and high levels of parent participation and were open to students throughout the city. Thus, for families who would not have considered sending their children to their assigned school, alternative schools provided a public school option. One outcome was that white students were represented in alternative schools at 200 to 300 percent their representation in the district as a whole.

This dynamic manifested itself in Metro2 in the low percentage (20–25 percent) of children from the surrounding working-class neighborhood. The student body as a whole was 39 percent Latino, but approximately half those students were from middle-class households, sometimes with biracial parents or with parents whose families had been in the United States for generations (or both). The school had made efforts in recent years to systematically reach out to the parents of Latino children in the Title I preschool located nearby.[2] Many of these children were the neighborhood students who had managed to get admitted. They were either recent immigrants themselves or children of recent immigrants (from Mexico and Central America). They were the students in the school who qualified as "limited-English proficient" and who were eligible for free or reduced-price lunch. As Valdes (1997: 395) discusses, such students are "at risk" not only because of their status as "limited-English speakers" but because they are "members of groups that researchers have described as 'recipients of varying degrees of socioeconomic marginality and racial or ethnic discrimination.'"

Though the largest group in the student body was Latino (39 percent), a significant minority of students (13 percent) were designated as "other nonwhite"; many of these students were biracial or multiracial, and most had one Latino parent (the mix was Latino-white, Latino-black-white, Latino-Asian).[3] These students, like the 33 percent of their peers designated as "other white," tended to be middle class and to have English as their first language. The remainder of the student body was African American, Asian, and American Indian. The certified staff of teachers and administrators were approximately half Latino and half white, while the classified staff, with the exception of a Chinese custodian and one white paraprofessional, were Latino.

The school is located in a working-class, Latino neighborhood where over 70 percent of households speak a language other than English at home and where the median family income sits at around $15,000 a year. The school building itself is rather plain from the outside but lively within. Parents had gone to great lengths to improve the interior spaces, decorating hallways and classroom entrances, setting up installations of artwork and photography exhibits, and mounting elaborate displays about Cinco de Mayo, black history month, and upcoming events. This effort was something one could take for granted after a while. After I had been at the school for some months, I almost ran into a delivery man stopped in the hallway one morning. After I excused myself, he turned to me saying, "Wow! They've got this place fixed up nice." Staff too had taken special pains to beautify the space, from decorating the adult restrooms to covering the hallway bulletin boards outside each room with displays of student work.

One of the city's publicly funded child-care centers was located inside the school. Parents could drop children off as early as 7:30 and pick them up as late as 6:30.[4] Early in the morning, students milled around near the hallway entrance and sat reading or playing in the child-care center or out in the yard. School personnel took over supervisory responsibilities from the child-care staff after the first buses arrived. Breakfast was offered and was consumed primarily by those students who also received a free or reduced-price lunch (almost without exception Latino and African American students). Unpaid Latina mother volunteers and one or two Latina school aides, who were paid by the hour, took care of most of the supervision in the cafeteria. Almost all the Latina paraprofessionals were from the neighborhood; some were also mothers of current or former Metro2 students. They created a familial atmosphere, reminding students to eat slowly, clear their places, and walk to the yard on their way out.

Most teachers regularly arrived several hours before the official beginning of school. Hallways were filled with music from classrooms as staff prepared for the upcoming day. Teachers moved in and out of each other's rooms clarifying schedules with their grade-level team members, chatting about weekend plans, or organizing all-school events. School personnel were collegial and spent a great deal of time talking about curricular issues. Because students never had the same teacher for Spanish- and English-language instruction, teachers worked in teams paired for language instruction and also worked on long-term planning in larger grade-level groupings. For example, grade-level meetings for the fourth and fifth grades were held weekly in the early morning before school began and involved long conversations about upcoming events, schedules, mainstreaming, concerns about particular students, the teachers' own group process, and school politics.

Inside the main office a tall divider separated the secretary's large administrative domain from the teachers' work area. The office was the location for the various sign-in books (for teachers, volunteers) and the binder of daily staff bulletins. At any point in the morning, one or more staff members usually stood while reading or writing comments onto the daily bulletins, which they all were required to initial every day. These bulletins served as reminders of staff meetings; notifications of absent staff, rearrangements in schedules, upcoming visitors, district opportunities, sales on classroom supplies, places to sign up for release time to observe other classrooms; notices about awards and accolades; and polls about upcoming decisions. One of the many modes for communication at Metro2, it enabled staff to be aware of what was going on in the school, and it helped to create a sense of community.

Spanish was the official language of shared space in the school. Thus, unless a speaker began a conversation in English (e.g., an English-speaking parent), school personnel spoke to visitors, to students, and to each other in Spanish. The two fourth-/fifth-grade English classrooms were the only spaces in which children were always encouraged or allowed to speak in English. Staff meetings were conducted alternately in Spanish and in English. In many formal and informal situations, however, English was the dominant if not the exclusive language. For example, school meetings that involved parents (e.g., PTA meetings or site-council meetings) were conducted either bilingually (everything said in both languages) or exclusively in English with translation available. This was one manifestation of the dominance of middle-class, white, and English-speaking households. The school had discussed the possibility of holding one meeting primarily in Spanish with English translation available, but the idea had been at least temporarily abandoned because of logistical issues. Moreover, students almost always spoke English in settings where they were allowed to or where they could get away with it (e.g., in the schoolyard, in the hallways, in the lunchroom)—even students for whom English was a second language. Despite the best efforts of the staff, English remained, as one teacher put it, "the language of status."

From my first visit to the school, personnel were open, interested, and eager to have me there. At no point during my introduction to the school or during my time there did the staff profess concern about a "negative" report or evaluation, unlike the staff at other schools I had visited. Teachers and administrators expressed interest in the subject of my study and in improving their performance. They thus saw me as a way to learn about areas for improvement and, from the beginning, spoke candidly about both areas of success and arenas where they were falling short.

When I first visited the school I met with Ms. Guavara, a founder of the school and still a member of the leadership team. She explained the school's status within the district and the competing demands it faced. The school received 250 requests every year for its 60 kindergarten openings (in practice the number of openings was lower because siblings of current students received top priority for kindergarten placement). As she described it, the complicated nature of the application and appeal process had historically affected the school's population significantly. The school district had not been too supportive of the schools' efforts to get the Title I preschool children into the program "for a number of complicated reasons." This lack of support was closely connected to the pressure alternative schools in the district felt to cater to middle-class families. There was tension in the district between the goal of having viable alternatives for white and middle-class families to keep them in the district and the goal of improving the school experiences and thus the test scores of Latino and African American students.

Ms. Guavara walked me upstairs to meet Ms. Wilson, the teacher in whose classroom I would mostly likely be located. My Spanish-language limitations meant I had to be in one of the two classrooms that were conducted in English—the fourth-/fifth-grade language arts/social studies classes. One of the two possible teachers was a subject of a great deal of controversy—essentially "forced" on the school by the district because her previous position had been eliminated and she had seniority. The school had fought her appointment for much of the previous spring. There was then, as far as the school leadership was concerned, only one good possibility for my research—Marina Wilson's class-room. Although Ms. Guavara said the school would "love to have me," she was clear that the final decision was "up to Ms. Wilson."

Ms. Guavara's introduction of me and the research project included her observation that "we [the school] could really use the input." Though Ms. Wilson expressed some nervousness at having me, she welcomed me immediately and seemed genuinely excited about the help and the possibility for feedback. From the beginning she expressed her deep interest in improving her practice and getting input from me about suggestions for growth. Ms. Wilson and I agreed that I would begin on the first day of school. She explained that in the upper grades, the English classroom focused on language arts and social studies, while the Spanish classroom focused on math and science. This was not a strict separation of curriculum. Teachers were careful to do some math and science lessons in the English room and some language arts in the Spanish room so that students would have access to academic language in all subjects in both languages. Ms. Wilson and her teaching partner, John Bridges, split two classes so that one group of students spent the morning with her and then switched with the other group from Mr. Bridges's room.

My last exchange of the day was with Nancy Lopez, the new principal. Like all the other staff members I had met, she was immediately friendly, open, and welcoming. "We would be glad to have you." My initial conversations with her and with the teachers were early indicators that the school's culture was neither guarded nor cautious.

The Classroom

On the first day of school, Ms. Wilson stood at the door of her room and greeted each child as he or she came in, asking them all to sit on the rug with their bags. Her classroom was large and was filled with an abundance of resources. By the end of the first week of school, one wall was covered with rows of students' first writing samples, each sample hung below a photograph of the particular student. The opposite wall was covered with student self-portraits done in "flesh tones" with the banner "We are a rainbow of beautiful colors" underneath. Ms. Wilson had gone to a local art store to find a variety of tans and browns for students to use for the self-portraits. Students had almost all used either a light "peachy" color or a deep brown for their skin color. All the white students and a few of the Latino students utilized the peachy color, while most of the Latino students and the few African American students used the deep brown. The choices were not entirely correlated with actual skin tone—particularly for Latino students. Several light-skinned students had elected to use the dark brown color. In practice, these were students whom I found, over time, to be more strongly identified with "Latino-ness."

All other wall space in the room was covered with recent student work; posters; maps and notes on large paper for current units; a large whiteboard for homework assignments, announcements, and reminders; and a schedule chart with the order of the day's events (e.g., writing, reading aloud, spelling, recess, special project). The room had full sets of fourth- and fifth-grade social studies textbooks; two almost complete sets of encyclopedias; three shelves of random literature, history, humor, and picture books; as well as five shelves filled with approximately 175 sets of literature and content-area books (from five to six copies of each, for literature circles, to almost full-class sets). The books ranged from short works on early American history, women's suffrage, and black history to longer books of poetry, literature, and autobiographies and covered a wide range of substantive areas as well as a great number of cultural groups. Books by and about Asian Americans, African Americans, Native Americans, and Latinos sat next to books about the Civil Rights Movement, about households with two moms or two dads, and about Chicano history. On more than one occasion, Ms. Wilson told me she felt both blessed and overwhelmed by all the resources she had available. In addition, the PTA provided each teacher with $500 each year to purchase literature for their classrooms. Compared with many other urban schools, Metro2 had an abundance of resources.

Ms. Wilson—a lean redhead—stood out among staff members, who were mostly shorter and generally dark-haired. Like other staff she dressed casually but nicely, wearing slacks, loose skirts, or long dresses most days. The only times I saw staff members in t-shirts was on Mondays and Fridays—"spirit days"—when they would wear the school shirt or sweatshirt. A former dancer, Ms. Wilson was full of energy and enthusiasm.

On the first day of school, after all the children had arrived, Ms. Wilson spent much of the morning discussing the students' ideas about the principles that would guide their "ideal class." Students rattled off "be responsible for your own stuff," "attentive listening," "have respect for teachers and other classmates," "treat one another like you want to be treated." After five boys in a row spoke, Ms. Wilson asked to hear from some girls. "Walk in the classroom so no one gets hurt," "don't interrupt," "no fighting," "no tattle talking." Ms. Wilson added "work together." After writing down all their suggestions Ms. Wilson reminded them of the four principles that guide all classrooms in the school: "mutual respect, no put-downs, attentive listening, and the right to pass." As the group collectively generated the list, nodding and expanding on suggestions, it was clear not only that these students were familiar with this democratic process of developing a guide for collective behavior but also that they already had some shared understanding of how to function in this community. Rather than being a battleground of competing conceptions, the school seemed to have built a solid foundation of understanding among community members about principles that would guide their interpersonal interactions.

Without appearing to be rigidly or strictly led, Ms. Wilson's classroom ran like clockwork. This efficiency seemed to be due both to her impressive skill and to the students' training. Ms. Wilson was always enthusiastic and clear and provided both a lot of direction and a lot of room for students to pursue their own interests. Students also seemed well versed in "school behavior" as they all proceeded to assigned tasks with minimal, if any, hesitation or protest. "Classroom management," the catch-all phrase for getting students do to what they are supposed to, was accomplished in Ms. Wilson's room through proactive strategies of creativity and variety in curriculum, combined with lots of direction. Everyone knew the tasks and could do them; help was always available. On more than one occasion, students walked in talking excitedly about a project they were in the middle of, trying to fill me in on what I'd missed the days I was not there. The classroom was a real learning community with all members working, often collectively, to write stories, research reports, dissect narratives, analyze history, pursue ideas, and succeed and achieve. Community building was not just a matter of managing the classroom, however, but a fundamental part of the curriculum. Though staff understandings of race were complicated, as I discuss in the next section, staff did understand that they were working with a diverse student body that would not necessarily coalesce without intervention.

Racial Logic and Discourse

At Metro2 understandings of race seemed coherent at times and at others scattered and inconsistent. For example, though staff recognized that issues of status and access were constantly operative in the school, they talked about these issues as relating to language, class, immigration status, and ethnicity but only rarely, explicitly, to race. For example, when I asked Mr. Bridges whether race was an issue in the school, he responded:

> You mean like ethnically or racially? Ethnically, um, in terms of . . . well we
> have uh, a lot of Latino students here who don't speak English, so if it's a racial
> thing . . . you know I, for one thing, being Latino is not a racial thing. I mean

it's just a word—maybe I'm just picking the word apart? Maybe it's more of an ethnic thing. . . . And then, we have a lot of children who come from families . . . who either come from mixed families or they come from families who have just been here for generations. So, I don't think it's really mixed up in terms of race. I would look at class—that is always my tendency. Class and it's immigration. 'Cause the people who speak Spanish are recent immigrants. And that, in this country, is usually a lower class, lower status. And that's where I think it comes in.

As is obvious in Mr. Bridges's discussion Latino was a confusing category because it included a diverse group economically, socially, linguistically, and in terms of status. Like Mr. Bridges, many understood Latino to be an ethnic group. Ethnicity here was a referent for common descent, for a connection to Latin America (either recent or distant). It was a matter of culture quite different from other markers of status, which Mr. Bridges labeled as immigrant status and class. People seemed to understand race less coherently, and they discussed it less coherently; though bodies in many shades of brown were present at Metro2, racial-group membership was regularly ascribed only to the few blacks in the school and occasionally to whites. For example, when I first visited the school and described my project to Mr. Camarena, a teacher in the early grades, he commented that Metro2 would not be the most appropriate location to study race "because there are not too many African American kids here." Yet in a society in which everyone is racialized, it is curious not only that race would be seen as irrelevant in regard to white students but especially that it would be seen so with regard to the many "brown" students at the school who, though neither black nor white, were not unaffected by racial issues or free from racial dynamics.

The ambiguity and ambivalence around the issue of race at Metro2 was possibly both a subtler form of the denial and silence at the other two schools and a sign that racial boundaries were operating more fluidly here so that race mattered differently if not less. Many of the patterns visible at the other schools were at least partially reversed at Metro2. Difference and equity were talked about regularly in reference to both internal practices and external politics. Though issues of status and power were talked about or, more probably, *because* they were talked about, they had a less potent influence on school practices. However, in many important ways traditional racial hierarchies remained relevant and powerful. Racial patterns in school outcomes, peer interactions, and parental roles still existed, even if in somewhat less coherent ways than at the other schools. Alternative racial narratives were present at the center, rather than at the margins, of school discourse. Yet, despite the staff's many efforts, they had not found a formula for fundamentally subverting the racial realities of which they were a part. Still it was a challenge they rarely backed down from.

In Pursuit of a Just and Equitable Education

As discussed earlier, staff members were quite open with me from the first. Regularly, several teachers would grab me during the day and say, "Make sure you get out to recess, that's where the [racial] separation [among students] *really* happens." "Notice that most of the kids use English on the playground. No matter what we do it's still the language of status among kids." These statements not only exemplified staff openness about shortcomings but also demonstrated that people were paying attention—looking, seeing, and talking about what they saw. Moreover, teachers put much effort into figuring out how to address these issues. For example, Ms. Wilson consistently asked me for feedback about what she could do better, how to improve her classroom practice in the interest of both equity and excellence.

Although the school pursued the goal of providing a socially just and equitable education, it did so within an unequal social context. This fact was not lost on Metro2 staff. Importantly, they seemed conscious of the impact of social context but aware of it in a different way than were the staffs at Foresthills and West City. As the teachers said in reference to language, English became the "status" language even if they did not want it to. But this perception did not become an excuse for giving up. As Mrs. Lopez, the principal, said to me in a conversation about race relations among students, "If society has a negative influence, it's not the excuse you need to do nothing, but the reason to do more." The recognition that external realities entered the school was not a justification for poor outcomes but a reminder to act more vigorously to intercede. Teachers undertook these responsibilities in relation to a curriculum aimed at educating students to be critical and engaged (e.g., a third-grade curriculum on stereotypes, a fifth-grade curriculum on the Civil Rights Movement) and also in an effort to educate all students well, to provide all their students with the knowledge and skills necessary to succeed. Thus, unlike the staff at many other schools, Metro2 personnel took ownership of their collective success and failure. When a student struggled, they understood it to be an instructional issue rather than a problem with the student. Even while recognizing that students had a range of academic abilities and proclivities, they had both an expressed and a demonstrated commitment to helping every student thrive.

Staff were also aware of the ways they were not living up to their goals. Mrs. Lopez's comment above about not making excuses was a reaction to a recent incident in which a white student had used a derogatory racial statement during an argument with an African American student. Mrs. Lopez talked about this not as the problem of an individual child but as a school problem, as evidence that they still had work to do. Similarly, various staff members made it regular practice to air "dirty laundry" at staff meetings, reminding their peers of the persisting shortcomings in their program. In this way, the culture of the school was uncommonly self-reflective and self-critical. This practice discouraged the staff from dismissing incidents like the one just described or explaining away unequal student outcomes; it also suggested a possibility for and a commitment to change that was not apparent in settings where these issues were ignored or avoided.

In many ways, the organization of the school as a dual-language immersion program put issues of race, power, and status on the agenda. As Valdes (1997) discusses, by their very design, these programs bring children from different racial, cultural, and language groups together in a single school building. They come together, however, with slightly different goals. In Valdes's (1997: 392) words: "The aim of these programs is for majority Anglophone children to achieve a high-level of proficiency in a 'foreign' language while receiving a first-rate education, and for minority children who do not speak English to benefit from having instruction in their mother tongue, as well as by interacting with English-speaking peers." Thus a central part of these programs is the bringing together institutionally of groups who would otherwise likely have little contact because of housing and language segregation.[5] Power and status become apparent in the different reasons children come to these schools. Though both groups come to school speaking one language and with the goal of learning another, some are there by choice to acquire a skill—Spanish—while others are there out of necessity—to learn English. Such programs thus bring together groups that are not only different but unequal in their access to social, economic, cultural, and symbolic resources.

The presence of issues of race, status, and power, however, does not necessarily mean that staff or students openly engage with such issues. As we saw in the previous two chapters and as other research discusses, such issues are more often ignored, avoided, and not talked about (Schofield 1982; Wells and Crain 1997). As discussed in the examination of Foresthills and West City, the silence around and the avoidance of such issues facilitates the reproduction of racial inequalities. In many ways Metro2 was trying to do something quite different. In relation to school practices, curriculum, and intergroup relations, the school community made an effort to engage and address these issues. The acts of denial and silence prevalent at Foresthills and West City were replaced with awareness and struggle at Metro2.

In almost every staff meeting I attended at Metro2, issues of equity either were on the official agenda or were raised by a member of the staff. One indicator of the school's willingness to engage came during the first staff-development day of the year. School language policy and practices were at the top of the agenda. The first item was a brief discussion of the Unz Initiative. As Mrs. Lopez explained it that morning, the Unz Initiative was a proposal being "pushed by the English Only movement" to, for all intents and purposes, "end bilingual education in the state."[6] Mrs. Lopez warned the group, "We should take it seriously because it would directly impact us." At the beginning of the meeting also, within a long but quick list of other announcements were both reminders about a meeting with the Lesbian and Gay Parents group to talk about lesson ideas for classrooms and a review of a trip planned for the next day to visit another immersion school an hour away. She encouraged the class-room aides also to go, offering them "comp time" to make up for the unsched-uled hours.

Within these first minutes, the principal had already engaged with multiple issues of power, politics, and status. She explained that the school would take up the issues of movements against bilingualism with the PTA. She mentioned that parents and teachers would get together to brainstorm developmentally appropriate lessons about the acceptance of different kinds of families. She encouraged classroom aides to participate as full members in the school's instructional community. The casualness with which she ran through this list signaled these as everyday kinds of issues and events.

In fact, the rest of the meeting was consumed by the whole staff engaging with key issues of equity and difference that lay at the core of their program. Mrs. Estevez, a first-grade teacher, brought along a recent *Harvard Educational Review* article by scholar Guadalupe Valdes titled "Dual-Language Immersion Programs: A Cautionary Note Concerning the Education of Language-Minority Students" and offered to copy it for anyone interested. She summarized the "cautionary" part briefly as taking up "power issues, language issues . . . things we've been discussing all along." Ms. Guavara suggested that, rather than just copying the article, they read and talk about the article together as part of their discussion of language policy that morning. Staff members were enthusiastic about the idea and agreed to take it up as soon as copies could be made. While Ms. Guavara headed off to photocopy the article, the rest of the staff turned to the task of revising the school's "Language Policy." Mrs. Estevez placed the lat-est draft on the overhead projector. It read:

With Students:
—Spanish always with your Spanish class inside and outside of your classroom. No code switching, no word dropping.

—English always with English class in classroom. Outside classroom, Spanish. Spanish always with students on premises.

With Parents:

—In Spanish Class—no direct out loud English with non-Spanish speaking parents. If you must speak English, whisper or step outside.

—Other parents (parents of ex-students, future students, English class)— Address in English; when student present, address the student in Spanish.

The policy generated a great deal of discussion about the competing needs of Anglophone and LEP (limited-English-proficient) students. Staff engaged in a back-and-forth discussion of how to balance the needs of the distinct groups in the school. The strictness of the language policy was intended primarily to assist the Anglophone students in the school in their acquisition of Spanish. Although enforcing Spanish usage in shared spaces provided good Spanish-language models for those learning Spanish, some were concerned that English-language learners were not getting enough English-language modeling. Spanish-language acquisition and Spanish-language maintenance were important goals of the school, but English-language acquisition was essential to the future success of Latino students. The staff struggled to find compromises that would serve both groups well. Some also expressed concern about how the language document might get "read" by those outside the school and requested that a section go at the beginning of the document explaining its purpose so that it did not "get out" and become misrepresented. The politically savvy staff recognized that they were working in a larger context that was hostile to bilingual education. This perception did not cause them to back off from their program, but, knowing that documents produced here could be misrepresented in the current climate, they initiated caution. This conversation was not merely about language groups but about advocating for groups with inequitable access to the power and resources necessary to make the school work for them. The parents of majority-language students (English-dominant students attending the school to learn Spanish) put a lot of effort into making sure their children were ably served. Staff members were aware of these efforts and pushed themselves to act also as advocates for the English-language learners.

The conversation about the language policy was cut short when Ms. Guavara returned with photocopies of sections of the Valdes article. The six tables of personnel were each to read a different section and summarize it for the whole group. In brief, the Valdes article offered a "cautionary note" on dual-language immersion programs like that in Metro2. As Valdes states, such schools are in part intended to bring middle-income majority children into the same schools as low-income minority children, and they may or may not serve the language-minority students well. For example, although dual-language programs may be useful for the ways in which they value minority culture, they may not provide the kinds of high-quality instruction that language-minority students need. Valdes states, "In dual-language immersion programs, therefore, special attention must be given to the quality of the primary language used with minority children. . . . Were the situation reversed, mainstream parents would vigorously protest having their children in classrooms in which the instructional needs of language-minority children required that English be used in ways that did not provide their children with the fullest possible exposure to school language" (1997: 416). Moreover, she states, the mix of students in these schools can lead to a number of important intergroup issues that teachers and staff need to be attentive to.

The group spent a large block of their meeting time that morning reading the article and collectively discussing Valdes's argument. Near the end of the conversation Ms. Guavara summarized the cautionary issues Valdes raised: "First, who are we serving? English-speaking kids learning Spanish, or Spanish-speaking kids learning English. Second, how are children from different groups interacting within the programs? . . . [We have to remember] language is inseparable from politics. . . . Language planning is never neutral." Several teachers reminded the group that they had been talking about the issues the article raised for some time.

Staff openly acknowledged the problematic reality that English-dominant students often outperformed minority-language students even in Spanish and recognized that at least one school practice—the use of sheltered Spanish—was contributing to these achievement gaps.[7] Though the teachers did not yet have any sense of how to confront these issues, openly naming them was arguably a necessary first step. Mr. Camarena and Ms. Guavara ended the conversation by reinforcing Valdes's final point, that it is the educators' job to "make society different," even though, as several other teachers pointed out, Valdes also said they probably could not.

The discussion of the article was a complex conversation full of emotion (confusion, frustration, inspiration). Of chief importance is the fact that the group had such a discussion. Using a research article as a way to reflect on and examine their own practices led the group to spend time collectively struggling with what they were actually doing as distinguished from what they wanted or hoped to be doing. The discussion also did not remain entirely at a removed or abstract level. As they began to put the article down, Mrs. Lopez asked, "Again, I ask where this leaves us with our language policy?" Mr. Camarena extended that concern: "We've dedicated an hour of our precious time to reading the article. If we leave it as theory, we're not respecting the time. I think we should apply it, take action . . . the article suggests that immersion programs though they look nice and are developed by [thoughtful] educators, don't necessarily deliver the goods to [LEP] students. . . . We need to make sure that we serve the needs of minority students." Although another teacher reminded Mr. Camarena that speaking Spanish was also important to the Spanish-dominant kids because it promotes cultural pride and makes it clear that Spanish is valued and important, she conceded, "It's true, we don't support [English as a Second Language]." The teachers recognized that the school's language policy was a crucial issue for the children's future success. Would they do well once they left the school? Though perhaps culturally supported, were they getting the skills and knowledge they needed to succeed? It was clearly no easy challenge to provide an equitable, multicultural, and rigorous education to the diverse students in Metro2.

This was not a one-time conversation. While I was there, I witnessed similar discussions among different staff members under varying circumstances (in the yard, in the teacher's lounge, in a grade-level meeting). It was more typical than unusual to hear staff asking themselves, Who are we really serving? What can we do about the social inequities among our students? What's our role going to be? Staff spoke openly about the power differences between families, the sense of entitlement some of their white students had. They talked about how easy it was for the needs of the English-dominant students to take over if the staff were not careful, how easily they were drawn in to responding to that group's needs, and even how easy it was to become focused on the students and parents who were active and engaged in school in ways that affirmed the teachers' effectiveness. Without specific thought and action to the contrary, the white and middle-class students' needs would drive the curriculum and practices. Not only did Anglophone Spanish-language learners outnumber Latino English-language learners in the school, the Anglophone parents were around daily, making requests, interceding on their children's behalf.[8] Theirs were also the most vocal children, and these children often made requests on their own behalf. The staff wanted to provide an educational setting in which both groups could thrive and knew it was a delicate balancing game. They also knew that there were lots of educational settings in which white and middle-class children could do well and few where racial-/ethnic-minority students (in terms of race, language, and class) could thrive. This recognition brought a special responsibility to live up to their expressed commitments to minority children.

Giving Voice to Hard Issues:
Talking about Race and Power in School

As the above episode illustrates, Metro2 staff were willing to acknowledge problems. I rarely uncovered an equity issue at the school that a staff member had not first pointed out to me in an interview or conversation. It may seem self-evident that people who work in an organization for long periods of time should be most aware of the ways they are or are not serving all clients. However, my work at the other schools indicates that school personnel often put considerable effort into not seeing such trends or into being prepared to justify them. At Metro2 the modus operandi was to be open about failings, to look for solutions, and to get help (e.g., to spend staff-development days visiting other dual-language programs or bringing people in to talk about issues around English as a Second Language). Despite this openness about problems, a certain ambivalence ran through much of the discourse about areas where the program was falling short. Because the school was relatively successful in many ways, staff held on to a sense of the school as a high-functioning and dynamic educational community. They were already doing better than most other places. Institutionalized racism was not a reality they worked to ignore but one they worked to manage in ways that would not impede the daily task of educating the children in their school.

Staff members were fairly politicized and seemed generally to recognize an outside world that shaped power and status issues and that was going to affect their school's outcomes no matter what they did. Nonetheless, they often focused on what they could do within the bounds of their school building day in and day out. In this way daily practices did and did not match up with their larger discourse about societal power inequities. In fact, the school's shortcomings were real—racial realities of unequal status were a part of Metro2. Staff could not completely overcome them. But they did make efforts to provide their students not only with traditional school skills and information but also with knowledge about the nature of the world in which they lived. Teachers raised issues in class that in other places were considered too political or not relevant enough to be classroom material. Teachers raised these issues not because they thought students should know about them but because they recognized that many students already did know and needed either to know more or to know that school was a place where such matters could be talked about.

For example, staff understood the role of state politics in shaping their students' lives. Recent years had seen a growing anti-immigrant movement in the state. One Latino parent told me that in response to tension and fear around state Proposition 187, members of the school had participated with families in demonstrations against the proposition:[9] "Their attitude in terms of Proposition

187 was really incredible. I went to a meeting in which the principal, Ms. Guavara, and the teachers explained what was going on and said that no one should be worried. They clearly said that—and this was very laudable—that in case this law passed, in the case that they were forced to turn the children in, they would refuse and they were ready to go to jail for that. They said: 'This is not going to be an Immigration Office.'" Students at the school also made calls to their schoolmates who had not been coming to school because they feared immigration authorities, assuring them it was safe. As this parent stated, it was important for his son to see the school confronting what was already an important issue in his own life.

During 1998, the year I was conducting research at Metro2, another ballot initiative was on the table—the Unz Initiative, or Proposition 227, attempting to outlaw most bilingual education. As Mrs. Lopez alluded to at the beginning of the staff meeting, parents and teachers were actively fighting this legislation outside school. The subject also came up often in class. Ms. Wilson and her students had numerous conversations about the Unz Initiative and issues of language and politics. They talked about why the children were glad to be bilingual, what it meant to them, and why people would oppose bilingual education. Interestingly, even though many white and biracial students talked about bilingualism as a good thing, primarily with regard to practical considerations like future job prospects, all the children understood that these larger political battles about bilingualism were also about race and citizenship. As the following exchange demonstrates, status differences between groups arose both in conversations about antibilingual education movements and in relation to the students themselves. What was for many of the students a threat to the "educational perk" of learning a second language was for others a threat to their very personhood and sense of membership in the social and school collective.

One day, Ms. Wilson was trying to explain to the class the dynamics behind the antibilingual initiative. She began by telling the students how lucky they were to be getting a bilingual education and learning to speak two languages. She did not learn Spanish until she was an adult, she said, and it was a lot harder that way. She explained that some people were trying to end bilingual education and asked the students what they thought about "them" trying to take bilingual education away. Enrique, a mixed black/Chicano student, yelled out, "They're taking away your culture." Earl, a middle-class, white student, followed, saying that he thought "they" were trying to stop "the Mexican or the Spanish so that the illegal immigrants won't come." When Ms. Wilson asked him to explain, he said that he thought that the immigrants were coming to the United States because they could learn in Spanish here. Jesus, himself an immigrant, replied in a frantic and breathless tone that not all immigrants were children, "and some [already] speak English." Walt, another white, middle-class child, offered, "If they stopped [bilingual education], then it would be like saying, 'Everyone who doesn't come from an English family has to get out of here.'" When Ms. Wilson ended the conversation by asking them whether they were proud to be bilingual, all hands went up. She suggested that for the rally they were going to attend the next day for Indigenous People's Day they should bring banners and signs saying things like "keep bilingual education." Enrique exclaimed, "Yeah, we should shout from the mountaintops that we're proud" and began chanting, "We are La-tin-o . . . we are La-tin-o." Jesus and Cesar joined in.[10]

These kinds of exchanges, full of complicated and contradictory understandings of language and status, were a part of daily life at the school. The two white students who spoke both understood that Proposition 227 was not only about language but about who was and was not allowed to be counted as a full citizen. As Earl said, the bilingual-education law was also about who should or should not come to this country. Like Walt, he seemed to understand that antibilingualism was anti-immigrant and specifically anti-Mexican or anti-Latino. As Walt said, "It would be like saying, 'Everyone who doesn't come from an English family has to get out of here.'" Though Walt's referent was "English," he was not talking merely about a language group. "English" as a category of people was, within school discourse, equivalent to Anglo or white. Jesus, the one immigrant child who spoke up, offered an interpretation similar to Walt's as he spoke from a defensive posture. He seemed to feel a different level of threat than the others. Although Enrique was quite vocal, neither of his parents was an immigrant, and both were politically progressive and active. Like Jesus, he took the issues quite personally but did not seem to feel as individually threatened. Rather than being defensive, he seemed clear about his rights. The class did, in fact, make signs for the rally. Although most of the students carried signs saying "save bilingual education," Enrique's read "Viva La Raza!"

Another day the class discussed the meaning of Dia de La Raza (Indigenous People's Day, or, as it is more traditionally known, Columbus Day). When Ms. Wilson told them that Dia de La Raza was coming up, she explained that "they used to call it Columbus Day." When she was in school, they talked about Columbus as a hero and did not talk about how he stole land from people and killed people. He could not, she contends, have discovered America as many claim because Native Americans were already here. When Kate asked about this view, Ms. Wilson stated that "Columbus wasn't a *bad* man," he was "just an explorer." Several minutes later Enrique raised his hand and seemed to disagree with Ms. Wilson when he said almost tearfully about Columbus, "I don't believe in him because he did bad things and hurt people." He talked about the many people who died at the hands of explorers. Ms. Wilson asked whether he just did not believe in him or whether he thought he was a bad man. Enrique said he thought he was a bad man. Ms. Wilson responded, "Well that's an opinion."

Here Ms. Wilson offered a much more historically complex understanding of Columbus's historical role than is usually offered in schools. As part of the lesson, she told the class about a conversation she had had with some people at a Native American educational organization the day before in which they had said it was okay to use either the term *Indian* or the term *Native American*. She told them that when she was in college, people said it was bad to say "Indian." "We just need to know that they aren't red with feathers." In this way she also engaged the students in a discussion about the importance of language in relation to how we name groups of people. In both examples she acknowledged the politics involved in education and in the knowledge-production and dissemination process, explaining that these were historical narratives that were told differently, incorrectly even, when she was a child. Her efforts to offer complex and critical understandings of history seemed partially muted in the effort to maintain comfort levels (e.g., her reaction to the passion with which Enrique argued that Columbus was, in fact, a bad man). Yet, she never shied away from issues. She and other teachers in some ways became models of white racial actors who were engaged in debates about and critical of racial inequities. Racism and social inequality became visible as subjects that everyone, including whites, should be concerned about, not just those who are victimized. These teachers thus provided models for all students of critical and engaged citizens.

From the beginning of the year Ms. Wilson made efforts to ensure that students were aware of important current events. On the Monday of the second week of school, Ms. Wilson reintroduced me to the class by reminding them about the anti-Proposition 209 march they had talked about last week, explaining that I had participated.[11] She asked me to talk about it a bit. I first talked mostly about the crowd and the experience of marching. Ms. Wilson then prodded me to explain a little about 209 and why I was at the march. I explained my concern about issues of equity and jobs. Ms. Wilson pushed me to say more, asking me, for instance, to explain what I meant by equity. Though I said a few more words, Ms. Wilson seemed frustrated at my hesitancy to talk in more specific ways and turned to the class and explained how 209 affected her personally "as a woman and as someone who has a lot of friends who are people of color." While she spoke, I noticed on the board a list of spelling words from Friday—*job, equality, march, affirmative, proposition,* and *education*.[12] As the conversation and spelling words showed, in both the formal and the informal curriculum, students were being engaged as critical citizens, encouraged to think about the world around them.

During the rest of the year, issues of equity, race, and power came up throughout the social studies curriculum in long units about Native Americans, the Constitution, and the Civil Rights Movement. Ms. Wilson repeatedly encouraged her students to be critical of popular historical narratives. Early in the year the class spent a few weeks talking about culture and ancestry. To follow up on some of that work, she showed a short cartoon titled "The Great American Melting Pot" from a video she had just purchased. As she introduced it to the class, she asked, "Who knows what a melting pot is? Why'd they call it that?" She asks the group, "Is it because we're all so hot we're melting? No." Walt guesses that it is because there's so much garbage. She tells him that's not it. Dennis says it is because "there are so many races immigrating to America and there's so much interracial marriage that they're all melting together." She says yes, they're marrying "or even just living near each other or sitting next to each other in school." She asks whether the melting is always peaceful and happy, and the class responds together, "No." "Right, there is still a lot of racism and prejudice and stuff like that, but I'm hopeful because of you."

The five-minute video consisted of a song with accompanying illustrations describing immigrants coming from the "Old World" (Europe) to the "New World" (America) for a better life. Without any reference to those who had been living in the "New World" when the immigrants arrived, or those who did not come voluntarily, the video ended with all the "immigrants" (including Chinese portrayed with stereotypic images, and blacks) jumping into a large cauldron labeled "The Great American Melting Pot." The story seemed contrary to much of what Ms. Wilson had been teaching, but, as she said, she liked the song and thought the video was "fun." Though she encouraged the students to enjoy the video and sing along, she also encouraged them to be critical of the narrative it offered—not as one that was necessarily wrong but as one that was too simple and left out important information. "Does it mention how difficult it was for people coming over on the boats, how many died and suffered?" No, it didn't mention all that. "Be careful with cartoons because they don't always tell the whole story."

Similarly, later in the year when the class read a short book on the writing of the Constitution, she pointed out that the picture depicting those at the convention showed only white men. This was not the beginning of a longer conversation about why only white men were present or how that fact affected the content of the Constitution, but it did raise questions. As with the video, the critique she offered was important, albeit not at the center of the narrative. Even if limited, her intervention was by no means meaningless. So many widely available popular historical narratives are incomplete if not wholly inaccurate. Ms.

Wilson could not avoid all narratives, but she did make an effort to challenge them. It is perhaps more powerful to read, critique, and challenge existing historical narratives than to merely avoid them. As Giroux (1991: 225) points out in quoting Toni Morrison, "The central question may not be why Afro-Americans are absent from dominant narratives, but 'what intellectual feats had to be performed by the author or his critic to erase [blacks] from a society seething with [their] presence, and what effect has that performance had on the work.'"

One test of critical multicultural curricula like that described above is whether students see any connection between this history and their present-day lives. As Wills (1994, 1996) argues, even the best multicultural history can remain distant for students and unconnected to the present. For example, students often understand lessons about slavery as stories about events that happened and were resolved a long time ago. In Ms. Wilson's class students sometimes made connections between history and the present and sometimes not. Although lessons about Native Americans remained singularly focused on distinct and distant groups who existed long ago, students did make connections between the present and what they had learned during the unit on the Civil Rights Movement.

The day after the antibilingual law passed, Ms. Wilson initiated another conversation with the class about bilingualism. After returning from a field trip, she found a set of handouts waiting to be distributed to the class; the material consisted of a press release from the school district about Proposition 227. Ms. Wilson immediately had the class sit in a circle on the rug. She began the discussion by explaining that Ms. Guavara was being interviewed down the hall by a local news crew about the law's passage. When the news crew asked Ms. Guavara what the school was going to do, she replied, "As the district mandates, [we're] going to keep on doing what we're doing now." When the reporter asked, "Even if that means breaking the law?" Ms. Guavara responded, "Even if that means breaking the law." Ms. Wilson explained how courageous it was for Ms. Guavara to say this, that Ms. Guavara was one of the founders of the immersion program at the school and that she believed in it strongly. Ms. Wilson then read the press release to the class; it explained that the district was going to file a countersuit challenging the constitutionality of the law. Trying to head off the students' growing concern, manifested in their worried murmurs and facial expressions and anxiety-filled questions, Ms. Wilson told them that "lots of powerful groups are going to fight the proposition." The students had many questions and were clearly worried. Ricky asked several frantic questions about what might happen next: "Is it going to [come to] blows, like the Civil Rights Movement? Is anyone going to get killed? . . . cause we'll fight it." The boy next to him jumped in, "Yeah we'll have a march." Ms. Wilson said, "It will never come to that. For now we are going to proceed as if nothing's changed." Still, as the day drew to a close at 3:30, the students' questions persisted, and they seemed stressed and worried. Trying to reassure them, Ms. Wilson reminded them that Proposition 187 never got implemented. "It's still in court."

In this conversation students seemed to identify with those who took part in the Civil Rights Movement. They saw their current situation as one in which their rights were being challenged and drew on examples they had recently studied about how to fight for themselves. In this way, these students saw the connections between their own lives and current situation and the lives and struggles of African Americans of earlier generations. Lessons they had learned about the Civil Rights Movement had not merely been filed away as stories about the past but were drawn on in the face of present-day confrontations concerning their own access to bilingual education.

Generally then, the school curriculum encouraged students to see and question wider realities—with some success. The white students in this school were the only white children I interviewed who were aware of and able to talk about discrimination and racism as factors in mobility and opportunity. In both informal conversations and interviews, they raised these issues as the reason some had lots of resources and others few. For example, in an interview with Walt, I asked why he thought some people were poor. He responded, "Because maybe their race. Because they don't get the job opportunities as other races." Yet, this general, abstract understanding did not always carry over into local understandings; these same white students could not see the exclusion of students in their school. I interviewed Walt and Johnny, right after interviewing Vanessa, an African American girl from their class. She had said that students sometimes treated other kids badly or would not play with them because of their color. In their interviews, Walt and Johnny assured me that such things would never happen at Metro2. They knew such things were probably common in other schools, "but not here." This pattern held true in the rest of student interviews at the school: some (mostly white) children viewed their school as an ideal racial community in which poor treatment was not allowed, and other (black and Latino) children viewed the school, at least with regard to peer interactions, as sometimes less than ideal. Thus though a majority of students were able to talk coherently about the impact race had on the lives of people far removed from them, they were less able to see the patterns of exclusionary behavior among students locally and in fact denied that these patterns even existed. Though it is a powerful testament to the school curriculum that most Metro2 students had a critical understanding of opportunity structures, it is also significant that white students and students of color evaluated the local realities differently.

Boundaries of Integration

As the statements by students of color in my interviews indicate, those students were not fully integrated in the school. No matter school personnel's intentions or how self-reflective they were able to be, there were reasons for concern. As the staff began to acknowledge in their discussion of the Valdes article, they had not managed to fully integrate their diverse student body socially or academically. As in the other schools in this study, African American and Latino students had different school experiences than did their white peers.

One day Metro2 had visitors from the state's Consent Decree office.[13] During lunch I asked Mrs. Lopez about the goals of the visit, and she explained that they were checking the schools throughout the district to see whether all children were being served equally. The visitors had quizzed her about how the African American students in the school were doing and why there were so few. She admitted to them and to me that it was the weakest part of their program.

In my time there, I found her observation to be quite true. In multiple ways, the few African American students were socially marginalized. A good example was Vanessa, a high-achieving fifth-grader, soft-spoken and amiable. At the beginning of the year, she became close friends with four white classmates. Though they all hung out together at lunch and in the yard, at numerous times throughout the year Vanessa was excluded from after-school or weekend events. As Valdes (1997: 417) states, "Children sense exclusion quite quickly, and minority children realize, when several of their mainstream friends talk about weekend excursions and out-of-school activities to which they were not invited, that they are not really part of the same group." When I spoke with the white girls in the group about friendship issues or weekend plans, Vanessa was rarely mentioned.

Just in the daily discourse of the other members of the small group she hung out with, Vanessa was often left out. For example, one day in class Karen and Natasha, two members of Vanessa's clique, came up to me saying they wished they were in the other class so they could have Ms. Wilson first thing in the morning. Natasha added, "Plus Sarah and Chris are in there." They did not mention Vanessa, who was also in the other class. Moreover, members of the group had several fallings-out during the year, and it was always Vanessa (sometimes in combination with one of the other children in the group) who was temporarily ostracized. During these times Vanessa would hang out with the few other black girls or dark-skinned Latinas. Though she identified the group of (white) children as her "best friends," she was clearly an outsider in the group. During an interview with Karen's mom, when I asked about Karen's friends, Karen walked into the room and listed Natasha, Chris, and Sarah. Her mother added, "And Vanessa, right?" Karen said, "Right, sure, Vanessa too." By the end of the year Vanessa had been permanently ousted from the group for reasons I could not get any of them to explain.

Part of the mystery in all these events was Vanessa's uniform popularity among all the children in her class. An affable and good-humored child, she was a strong student and came from a stable and supportive home. In regard to language, interests, and socioeconomic status, she was more like the white peers she began the year spending time with than like the low-income, Spanish-dominant Latinas she was friends with at the end of the year. Yet she was never able to become a full member of the white peer group and was welcomed warmly by the others.

When I spoke to Mrs. Lopez about the school's demographics, she was clear and articulate about the problem of having too few African American students in the school:

> We only have 8 percent. And a lot of them are achieving, but they are such a minority, like maybe one per classroom, it's really hard to deal with any of their specific needs except for a "joe-blow" [a generic] student. Culturally it's very hard. . . . Along with, it's so noticeable like, I see Mark out in the yard being the only noticeably African American playing. That just sends the wrong picture to the kids . . . it's a just, a mixed message that you're fighting for integration of the schools but yet we're not integrated. I mean, that's a contradiction and also, it would show respect for the Spanish language if there were African Americans also learning Spanish and not just whites and Latinos.

Within the first few weeks of school, I knew who all the African American students in the upper grades were. There was literally one in each class (one class also had Enrique, a biracial African American/Chicano student whom teachers referred to as black). Although the few African American boys usually played basketball with white peers, the few black girls could usually be found in the yard jumping rope together or playing with the darker-skinned Latinas. Aside from Vanessa, girls in the school rarely crossed lines of social separation. These lines were more racial than ethnic as white and biracial light-skinned Latinas played together, separate from Latinas who were darker-skinned and from the neighborhood. Though the boys were more integrated, even within their ranks the darker-skinned Latinos tended to play separately.

One morning Mrs. Lopez asked me to supervise the yard while the teachers had their yearly staff photo taken. When I came out, a group of mostly middle-class, light-skinned Latino and white boys were playing a modified baseball game with a tennis ball. A long line of boys, almost all dark-skinned Latinos, stood and watched. I asked several of them whether they wanted to play also, and they nodded. As I knew to be the general rule in the yard, I announced to the boys playing that they would have to let the other boys join them at the end of the game (the current game was almost over). As soon as it ended, the boys who had been playing all walked off. Their exit was rather dramatic, so I asked Walt, Jorge, and Johnny (boys I knew from class who had been playing) why they had walked off like that. They expressed in exaggerated tones that they had no idea what I was talking about. As one put it, "No big deal. We played, we finished, and we left." When I told them to imagine how it might make the other kids feel for them to walk off like that, Johnny said, "They look like they're having fun to me." This was the first time I experienced these boys as even remotely disrespectful. When I returned to the baseball diamond, the new boys were not even playing because they did not have the tennis ball anymore. The boy whose ball it was decided not to play and had joined the group of defectors. Though I had always noticed racial separation in student games in the yard, this was the first time I (or anyone else in my presence) intervened—in this case with little success.[14]

In the classroom later I related the story to Ms. Wilson, who was upset. She said there had been a lot of exclusivity in the yard lately, with closed social clubs and other restricted groups. As soon as the students settled in, she brought the matter up. Ms. Wilson started by saying how it upset her to see kids on the playground getting their feelings hurt—especially when people formed clubs that others could not join. "People's feelings get hurt. . . . Do not form clubs on the playground that don't include everyone—they're cliquey and mean." She said she had not seen them be mean to each other in the classroom at all—it was remarkable how much they helped each other—but on the playground they were cliquey. "You have to take a look deep inside and see if that's the kind of kid you want to be. . . . What goes around comes around. If you're going to dish it out and be mean, be prepared for it to come back around to you. If you're nice, then others will be nice. If you want a good friend, be a good friend." Vanessa asked whether it was okay if people are friends and it's private. "That's different, but remember there are soft ways and mean ways to say that you need some privacy." Ms. Wilson told them that she wanted the kids in her class to set an example for others. With somber expressions most nodded and listened attentively.

Although the boundaries on the playground and in the lunchroom were clearly drawn, Ms. Wilson was right that students were more likely to interact and to be kind to each other in class. Cooperative learning was a central part of Metro2's pedagogical practices, and I rarely witnessed any negative student response to the many groupings and pairings in which they were placed. For example, for a large and lengthy "State Report" project, Ms. Wilson paired white or light-skinned biracial students with dark-skinned Latino or African American students. After being assigned partners, students chose a state out of a hat, grabbed the relevant encyclopedia, and went to work. One after another, pairs of students got together and began working without any complaints. Eddie, a GATE (Gifted and Talented Education)-designated Filipino-Mexican fifth-grader, was paired with Cindy, a white fourth-grade girl.[15] He scooted over next to her on the rug as soon as he heard she was his partner. They had the following exchange:

> Eddie leans over and whispers to Cindy asking her if she's a good reader. She shakes her head no. "So you're not a good reader, can you write?" "No." "Can you write neat?" "No." They decide she'll be the draw-er. As Alex goes off to get the encyclopedia, Cindy turns to me and says, "I suck at drawing."

Almost every day of class involved students working together on tasks or in groups. But although they worked well whenever placed together, even in the classroom, voluntary interactions were rare. Thus, though the school was successful at having students work cooperatively and well together during a variety of organized activities (e.g., reports, dance classes, art projects, reading groups), students still seemed to remain more strangers than friends during informal time, and boundaries generally fell along racial lines.

Variations in levels of social integration were mirrored in academic integration. In most cooperative work, English-dominant students (generally white or biracial and light-skinned and middle-class) almost inevitably took over, even if they were younger. These were almost always the only students who volunteered to read aloud in class. Their deportment in class and their relation to teachers and to lessons were distinct from those of their dark-skinned Latino peers. I spent some time in the Spanish math/science class to see whether class participation and interaction patterns differed across language of instruction. Though at least one Latino student participated more in the Spanish-instruction class than in the English-language room, high-status children (white or biracial and middle-class) did not participate any less. In both classrooms high-status students were most likely to raise their hands, volunteer answers, and take over in small groups. There was only minor gender variation overall (boys did participate slightly more than girls).

After our first formal interview, Ms. Wilson asked me whether I had any feedback for her related to issues of race and equity. I explained that I could not give her any analysis because I was just in the process of recording data. She pressed me more to tell her whether there were any areas for concern, and I said that I had not seen a Latina raise a hand or get called on in over a week. Similar to patterns found in other schools and in other settings within the school (e.g., the playground), patterns of classroom participation at Metro2 were in this way not only racialized but gendered. Although boys were vocal at least in between lessons if not during them, Latinas remained silent during most of the day. As they did at West City, Latinas remained off the radar much of the time, obeying the rules, rarely volunteering. However, unlike at West City, the structure of the class meant that even if these students were not participating in the whole-group activities, they still had opportunities (and sometimes were required) to engage in small-group activities. Nonetheless, Latinas' ideas, input, interests, and needs were rarely at the center of what was going on. The next morning I walked in to class to find Ms. Wilson rubbing her hands together. "I'm going on a campaign starting today, the Latina girls' campaign. . . . I told Mr. Bridges that this morning and he said, 'Oh shit, whenever you go on one of your campaigns you win.'" Patterns in the class did change. Ms. Wilson was much more likely to call on Latinas during discussions and to encourage their active participation. Her commitment to equity did not mean that her classroom was free of problems; it did mean however that she was eager to get input on how to improve the classroom experience for all the students.

Though willing to talk about general issues of race and equity, the staff never seemed very comfortable talking about students of color in the school who were not doing well academically. As Mr. Bridges stated in a conversation one day, "The huge challenge is why our African American students, . . . as a general rule, are failing our program." Though he was quick to clarify that there were exceptions to this "general rule," he was distressed by the overall pattern. Vicki, for example, a fifth-grade African American girl, was reading and writing far below grade level. Midway through the first semester, Mr. Bridges called a meeting of the student study team (consisting of the principal, a resource teacher, and the regular classroom teachers) to talk about her status. He began the meeting saying he thought that "the school had chumped Vicki out of an education. . . . She's not reading or writing much in English, not at all in Spanish, her math is also very low . . . she essentially dropped out of Spanish last year." Ms. Wilson concurred that Vicki's spelling, language, and punctuation were all low and suggested that maybe it was a "linguistics thing coming in, maybe it's an Ebonics issue." After Ms. Wilson showed some recent writing samples to the group, Mrs. Lopez, who was Vicki's teacher last year, pointed out that there had been some progress. "Last year she was doing first-grade writing, we could not decipher it. What I see is that with help she can progress. In the appropriate environment she might move quite a bit." Mr. Bridges again raised concerns about whether Metro2 was the best place for her and whether, in fact, they had been clear enough with Vicki's parents: "I wonder if we've been strong enough. The parents have the ultimate power. As teachers, we tend to want to say that kids are okay, but this is not okay. It's keeping me up at night." Mrs. Lopez agreed, reiterating that because Vicki was going to middle school next year, they needed to get her some help soon: "Otherwise [her report card next year] is going to be, F, F, F, F, F." Vicki herself did not want to leave the school, so her parents had been interested in working with the staff to keep her there for the final year.

As a result of this meeting, Mr. Bridges, Ms. Wilson, and the resource teacher arranged a new schedule for Vicki that would essentially pull her out of Spanish and give her more English reading and writing help. These dedicated and committed teachers were trying to do the best for their student. However, as this meeting highlighted, some of this concern came a little late—Vicki's needs had been clear for some time and could, perhaps, have been addressed sooner. The strong undercurrent of the conversation was that they might have moved slowly in this case because of their own discomfort with the racial patterns in underperformance that Mr. Bridges described. Even in this case, however, the student study team discussed Vicki's struggles as school and instructional issues rather than as problems that resided within Vicki or her family. The team members made an effort to hold themselves accountable for having, in certain ways, failed this child.

Interestingly, the small number of African American students in the school indirectly took up the rest of the meeting of the student study team that morning as the teachers struggled with how to rearrange Vicki's schedule in a way that would maintain current levels of "integration." If they switched the group Vicki was based in, one class would have three African American children and the other none.

Staff consistently made efforts to integrate groups across and within classes. The only places this did not happen were the few instances of within-class ability grouping. For example, Ms. Wilson had divided her class into three spelling groups, each named after a character from a book they had read at the beginning of the year (the "Aunt Magnolias," the "Mr. Breedloves," and the "Mama Youngs"). Ms. Wilson expressed some reservations about this kind of ability grouping, but she had not figured out another efficient way of handling the spelling curriculum. Though she always referred to these groups only as the Magnolias, the Breedloves, and the Youngs and never talked about them as low, medium, and high groups, the students clearly recognized the hierarchy. Not long after the creation of these groups, I overheard a Latino and a biracial student talking about their groups. The Latino boy said he was in the Aunt Magnolias because "I'm weak." In some ways the children in the high group, the Mama Youngs, seemed most aware of the hierarchy. Earl, a member of the Youngs, came in one morning and looked at the new spelling words. He walked over to Ms. Wilson and told her that he thought she had gotten the words mixed up. "The Youngs look too easy, so it must be for the Magnolias." Ms. Wil-

_____ Table 4.1. _____
Racial breakdown of morning spelling groups at Metro2

	White	Biracial	Latino	Black
Total number in class	9	6	6	2
High group (Mama Youngs)	44%	25%	17%	—
Medium group (Mr. Breedloves)	33%	50%	17%	—
Low group (Aunt Magnolias)	22%	25%	67%	100%

_____

Note: Totals may not equal 100 percent because of rounding. Two learning-disabled students (one white and one Latino) are excluded from this table.

son looked and, realizing he was right, fixed the posting. Another day Mark, also one of the Youngs, compared his test grade with others at his table; he bragged about being the only one to get 100 percent. Omar, sitting at the next table, showed his paper—also with a sticker signifying no mistakes. Mark replied, "Yeah but the Breedloves' words are easier."

Importantly, these were not fixed groups; students were able to move up if they got six perfect spelling tests in a row. But they were also the least integrated groupings I ever saw at Metro2. The morning group included ten white students, six biracial students (all Latino and white), seven Latino (all dark-skinned, working-class students), and two black students. As Table 4.1 shows, whites were overrepresented in the high group, while Latino and black students were overrepresented in the low group.[16] During spelling tests, each group would be called up one at a time to take their test while the other groups read quietly on the rug. As the groups were separately called up, it was hard not to see the differences in the demographics.

In many ways this distribution captures the problems the teachers themselves highlighted—the general failure of African American students and the lack of coherent English as a Second Language instruction, which left English-language learners short on language skills in later grades. The way this breakdown graphically captures the social geography of race, with darker groups overrepresented at the bottom, is still, however, disturbing. Even if these groups were put together for pedagogically sound reasons in relation to spelling, they inevitably convey other kinds of messages and lessons. Students see and understand the distinctions among groups. The few white students in the low group seemed regularly embarrassed about their categorization and seemed to have much more anxiety about it than their Latino or black peers did. The structure of the spelling groups was one of the few ways Ms. Wilson's class mirrored the organizational pattern of typical elementary school classrooms. It was one of the few places where hierarchy ever entered the picture. Once it did, racial patterns were clear and were meaningful not only for what they suggested about who was best thriving in the school but also for the larger lessons the structure conveyed to students.

Patterns of social and academic integration (or segregation) are produced by and themselves produce students' understandings about group differences. For example, during interviews, a number of parents talked about how nice it was to see their children at Metro2 interacting with diverse groups of students. They talked proudly about the school as an integrated space. Almost inevitably, however, as we discussed their children's school experiences, parents of white and biracial students would pause at some point and remember a story or a comment their child had made that forced them to qualify what they had said. Perhaps, as one white mother put it, her daughter did think of herself as different from the "Spanish girls": "like I don't think she'd invite them over." Or as others put it, their children thought of themselves as different from the "Latino kids," "neighborhood kids," "immigrant children." Not only did these white children think of themselves as different, but they remained largely separate in informal activities. For example, as I was talking to Ms. Lawrence, the white mother of a biracial (Latino-white) student, she remarked that her son's friends were "not kids who are from primarily Spanish-speaking families." She was struggling with how to think about it: "So you know, at first you say, 'Oh I think [the school] deals with [racial diversity] really well,' but I don't know, I mean if there's something that I circle as slightly off, but maybe it's not the school's fault, I mean it's so hard for an institution to deal with that but it still seems like kids in some ways are very cliquish."

Mrs. Lawrence was not the only mother who discussed this lack of informal integration. When talking about her biracial son, Ms. Velez hesitated before remarking, "He and his friends, they are all 'white-ish.'" As others have mentioned in other contexts, certain light-skinned Latinos were able to move across boundaries and were even treated almost as "honorary whites" (Almaguer 1999; Bonilla-Silva and Glover forthcoming). Similarly, Ms. Hivert reported about her white son Mark, "Yeah, actually, some, I mean, his best friends happen to be white." These patterns recurred throughout interviews with parents of white and biracial children. Certain children were clearly different, or racial "others," in a setting that despite multiple efforts to the contrary still often functioned as a "white space." Maureen and Larry Brodski, the parents of Walt (a white fifth-grader), described their impression:

Maureen: When kids are in specific activities together, it seems to be a pretty harmonious place. But I think that in their private time they really break down racially, and I think that it's probably like that in every school.

Amanda: Why do you think that is?

Maureen: Shared culture.

Larry: Well, safe.

Maureen: Comfort, yeah.

Though children were able to work together, they still did not cross racial boundaries in "private time" inside or outside school boundaries.

Resources and Race

White and light-skinned, middle-class children were privileged at school in many ways. As I illustrate below, this situation is not just about class or about race but about the interaction of the two. Racial differences were often utilized as quick and easy signifiers of those who did or did not have cultural capital or access to resources. Moreover, it is no mere happenstance that white, biracial, and light-skinned third- or fourth-generation Latino children were middle-class. At issue here is the convergence of differences in culture, concerns, and priorities with differences in power and resources. Some families had more control than others. Mr. Bridges remarked:

> It's definitely Anglo parents over, over Latino parents. I don't mean "over." It's not like they're squashing them down although maybe—I think they are in— well you saw the Back to School Night. What happens is like this brouhaha develops in English. And it becomes just like this growing wave, and it's hard to fight it in Spanish. It's hard to keep the Spanish part in place. So yeah, it is run by English, run by Anglo parents . . . generally it is, I think they're the ones that—well, they tend to be middle-class. But not all of them. I mean there's more middle-class Anglo people than there are middle-class Latino people, right. And so um, so like our committee to go to Mexico is a great example, I mean they're all like . . . there's two Latino people but, um, they're not Spanish-speaking Latinos, you know. [laughs]

These power struggles worked themselves out both in relation to schoolwide politics and in classroom practices.

School Policy

Two controversial school issues had parents firmly divided. Several years before my study, a number of Latino parents had proposed having school uniforms. In relating the story to me, teachers explained that white and middle-class parents thought the plan too regimented and likely to squash their children's creativity. For Latino parents the issues were cost and equity. In the end the uniform initiative failed. In what Mrs. Lopez called "a pretty weak compromise," the school had "spirit days" on Monday and Friday, when students were encouraged to wear school shirts.

Early in my time at the school, the second controversial issue arose. Teachers had adopted a new policy to assign students who had not completed their homework to "detention" during recess. The issue was the subject of a heated discussion during Back to School Night. A group of parents who were almost entirely white voiced strong opinions that the policy was draconian if not contrary to school district regulations. After the meeting I spoke to a Latino father who strongly supported the policy and laughed at the other parents' "sensitivity," saying, "It's gonna be just like the uniforms thing," meaning that the white parents (who in this case were afraid of their children getting their "feelings hurt" by the public punishment) were going to dominate the debate and the result. Eventually teachers took a poll; almost all the forms filled out in Spanish supported the policy, while those in English were against it. The policy was abandoned within the first month of school. As the Latino father had predicted, the differential access to social networks and power of the different parent groups led white concerns to dominate school policy.

Though, as one white mother put it, the school was full of "political people . . . like the white sort of left-leaning people" who want their children to learn Spanish, who value a diverse learning environment, and who value a multicultural curriculum, in political struggles like these over school policy we see at play not merely cultural differences but differences in resources and power. Here the confrontations involve different understandings of discipline and different priorities. A white liberal commitment to individual freedom of expression comes up against concerns about cost, discipline, and equity. These school battles are in the end won or lost not on principle but on power. In this case white and biracial or bicultural middle-class families pursued the policy they believed was in their children's best interests, and the priorities of lower-status families lost out.

Extracurricular Clout: Knowledge, Skills, and Capital

The relatively empowered students had access to certain kinds of knowledge, skills, and cultural capital that paid off within the classroom. Some curricula were clearly suited to middle-class cultural knowledge. One day, for example, as an introduction to a new unit on U.S. geography, the class played several rounds of a game called USA Bingo. Ms. Wilson read clues about a state, and students raised their hands to answer. Prizes were awarded to those who correctly named the state and to those who got Bingo (not related to answering questions). Ms. Wilson went through twenty to twenty-five cards before someone called out "Bingo!" Of the more than twenty students playing, only two dark-skinned Latino students even raised their hands to guess. Many white and middle-class students who answered talked about the states as places they had traveled to or where relatives lived or where a parent had gone to college. Although a Latina was the one to eventually call out "Bingo!" she, along with many of her Latino peers, had otherwise sat silent for twenty minutes. Here, knowledge from nonschool sources provided school benefits. Although students were not directly penalized in this case for not having such information, as they are on standardized tests, they did indirectly lose out: students who had resources received benefits, either in the form of prizes or in increased teacher expectations.

Knowledge from households was important in other ways also. Some of the effects were beyond the control of the school. On more than one occasion, white students talked about help a parent had given them with their homework. One day four white or biracial boys were the only ones to complete a long, complicated math assignment; all four talked about getting some assistance from a parent. In contrast Marlyn, a Latina, arrived with a note from her mother saying, "Dear teacher: we were unable to do the homework. my daughter she didn't understand and also me, I've tried but I couldn't explain it to her." Although Marlyn was not penalized, the boys were rewarded for their completed work.

One might expect Spanish-dominant children to be able to utilize their skills with Spanish to secure some advantage. Yet, when Ms. Wilson described which students did best in the school, she spoke more about the cultural resources in Anglo and English-dominant homes. She referred to Spanish-speaking students' language skills as a resource only in the context of their serving as language models for others.

> Yeah, I think the kids that do best are the kids that, the kids that come from bilingual or Anglo homes that are very involved and that are warm nurturing places where they get a lot of extra help . . . kids coming from, I don't even know if I think the kids coming from Spanish-speaking homes do that well, in a lot of ways, I don't think they do nearly as well as some of the higher-end English-dominating kids because [English as a Second Language] is a major element that is missing from this program, so it's almost like Spanish-speaking kids serve as models [for Anglo students], and then they don't get the support when it comes time for them to acquire their English, not in later years or even in their earlier years.

Not only parental knowledge of the kind Ms. Wilson referred to but also parental action was at play in school outcomes. For example, parents who felt able to challenge the teacher's evaluation of their children often had immediate success. In one parent-teacher conference, Sarah's mother challenged Ms.

Wilson gently but firmly several times about Ms. Wilson's assessments of her daughter. As Ms. Wilson was explaining Sarah's reading grade, Sarah's mother stopped her and expressed some surprise, explaining how much Sarah liked to read. Ms. Wilson stumbled for a moment and then decided to raise the reading grade, explaining that it could have gone either way. Though Sarah's mother consistently questioned her judgment during the meeting, Ms. Wilson listened to her input and took it to heart. In contrast, during their conference with Ms. Wilson, Vicki's parents' equally gentle and also firm efforts to intervene in the assessment of their daughter's social problems were completely unsuccessful. Ms. Wilson repeatedly reasserted what she was seeing as the "facts" about what was going on and the need for Vicki to work on her attitude. Ms. Wilson thus seemed much more comfortable asserting her expertise and authority with some parents than with others.

As Lareau and Horvat (1999) discuss, the relative success of parents' actions on behalf of their children depends at least in part on how those actions are read or received (or both) by school personnel. Also important is having either the knowledge necessary to force the school to respond or the financial resources to get a child's needs met elsewhere. The few white students in the class who were struggling academically received extensive extra resources. One white student who had been classified as learning disabled had a mother who worked as a special education teacher. She often met with school personnel to explain her child's rights and the school's responsibility to provide him with services. His individual educational plan (unlike those of the Latino and black special education students) reflected this active intervention on her part. Another white student who had no special education designation but was a slow reader attended an expensive after-school supplemental program.

Aside from formal curricular issues, white and middle-class students seemed to have many more informal interactions with staff. They were more often helping out in the classroom before or after school, talking to a teacher at recess, or corresponding with old teachers via email. When I asked Ms. Wilson whether she thought her race had any impact on her relationships with students, she hesitated but eventually responded that it probably did:

> Well, I guess um, I don't know, no. I don't know, maybe it could be . . . I think I'm pretty fair to all the students. I mean at least I try to be as fair as I can to all the students. I would not deny though that I definitely have more conversations with, or the kids that seek me out more tend to be the more Anglo kids. And I think that it's two things, one is their English is strong and I'm their English model and so they feel like you know, whatever. Two is, I think it's a personality thing that they really identify with me or whatever and they

reach out to all their other teachers as well. We have like a certain group of Anglo kids that are always very verbal, so yeah, I guess in some ways it does.

We can see how an otherwise articulate Ms. Wilson stumbles through this explanation that her stronger connections with Anglo students were not necessarily how she wanted it to be but the way it was. Given the multiple demands on her time and energy, she did not seem to have much energy left to worry about who was stopping by to chat. Yet her estimation of some children as more, as she put it, "verbal" than others was not without implications. For example, on the first day of school two white female students helped to organize books in the classroom before school. Ms. Wilson was telling me about her class and whispered to me while gesturing toward the girls, "You'd be amazed at the intellectual capacity of some of these children. It blows me away sometimes." The range of student ability is really wide, she continued, "from LEP kids to middle-class white kids like them."

Particularly in a Spanish-immersion program such as that at Metro2, limited skill with English should not so easily serve as a proxy for low school performance. The label *LEP* is supposed to be a notation of a skill—English-language proficiency—not a measure of academic ability or proclivity. Yet, as the quote above demonstrates, terms like *LEP, Spanish,* and *English* were often used as shorthand designations of status that signified much more than language mastery. Given group-level differences in whom students of different races spent time with, the ways parents of different races interacted with the school, the amount of class participation by students of different races, and the racial make-up of the spelling groups, race clearly shaped school outcomes in a number of ways (including access to power, cultural capital, skills or human capital, and the resulting benefits).

Making Sense of Race

As discussed, Metro2 staff were actively engaged with issues of equity in their school. Yet, the exact way those issues were understood and articulated may well perpetuate them as problems and issues that need to be talked about in the school. For example, though many Latino Metro2 students had dark-brown skin and Mestizo features, the category Latino was often talked about solely as an ethnic or cultural rather than a racial designation. As Mr. Camarena, a lower-grade teacher demonstrated in his first comment to me (that race was not relevant at the school because of the small number of African Americans), the large group of Latino students were understood to constitute a cultural or ethnic group rather than a racial one. As a result, group differences in access to power and resources often received less attention than did issues of cultural distinctiveness. Though teachers did talk about power, they did so most often in reference only to class status. For example, in early conversations, Mr. Bridges suggested there were achievement gaps among groups, but he believed the gaps to be class-based rather than racial. However, race and class were highly correlated: the underperforming working-class and poor students were almost exclusively either African Americans or dark-skinned Latinos. Though many markers of difference were explicitly read as cultural markers— less imbued with power, more a signal of diversity—they in fact functioned also as racial signifiers that carried multiple layers of meaning. In many ways staff, parents, and students were less than clear about how race was shaping their own understandings and interactions. Explicit local discourses about differ- ence operated in the realm of culture, expressed support for diversity and cul- tural distinctiveness, and helped to generate a collective narrative of acceptance and openness. At the same time implicit discourses of difference, which oper- ated in the realm of racial categories, were imbued with meaning and power and, although (or sometimes because) they remained unstated, continued to shape practices in ways that benefited some more than others.

This dynamic could be seen in the different ways various Latino students were positioned in the school. It became clear over time, as exemplified in the patterns discussed above, that there were two group of Latinos in Metro2. In school district terms, they were officially categorized either as Latino or as "other nonwhite." These categories were less clear in practice. For all those stu- dents who were labeled by parents, teachers, or peers or who self-identified (or both) as Latino, skin tone, class, and language status were significant. In many ways the label *Latino* operated for some as an ethnic category and for others as a racial category. Although one group was viewed as Latino in relation to Anglos (a cultural category) in regard to issues of culture and heritage, only a subset of this group was viewed as Latino in relation to whites (a racial category) in regard to differences in race and power. In practice these two groups were dis- tinguished by several overlapping and closely correlated markers of differ- ence—language, class, and particularly phenotype (physical, observable features such as skin tone, hair texture, facial features). Because class, lan- guage, and phenotype were so highly correlated and because class and lan- guage are more difficult to "see," phenotype often functioned as a shorthand way of delineating who was who.

In general, racial membership is often not as important as whether one sig- nals racial difference—a particular racial membership—to others. For example, historically, light-skinned African Americans who were able to "pass" secured access to many opportunities and resources that would have been denied them otherwise (Davis 1991). Thus, "passing" meant that those who might legally have been defined as black under the "one-drop rule" could avoid the many negative character ascriptions and material penalties associated with "blackness." Here, I am not concerned with one's internal sense of self or with how one would be legally classified if genealogical charts were brought to bear in a court hearing but with the external assignment of identity that occurs in interpersonal interactions.[17]

Issues of sameness and difference are central to processes of social identification and differentiation. Social identities are inherently relational: one both identifies with like and defines oneself against difference (Jenkins 1996; Phoenix 1998). We are partly who we are because we are not something else. In regard to racial identity, our understandings of categories and boundaries depend on our knowing where both we and others fit in. We use various inputs as signals of racial status in processes of racial identification and differentiation. Drawing on available information about skin color, facial features, language, and cultural styles, we determine how people we interact with fit into the available racial schemes. This information is also understood to convey or signal who a person is in more profound ways (Omi and Winant 1994). These racial differences are important only because, as Hall (1986a) argues, racial categorization and issues of power and access are inseparable. Unlike dissimilarities that make little to no difference (e.g., shoe size), the racial category in which one is placed has implications for both identity and life chances.

Issues of racial classification have been contested in relation to Latinos and Asians, particularly Latinos (Almaguer and Jung 1999; Falcón 1995; Gonzalez 1998; Jones-Correa and Leal 1996; Melville 1988; Nelson and Tienda 1985; Rodriguez 1991; 1992; Rodriguez and Cordero-Guzman 1992; Zimmerman et al. 1994). "Latino" incorporates a wide range of groups from distinct geographical, political, and social contexts.[18] Although Latinos share a language (though there are certainly variations in the kind of Spanish spoken), they do not share a country of origin, a history outside the United States, or a mode of incorporation into the United States. Asians have generally been categorized as a distinct racial group, but Latino has been utilized primarily as a panethnic category encapsulating those who are racially white, black, and "other." These within-group racial differences are particularly pronounced in relation to Caribbean Latinos from Puerto Rico, the Dominican Republic, and Cuba—countries that have a history of African presence. Though Latinos in the United States are pressed into our existing racial categories (more or less successfully), they come from societies in which racialization is a far more diverse and complex phenomenon (Almaguer and Jung 1999; Rodriguez 1991). In contrast with the bifurcated racial scheme in the United States, which is determined by blood or descent, racial categorization in Latin American countries involves more layers of gradation and incorporates a variety of factors, including skin tone, class, and other status markers.

In some ways this more complex, Latin American–style racialization scheme was operating at Metro2. The confusion around the category Latino was not surprising in this setting, in which many self-designated Latino students did not readily signal nonwhite status. Some Latino students were phenotypically white, were clearly empowered, and had access to middle-class cultural, social, and economic resources. Others came to school with poor English-language skills, few economic resources, and few prerequisite skills and understandings. As Ms. Wilson indicated, most of these students, often captured with the "LEP" designation, were by the fourth and fifth grades also in a separate academic category from their middle-class white, biracial, or Latino peers. Class, race, ethnicity, and language converged here in a muddled but complex set of understandings about difference.

Race is not a real or innate characteristic of bodies but a set of signifiers projected onto these bodies. Unlike other physical differences, phenotypic differences that signal racial difference are imbued with meaning. Because of the depth and pervasiveness of these racial meanings, because of the persistence and strength of racial boundaries, and because race and power have been so inextricably intertwined throughout the history of the category, racial designations have an impact on social location. The issue then is not whether these students were really racially different or whether "Latino" is really a racial group. One could quite correctly answer no (or yes) to both issues. However, in daily interactions, a group of students labeled *Latino* were interacted with as if they were racially "other." Thus, the staff's complex notions of who was racially "different," where the boundaries fell, were based not only on students' skin color (a form of symbolic capital) but also on their cultural styles, performances, and tastes—all signals of "outsiderness." The black/white binary seemed to be in effect even in this setting: light-skinned, middle-class, English-speaking Latino students who did not signal "nonwhiteness" were generally interacted with as white and received the benefits attached to that category. To the extent that students did not easily fit into the white or black categories, they were situated somewhere in between; dark-skinned, working-class, Spanish-dominant students existed in the territory of "neither black nor white"—racial "others" who signaled the kind of racial difference that has multiple ramifications but who did not fit neatly into dominant schemes.

Thus the process of racialization or racial categorization was perhaps more complex at Metro2 than in the other schools, but it still operated and did so in important ways. To illustrate some of these processes of categorization and ascription, I discuss here the circumstances of several students who existed on the borders of traditional racial/ethnic categories.

Héctor was the son of an El Salvadoran father and a white (European American) mother. Both parents had low-income origins and worked in low-paid, white-collar jobs. In a conversation, Héctor's mother reported her son's regular frustration that teachers considered him white and assumed that his first language was English. Héctor's El Salvadoran grandmother, who spoke only Spanish, had provided full-time child care for him since he was three weeks old. Thus Héctor was truly bilingual from a young age. If he had a first language, it was Spanish. Though Héctor was read as white, he was proud of his Latino heritage and of his skill with Spanish. Though his teachers might not deny his Latino ethnicity, in casual classroom exchanges he was regarded as distinct from the dark-skinned, working-class Latino children. Thus, no matter how he envisioned himself, Héctor was generally associated with whiteness. For instance, in class, when teachers were calling on native Spanish speakers, he was functionally excluded from a group of which he was, in reality, a part. He was sometimes referred to by other kids on the soccer field as "Gringo," a nickname that pained and embarrassed him.

Héctor's status contrasted interestingly with Omar's. Though similar to Héctor in parental heritage, Omar was categorized quite differently by teachers and peers. He was, like Héctor, the son of a Latino father and a white mother. He lived with his father in the heart of the large Latino neighborhood surrounding the school. He and his best friend, Eduardo, a dark-skinned Latino boy, were inseparable. Though Omar regularly talked ambiguously about his own identity, he was externally situated as Latino, as "nonwhite." Though he often referred to himself as a European American, as a brown-skinned boy from the neighborhood, whose social networks included other brown-skinned boys, he was externally situated as Latino, in this case a racial designation as much as an ethnic one. This process was not passive but occasionally incorporated direct action or ascription. For example, one class project, called a "culture bag," involved students' bringing in items from their "culture" and sharing them with the class. At the beginning of their presentation, children introduced themselves and described their ethnic origins. Omar's presentation was the only one in which I saw the teacher prompt or correct a student's self-description. When Omar described himself as "European American," Ms. Wilson interrupted him and asked in a perplexed tone where in Europe his parents were from. He explained that his mother was from Germany and his father from Bolivia. "So you're Latino also?" "Yes."

In a different way, Enrique's Latino-ness was rarely referenced or acknowledged. The child of an African American father and a Chicana mother, in most official capacities Enrique was referred to as African American or black. Enrique was quite proud to be black, but he was also quite proud to be Chicano. His blackness, however, as is traditional in U.S. racial schemes, trumped his other bloodlines, and he was in practice regarded as black, even as he led chants of "Viva La Raza!"

Pushing the boundaries of all racial categorization, Benjamin was the son of an Indonesian father and a Colombian mother. He was particularly uncomfortable with ethnic and racial classifications, ducking and resisting moments when he was asked to describe himself. Despite his ambivalence, peers often quickly and easily ascribed to him to an exclusively Asian identity, specifically as "Chinese."

Héctor thought of himself as Latino but was considered white by his teachers. Omar seemed to think of himself as racially white, but all signals suggested he was externally categorized as racially "other"—Latino. Enrique thought of himself as black and Latino but was referred to as black or African American. Benjamin did his best to avoid the existing racial schemes but was nevertheless mapped into them by his peers. Each of the four boys was in practice ascribed to a specific racial category different from the one with which he identified. These are just a few examples of students whose own identities and those ascribed to them by their teachers and peers did not match up perfectly. In many ways, these sorts of identifications were much more fluid and flexible at Metro2 than in the other schools. In other ways, the exact system by which boundaries were understood, interpreted, or drawn in daily exchange demonstrates the persistent power of racial difference.

These are differences that matter. As demonstrated throughout this work, a relationship exists between race and power such that those in certain groups collectively have more financial, social, and cultural resources as a result of long histories of racism and oppression. Even in a place like Metro2, where people imagined themselves to be antiracist, whiteness still functioned as a symbolic resource, providing all those who possessed it with the benefit of assumed knowledge and ability. Not only did race directly and indirectly influence which students got into Metro2, which ones were able to get the school to serve them most directly, and what kind of resources families could draw on once there, it also affected how people were read and understood by others in the school community. For instance, Enrique's being read as black affected the holidays he was asked to talk to the class about (e.g., Kwanza) and the group he was assigned to for integration purposes, in addition to influencing whom he identified with and was friends with. In this way, despite the ambiguity surrounded the category Latino, staff clearly understood both white and black as mutually exclusive racial categories.

White became a signifier for enfranchised, middle-class, influential families and children. Partly this association concerned social class, but white was also used to represent the relatively empowered, the category of parents who controlled much of what happened in the school, the category of children who had cultural capital and relatively higher skills. White was not used to describe all that was good and virtuous, nor all that was oppressive. It was a description of a social location. In this way, on a continuum from white to black the school was whiter than it was anything else. Academic programs predominantly benefited white, English-dominant children. Middle-class, mostly white parents ruled the PTA and the site council. English was the unofficial high-status language. The staff signaled these consequences to me when they described Metro2 as a white school. It was not an admission by the staff of a desired outcome but an admission of the workings of power and status and of the school's shortcomings. Thus, though Metro2 was in many ways a progressive space in which current racial realities were at least partially confronted, those challenges were only partially successful. As a community collectively engaged in self-reflection and with issues of equity, however, Metro2 did offer reason to be hopeful about different future outcomes.

Five

Learning and Living Racial Boundaries

Constructing and Negotiating Racial Identity in School

One day during recess at Metro2 I observed an exchange that I recorded in my fieldnotes as follows:

> Lily and Kate, two fourth-grade girls, stand on the schoolyard talking. As part of a class presentation that morning, Lily had described her ethnic heritage as "Mexican American and European American." She is asking Kate about her own background—"just Caucasian." Seeing Benjamin (a biracial/bicultural Columbian and Indonesian fifth-grader) sitting nearby eating his morning snack, Lily turns to him and asks, "What are you?" He looks at the two girls for several moments without replying. Eventually he responds that he would "rather not say." Trying to be helpful, one of the girls offers, "You're Chinese, right?" When he does not respond to either confirm or deny their suggestion, the girls turn away.

Like Benjamin, all adults and children must contend with others' racial ascriptions—external racial identifications that may or may not match individuals' own self-identifications. In daily interactions like the one here, people regularly go through the same process as Lily and Kate—they work with available racial categories and meanings, draw on available cues, and make decisions about who they think someone is, where in the racial schema the person they are observing fits. In this chapter I discuss these issues of racial signification as they operated in all three school communities. By *racial signification,* I mean the way race comes to affect our understandings of ourselves and others and how, as part of that process, it simultaneously shapes our interactions and opportunities.

Schools provide a venue in which to study larger social processes as well as a unique setting in which to study identity formation—they are one of the central places where notions of self are formed. Confrontations over difference often happen for the first time in school, and they tend to happen over an extended period. The data collected in this study give us a window into racialization processes, and they allow us to examine these processes at work in the place where we often first learn about difference and about who we are in the larger world. Schools are the context in which we land when we first leave the family. Moreover, because the schools in this study are elementary schools, we are able to study them as communities in which families are still integrally involved. In this way I am envisioning schools as functioning in relation to family rather than separately from family. Thus, in this chapter, I draw on data not only from interviews and observations within school buildings but also from interviews with parents and other school community members.

In previous chapters I described how race is part of the normal operation of schools; as Omi and Winant (1994: 60) describe it, race is "a way of comprehending, explaining, and acting in the world." Race, for example, shapes how teachers understand and interact with the children in their classrooms, how adults and children make decisions about who would make a good friend, classmate, or neighbor, and, as in the example above, how peers make sense of each other. In this chapter I analyze how racialization processes played out in the three school communities. These processes include how people get racially categorized; how boundaries between racial categories are formed, negotiated, and interpreted; and how those first two processes (racialization and boundary formation) affect interactions and opportunities. Drawing on observational and interview data from all three schools, I analyze the ways race shapes interpretations of the world and how people understand their experiences in racial terms.

Racial-Ascription Processes

Racial-ascription processes are in operation most of the time; they are part of the backdrop to interpersonal interactions. We utilize familiar social categories to anticipate what to expect from strangers and strange situations. "The ability to identify unfamiliar individuals with reference to known social categories allows us at least the illusion that we know what to expect from them" (Jenkins 1996: 83). Categorization usually takes place automatically and unconsciously except when we confront someone who is racially ambiguous; in such cases categorization becomes more conscious and deliberate. As in the well-known *Saturday Night Live* skit involving a character named Pat, who has a number of ambiguous gender characteristics, when we encounter people who seem to straddle several racial categories or who do not easily fit into our existing schema, we draw on all available information to try to determine where they fit. The process of racial categorization in such situations is not necessarily different from the more common unconscious and automatic processes taking place when someone's race is seemingly obvious, but it is more explicit. Therefore these ambiguous situations often provide insight into how categorization works more generally—what cues or indicators we look for, how we interpret them, what we do with conflicting information. Once categorization is complete, once we have utilized available clues or signs to decide where someone fits, we have, in fact, created a relationship with that person—one imbued with perceived lines of sameness and difference, in which the person is variously "like us" or "different."

In addition to categorizing others, we must, both interpersonally and in our interactions with official institutions, contend with others' evaluations of who or what we are. For example, Rodney, an African American fourth-grader at West City, made the following evaluation of his Latino fifth-grade peer Mike:

Amanda: What about Mike, what is he?
Rodney: White.
Amanda: He's white?
Rodney: He white to me.

It is safe to say that Mike would have been quite upset had he heard Rodney's ascription of majority identity to him. Yet in his use of the phrase "He white to me," Rodney astutely recognized the reality that external racial ascriptions in many ways matter as much as one's self-identification, if not more. Thus though what Mike thought (how he self-identified) mattered, it did not necessarily trump the identity ascribed to him externally. Rodney was reading the world and mapping those he saw into the schema as he understood it, and as far as he was concerned, Mike was white. As Jenkins (1996: 2) states, "Identity is often in the eye of the beholder." Though Rodney's reading may have mattered less to Mike than that of Mike's teacher, a store owner, or a future employer, peer judgments of racial categorization and performance are far from unimportant or meaningless.[1]

The examples of Lily, Kate, and Benjamin from Metro2 and of Mike and Rodney from West City illustrate the kinds of external ascriptions that are a daily part of peer interactions in school. Racial ascriptions also are a part of interactions between teachers and students. In a case involving Metro2 school personnel, Ms. Lawrence discussed her son Héctor's struggle to be "recognized" at school. In my interview with him, Héctor had unequivocally identified himself as Latino, but as his mother reported, he was not necessarily read as Latino at school.

Well, let's see, well his father is originally from El Salvador and Héctor, Spanish is really his first language, although I've never been able to convince anybody at Metro2 of that. I think they look at him and they think he's white, basically and don't want to hear otherwise. . . . My concerns stem more from, have people been able to see my son as I see him or how I think he is? And I don't think that's always happened. . . . He had two kindergarten teachers, one of them didn't even know that he spoke Spanish . . . and they're suppose to assess him and they're like writing a report card, you know, "Spanish coming along . . . " and to me that is just so annoying and I try to talk to them but it's like they think he's white. Whenever [my ex-husband and I] talk to him about being in two different cultures, Héctor goes "yes, but I'm not white, look at my skin," his skin's like very very pale but he's saying it's brown.

As we can see from Ms. Lawrence's discussion of her son's defense of his own self-identification, skin color was a key factor both in his teachers' identifying him as white and in his own claims to be otherwise. That skin color was used both in the teachers' reading of him as white and in his own defense of his brownness highlights the often subjective quality of this category. Yet, skin color is not the only factor at play in racial ascription. As Héctor's relationships with his teachers illustrate, language is closely linked to, and often works in interaction with, readings of external physical features (phenotype). Héctor's teachers' mistaken assumptions about his Spanish-language proficiency were tightly interwoven with their reading of him as white (a speculation on Mrs. Lawrence's part that my observations largely affirmed). Language and physical features often interact with other factors to mark someone as similar or different ("of color").

Markers of Difference/Otherness

When Ms. Harrison, an African American first-grade teacher at West City, reflected on her experiences growing up and what had made her feel different, she talked not only about skin color and language but also about other factors.

It came up with skin color and hair, and a lot of that has to do with being female and growing up you know, with no TV and not having a lot of white folks around me necessarily, but you know, wanting to be like the more fair-skin, long-hair children and stuff. So that was a message . . . I don't know, but those were issues that came out. And language—either black people say "you talk like a white girl" or feeling uncomfortable, talking in front of white people and stuff, you know, all of that. Those were some real important messages.

Ms. Harrison experienced being different in relation to color, hair, racially coded standards of beauty, and racially coded ways of talking. She described struggling while growing up to find ways of speaking that would allow her to be successful in school but not leave her feeling like an outsider in her own community. In this way, language is not a neutral mode of communication but a way of telling who people are, where they are from, whether they are in some way collectively different or whether they are "like us" and therefore are people to whom we can easily relate. Not only is language racialized (certain ways of talking are thought of as black or white), language itself racializes (certain ways of talking can mark one as racially other).

In making decisions about who is white and who is not, language, accent, cultural performances, and other signals of social location regularly come into play. All these are somehow indicators of difference and perhaps nonwhiteness. These various markers of otherness operate interactively to move people further or closer on the continuum of difference. For example, when I asked Anne Velez, the white mother of Jorge, a biracial white/Latino fifth-grader at Metro2, how he racially self-identified, she raised issues of cultural performance as key to racial identification. Initially she signaled her son's Latino-ness by stating, "Well, he's a *Velez*." Almost immediately, however, she began to backtrack as she remembered a recent incident. Ms. Velez's Latina sister-in-law, Aunt Maribel, took Ms. Velez's boys and her own children to the amusement park every summer; in the past Jorge had had trouble getting on the roller coasters because of his height. This year Maribel gelled Jorge's hair back to make him appear taller. As Ms. Velez stated, "It worked, and he got on, and it was fabulous." Yet, as she reported, when he looked at himself in the mirror with his new hairdo, Jorge's reaction was to laugh as he said, "'I look like a Latino kid,' and [his aunt] goes, 'Well what do you think you are?'" This incident highlights the performative nature of race; when it comes to everyday interactions, certain kinds of performances, styles, or costumes may determine what one "is" or how one is seen and categorized as much as if not more than "blood," ancestry, or phenotype.

In fact, later in our conversation this same mother raised an additional possible marker of racial difference when she described what she perceived as a private school's somewhat hypocritical attempt to recruit her children as a way of bringing in more students of color. Though the school was interested in them as part of an effort to diversify their student body, Ms. Velez talked about her family as more "pseudo-color" than real color. When I asked her what she meant by this term, she replied:

Well, I mean, you know—pseudo-color. I think [my husband] and I are, I mean, we're, [our sons are] a *Velez,* but, you know, I mean [they are] a blend.

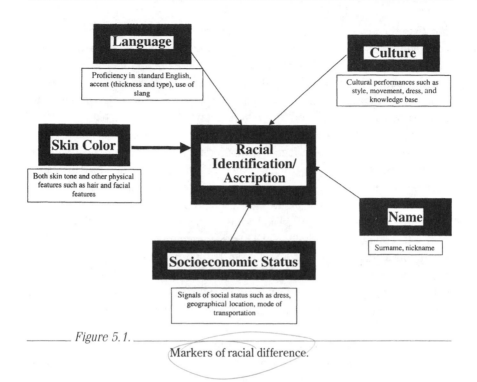

_____ *Figure 5.1.* _____

Markers of racial difference.

I mean I feel like everybody's blended, I mean we're getting more and more blended so, I feel . . . what did I mean by pseudo-color? I meant maybe economically, we're not, you know, we're definitely, there's a certain level of economically advantaged people that go there and, we're not at that [level], we're not up there, but we're fine and we're not poor and so I guess that I was making us this break—they were trying to diversify the people that [go to the school] but that diversification only went a certain distance.

As she expressed it, her children were not very different from those already attending the school, and that understanding led her to question the school's commitment to diversity. Thus, in her lexicon, her family's "pseudo-color" status was not only about skin tone or being biracial or "blended" but about being financially secure—a status not symbolically associated with being a "minority." I am not suggesting that money necessarily has the power to "whiten," as it does in some Latin American countries, but that a complex set of criteria is used to signal racial difference. These markers of difference combine to position one symbolically as close or distant.

As Figure 5.1 shows, a collection of factors provides the information for making racial identifications. The thicker arrow connecting skin color to ascription points to the fact that in many ways phenotype functions as a trump card: skin color and other physical features can unambiguously mark one as being racially other. In these unambiguous cases other factors are not unimportant; they often function as modifiers, answering the question "how other" or "how different." These factors may shape the kinds of racial stereotypes that come into play; for example, dress, language, and style may affect whether an Asian teenager is read as a dangerous gang-banger or a brainy overachiever. However, as many African Americans experience daily, in many situations (say, trying to hail a cab) few factors besides skin tone matter much at all (dress, language, and other indicators cannot protect one from negative outcomes of racial categorization).

When external physical features are ambiguous, people draw on other markers of difference (e.g., language and name) to figure out how to read those they confront. The mere introduction of a name, for example, can shift racial/ethnic ascription instantaneously from white to Latina or Native American. In other cases, markers such as accent or cultural performance can themselves introduce ambiguity and confusion where it did not previously exist (maybe the initial reading was incorrect? maybe they are not really what we thought?).

This process works not only in external ascriptions but in people's self-identifications. When Ms. Velez and other parents of biracial and bicultural children discussed their own and their children's flexible and changing identifications, they talked about language and culture as much as they did about color. For example, when Ms. Guerrero, who is Latina, indicated that her children would identify themselves as both Latino and Filipino, I asked which they would select if they had to pick one. "Latino. It's just they are more and more interested in it, you know. I mean, you know, Mom is around and Dad hasn't taught them his language. That makes a difference, he hasn't taught them his music, you know." As she indicated, her children's choice was driven partly by language and culture, factors that led them to feel closer to one identity than to the other. On meeting them, people would not automatically or necessarily identify them as Latino, but, given the children's somewhat ambiguous appearance, their speaking fluent Spanish might be enough to clear up categorical confusion.

As these examples demonstrate, racialization processes are often easiest to see and identify at the borders between categories. In these cases such processes become conscious, and explanation is required. In regard to both self-identification and the categorization of others, processes that are in effect in all cases become more self-evident and explicit as people navigate through ambiguous racial terrain. Thus, though I give many examples of biracial children and multiracial families who exist on the borders between racial categories, the process they grapple with is operating in interpersonal interactions generally—although it may be only implicit or assumed.[2]

The Confrontation of Internal and External Identifications

Choices about self-identification must necessarily be made in interaction with an external world that regularly assigns identities. Omar, a Metro2 fifth-grader whose father was Latino and whose mother was German, struggled with these issues. His experience exemplifies some of the complexity in the confrontation of internal and external identifications. Omar's father, Mr. Morales, who was Latino, described his son's self-identification:

> I think that Omar identifies himself more with Latinos, in part because he lives with me, and all his life he has lived with me, so, you can't obviate that fact. At the same time, he feels part of the whole American culture. He speaks more English than Spanish, for example. But I don't even think that he has determined what he wants to be, and I think that it's definitely up to him, and what he wants. If he wants to be, to determine himself as white, American, or white-Latino or Latino-Latino, or Hispanic, I think that will come later.

As I discussed in Chapter 4, Omar did identify as both white and Latino in different moments, but he was externally identified almost exclusively as Latino. He was, in practice, not really able to choose. Omar understood this reality to some extent. As his father explained, Omar recognized his own status when it came to various political issues. For example, he and his father had participated in marches and protests against the anti-immigrant Proposition 187, and Omar, despite his U.S. citizenship, had identified with the group being collectively targeted and unwanted—Latinos.

As many adults and children in this study described, they most often thought self-consciously about their identities in moments of confrontation with other individuals, institutions, or situations—moments where an external identification was made. For instance, Mr. Ortiz, who did not necessarily signal any nonwhiteness in his physical appearance, regularly had people define him as white. It was mostly at these moments, he reported, that he thought about his own identity.

Amanda: How often do you think about your racial identity in your life these days?
Mr. Ortiz: Not a whole lot, unless it's asked.
Amanda: What kind of things make, bring it up?
Mr. Ortiz: Oh—the most apparent is, when I'm at a store, or outdoors. Any location, I believe, where there are people. And . . . they will assume that I'm Anglo or whatever. And they'll make some comment in regards to immigrants or Hispanics or Southeast Asian or whatever that . . . and then I speak to them in Spanish, and then they get embarrassed.

Mr. Ortiz indicated that the issue was not only that people saw him as white but that when they did read him as Anglo, they were reading him as someone likely to be sympathetic to racist or xenophobic remarks. They were making a categorical mistake in assuming he was like them. His response, to speak in Spanish, was to automatically invalidate that assumption and at least symbolically distance himself.

Although many whites explained that they thought about their racial identifications only in confrontations with others, for many African Americans and dark-skinned Latinos this kind of confrontation with external racial ascriptions was such a part of daily interactions that they had come to understand it as a regular factor—whether the ascriptions were made explicit or not. Thus, thinking about their own racial identities was an everyday thing, not an unusual occurrence. Both positively (e.g., having pride in their racial heritage) and negatively (e.g., dealing with racism), they had come to understand their racial identity as a part of daily life.

Racial Boundary Formation

The various interactions described earlier—between Lily and Kate and Benjamin, between Héctor and his teachers—are skirmishes along the borders between racial categories. As categories are applied in interpersonal interactions, the boundaries between categories are simultaneously created or reinforced. One cannot determine who one is without determining simultaneously who one is not and in some manner, at least metaphorically, drawing a boundary. But these racial boundaries are not fixed. They are in flux, the ongoing products of social interaction in which identities are produced and reproduced.

The borders between groups were not the same in each school. As Figure 5.2 illustrates, some of the schools had a fair amount of fluidity between certain racial categories, a moderate amount of border crossing, while at others boundaries were more fixed and borders were less permeable. For example, at West City racial categorization was an either/or process of identifying which single category a person belonged to. In contrast, both Metro2 and Foresthills had some room for movement between white and Asian and white and Latino categories. In every context however, white and black still functioned as mutually exclusive and distinct categories, with little to no crossing or fluidity, and thus no overlap. For example, Sylvie was a black child regardless of the fact that she had a white mother. Enrique, at Metro2, was a black child no matter how he self-identified ethnically. Moreover, white and black were still the primary referential categories—the two poles that other categories were defined in reference to. For example, when Crystal, a white Foresthills fourth-grader, described several of her classmates she said: "Well Cedric [a Filipino fourth-grader] is kind of black kind of. Unless he's really really tan, but . . . um . . . otherwise that's

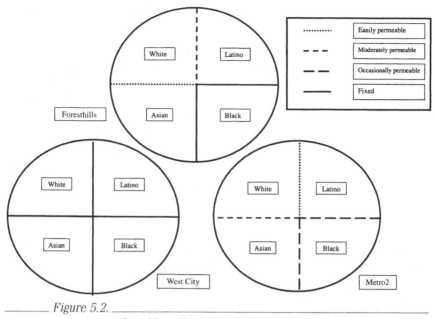

_____ *Figure 5.2.* _____

Racial boundaries in the three schools.

kind of it. Jake [a Korean fourth-grader] is kinda white. But kinda tan, but he's more on the white side kind of." Whether students were seen as kind of white or kind of black depended not only on phenotypic variation but also on relative acculturation and socioeconomic status—all those factors indicated in Figure 5.1 that play into racial identification and serve as markers of racial difference.

Racial Meaning, Power, and Exclusion

In regard to race, the delineation of same and different that transpires during ascription is not a neutral or benign process but one imbued with power. People experience not merely being identified or labeled but, as boundaries are drawn, being simultaneously included or excluded—they are treated in a particular way because someone has identified them as a member of a particular racial group. Racial identifications thus are not merely about thought processes but about action; acts of inclusion and exclusion are part of the racialization process. These acts range from explicit exclusion or racial violence (e.g., racial discrimination) to subtle inclusion (e.g., Mr. Ortiz's being included in a white "we" who are hostile to immigration). In truth, the process of being confronted with external ascriptions and the many accompanying stereotypes and assumptions is one that we all deal with, but it affects various groups quite differently.

Racial minorities are much more often confronted with negative assumptions and exclusionary practices as a result of racial-ascription processes, while whites often reap advantages from their categorization.

One Latina mother, Ms. Carillo, described what often happened when her Latino-ness was recognized: "Oh, yes, yes, right off the bat [people] recognize the Latino, don't you think? The Hispanic. Not that one feels bad about it, you know, but some people give us bad looks sometimes or . . . or they do not answer the way they should. I have seen racism in that sense particularly. A certain look sometimes says it all." This subtle exclusion plays out not only in "a certain look" but also at times in a certain tone of voice. As London, an African American nine-year-old explained, sometimes a way of speaking says it all:

Amanda: Has anybody ever been mean to you or treated you differently because of your color?

London: Yeah.

Amanda: How so?

London: People in the store.

Amanda: What happened?

London: A month ago. He accused me because he just, he just start yelling but I don't know why though.

Amanda: Do you think he was yelling at you because you were black?

London: Yes.

Amanda: How do you know?

London: I don't know, it just sounded like it.

Ms. Carillo and London recognized through subtle (or not so subtle) interactional cues that someone had made assessments of them based on a racial ascription. They had behaved or appeared in ways that marked them as qualitatively different, as lesser. In these cases the subjects became aware of ways that others had read them racially and the maltreatment that followed. These kinds of daily microaggressions take a toll on those who experience them (Lewis, Chesler, and Forman 2000; Solórzano, Ceja, and Yosso 2000).

This process of being marked, of being placed in a category and bounded-off, operates in multiple ways in multiple spheres of social interaction. As another Latino father discussed, he was regularly forced to think about his own race as he tried to negotiate successfully through the world:

Yes, I don't think about it constantly, I don't go out thinking "I'm Latino" but it is true that frequently, one is forced to do so. For example, when I go to Batista Valley, when I think about [going], I think about, "what time it is and where you are going, and why?"[3] Because I'm Latino, and it just so happens that they have a history of racism over there. For example, at the train station [there], they hanged a black man, about six years ago, maybe five. So then . . . there are certain places where there are certain organizations like the skinheads, or people like the KKK, there are certain cities which have a certain history, and when there is a certain history, one necessarily has to think about one's color and everything, because you have certain defenses which immediately tell you that you are at risk. When the police appears, that's really obvious, any Latino can tell you that—that he had problems with the police—so you think that it's your race, in the sense that you are running a higher risk than if you were white. At work also [in lots of ways, like the story I told of being called a wetback]. Then, the accent you have, that makes you think a lot about what you are because it's really . . . if I call the bank for some information, I obtain less information than if, for example, Jennifer, my loved one, calls. Because she has no accent or anything, but if I call, I get less information, why? So that makes you think, "Oh, of course, it's because I'm Latino." Sometimes I have, just to be practical, if I need any information, if we need tickets to go and visit someone in Los Angeles or whatever, to facilitate and make thinks quicker, "Why don't you call? That way, we'll be done more quickly." Because otherwise, there's always a problem, and that's obviously a racial issue. So yes, Latinos, particularly me, sometimes I am forced to think about the racial issue or to look at the color of my skin, because you are forced into that situation.

As this example illustrates, less subtle kinds of exclusion can take the form of a selective distribution of information, police harassment, or threats of physical violence. In a matter of moments this father rattled off the daily experiences of exclusion—all the ways his race put him at risk, at a disadvantage. In each exchange, visual or aural cues (or both) marked him as "other"; boundaries were drawn, and he was then treated poorly, put in danger, or otherwise excluded. Moreover, as his statement indicates, to negotiate the world successfully and safely, he had to pay attention not only to his personal experiences but also to the racial dangers others had faced (e.g., racial hostility in Batista Valley). To get full information, to get to a destination safely, to be treated properly at work, he had to be on the alert for signals of racial discrimination or danger.

For this parent (and for others raising children in a multiracial metropolis) this kind of knowledge was important not only for thinking about how to negotiate his own life but for anticipating the experiences his children were likely to have both in school and in the larger world. Mrs. Macias, a Latina mother from West City, related a long story of teachers and school administrators repeatedly and falsely accusing her older sons of writing graffiti and of vandalism, of essentially reading them as "cholos" and therefore as likely to be responsible for the destruction of school property. None of the charges held up once police investigated; they found that these boys lived in a strict Catholic home, in which their father did not let them leave the house after school. Nonetheless, their mother found it extremely frustrating to have these accusations leveled at her children year after year.

Other Latino and black parents told many stories of poor treatment they or their children had experienced at a range of public-service institutions from the Department of Motor Vehicles to the hospital. Almost all had stories of exclusion from their own school days. Mrs. Jones-Washington, Darnell's mother (Chapter 3), said:

> In high school mainly, um, my self-esteem was just trampled on, it was just horrible because I mean I got things like, not from the kids, interesting enough, but from the teachers, that I wasn't smart, that I was a dummy in fact, I got called dummy . . . it was just really horrible um, my counselor that was supposed to be helping me pick the right college or whatever told me "you are not college material, but if you really want to go to college, why don't you go to one of those black colleges down South." . . . There were only ten of us [African Americans], out of four hundred, so I was convinced that I was nothing, that I wasn't smart, there was no point in me even doing anything, so um, and I can't really tell you how I got out of that, years of therapy.

Mr. Valenzula reported institutional practices that regularly left Latinos and blacks excluded and segregated:

> Oh, a lot of racism, a lot of racism you know. The way I look at it, Latinos and blacks get discriminated from left and right and you just have to deal with it. [Like] how kids get treated when something happened. When you get in trouble, how was the issue dealt with if you're black or Latino versus if you're white. And you've seen the difference. Then if you're in a classroom and you don't like the classroom and you want to be changed to another class, you can tell the difference there with who gets preferences. All that was there. How kids got treated when they got in trouble or when they wanted to get into electives. If you wanted something bad, you wanted to go to a class, you wouldn't get it. I mean they would tell you "no, that one's full." And you can tell when you go to a class [and there are only] one black or a few Latinos here and then you got all these Latinos in this other class, you can tell.

Here Mr. Valenzula is relating not only the daily experience of being tracked but the full recognition on the part of the students involved of what was going on: "You can tell."

These experiences, in which youth learn what it means to be black and Latino, provide further evidence of the role of schools in shaping racial identities and understandings. These kinds of memories of school as a place of injustice and pain necessarily made parents like Mr. Valenzula and Mrs. Jones-Washington cautious and concerned when thinking about their own children's schooling. Although they recognized that times had changed, that some improvements had been made, they generally believed that the situation had not changed as much as they had hoped. As a result, they felt that one of their jobs as parents was to prepare their children for the racism they would inevitably face. As Mr. Jackson, the father of a black/Chicano son, put it:

> I think being . . . a man of color, will be one of the greatest challenges [he'll face growing up], because this country's not set up for men of color to succeed. That's why I feel, as his father, that the preparation that you do, here— see my thing for him is, you come home, you do your homework, you prepare yourself. Because someone's gonna always challenge you. You know, someone's gonna always see you as less than. So I think what Enrique has to do, and I tell him that you got to be prepared—you have to study. You have to not be concerned about what other people say or do, you've got to be concerned about yourself . . . I would just hope that our society will change. But, in my lifetime it hasn't changed, and . . . you know I don't think it's gonna happen, so I think he just has to be prepared to be, to be a man of color.

These subtle and not-so-subtle exclusionary exchanges result in part from the understandings that are associated with a particular category, the "content" associated with the categories white, black, and Latino. As a number of people related in various ways, racial categories are imbued with meaning. Mrs. Bonilla, a Latina mother of a West City student, described her responses to early work experiences in the United States:

Interviewer:[4] How was your first contact with people with a different skin color?

Mrs. Bonilla: Me? . . . well when I came here I started to clean houses, and regularly, the majority of the people were Americans.

Interviewer: You mean white?

Mrs. Bonilla: Yes . . . up until now, I am cleaning houses and they are all Americans, and they are beautiful people. Sometimes I also clean the house for a couple of blacks [laughs].[5] It seemed very funny to me, I would say "Wow!"

Interviewer: Why?

Mrs. Bonilla: Because I have always known that blacks were slaves before, right? And then I would say, "Hmh, and now these people are paying me to clean their house!"

Though it made perfect sense to her to be cleaning the houses of whites, she experienced dissonance in being hired by blacks for the same purpose. In this case, she understood blackness to be attached to a particular social location— one in which people could not afford to pay others to clean their houses. In her mind, low status was not a condition of blacks just in a previous time during which they were forcibly subjugated but a position they still occupied.

Ms. Hivert, a white mother originally from New York, related her strategic choice to lie about her own racial background (essentially to "pass" as Latina) so people would accept her low-status job.

Ms. Hivert: At one point in New York I was working in a garment factory, and I wasn't comfortable saying I was white so I passed as Puerto Rican . . . and that was my thing, I couldn't really fit in, I just felt it too much, so I just said my dad was Puerto Rican. . . . Everybody else was [a Latina]. [People kept asking] "what I was doing in this garment factory, a smart white girl like you," what was I doing there, it didn't make sense. . . .

Amanda: Until you said you were half Puerto Rican? That made it make sense to people that you were there?

Ms. Hivert: It seemed to open the door that um made it more acceptable for them.

It is not merely that poverty, danger, and other negative characteristics are associated with being of color, but that power, wealth, and other characteristics of high status are associated with being white. This is a set of understandings that whites and people of color shared. As a Latino father stated, "Well, the fact is that you cannot forget about the clear fact that the people who have money are white, and there's no dispute in that. . . . You can find people who are black and have a lot of money, but that doesn't imply that the police won't stop them if they're driving a Ferrari or something, thinking that they stole the car just because they are black." As reported in Chapters 3 and 4, students also regularly talked about whites as people with money and authority. At one point Rodney, an African American fourth-grader, tried to explain what he would do if he were going to imitate a white person: "I would just put some white make-up on and dress up kind of like." When I asked him why he would dress up, he replied, "Because white people have more money."

Racialized understandings shape our impressions not only of other groups but also of our own, as in Rodney's explanation of why he thought white people had more money:

Amanda: Why do you think [white people have more money]?

Rodney: Because mostly black people is on the streets and white people have cars, houses, big houses, and everything.

Amanda: Why do you think they have big houses and stuff though?

Rodney: Because they have money.

Amanda: Where do they get the money?

Rodney: Job, working, or . . .

Amanda: Why do black people have less money?

Rodney: Because mostly black people is [too] lazy to go find something else so they can get something.

As reported in Chapter 3, Rodney was also the student who explained his understanding that "all black men" must go to prison at some point in their lives and his opinion that it was better to go before college.

Children, like adults, are working to make sense of the world around them. They are reading the world, taking in what they see and experience and interpreting the meaning, the patterns, and the order. Rodney's belief that "all black men" must go to prison at some point in their lives, though troubling to his teachers, was merely part of his strategic attempts to assess the world he had to negotiate. Race is one lens through which this reading of the world occurs; it is at least in part how we decide who is friend or foe or, as Peshkin (1991) talked about it, who is a friend and who is a stranger.

The Influence of Context

Though racialization processes exist in all settings, they do not operate uniformly across time and space. Thus, local contexts, although existing within a larger racial formation, have some impact on the shape of racial boundaries and on how they operate in everyday life. The way people get categorized varies from setting to setting (e.g., the same person may be read differently in different settings). And the meaning of particular labels (e.g., the meanings associated with *black* or *Latino*), as well as the experiential aspects of group membership (e.g., how Latino-ness or blackness is experienced), varies from place to place. Being black in a setting where you are one of many is quite different from being one of eight black students in a school of six hundred. Context clearly matters in at least three ways: spaces themselves can be racially coded, local contexts and institutions can have both direct and indirect influences on identification processes, and the effects of being categorized as well as understandings of the meaning of race can vary by context.

Racially Coded Spaces

People frequently talked about schools as racially coded institutions. At different times each school in this study was described as a socially or culturally "white" space (even if it was not demographically white). In this way, all institutions, neighborhoods, parks, and cities function as racial spaces with their own set of dynamics, rules, associated meaning structures, and cultural repertoires (e.g., the Latino father's caution about going to Batista Valley). Schools are not only racial spaces but also spaces in which racial politics are fought out. Mrs. Clive, an African American parent, talked about educational institutions as racially coded. She was describing her experience as a student at a formerly "white" school that was suddenly integrated:

> It was kinda hard the very first year [at Foster—my new high school—] because it was the very first year [mid-1980s] that there was a lot of African Americans and Pacific Islanders going there. And I think it was kinda overwhelming to the staff, they knew we were coming but I think it was kinda overwhelming. Then we as a group that was bused had to adjust [ourselves]; "dang this is so different from East High School!" You know. I mean people put schools into categories. East High School used to be considered a high school for the ghetto kids you know, and Foster was considered a school for the white kids, and that's how it was, and I think that was kinda just accepted at the time.

As a student who was part of the school transition, Mrs. Clive was aware of the racial transformation she and her peers were participating in. She was also the parent who, in her multiple and various efforts to get her children into high-performing nonghetto schools, had decided that persisting patterns of racial segregation were not acceptable (Chapter 3).

Children and parents of color were not the only ones who recognized the ways schools were racially coded. Mr. Hargrove, the white father of Alex, a West City fourth-grader, explained why he was trying to get his son out of West City and into an alternative school nearby:

Amanda: What are the differences between West City and [the alternative school]?

Mr. Hargrove: Um basically parent participation. I would have to say that [pause] I think a lot of the kids that come from [pause] that are in West City, their parents aren't involved with their kids' education. It's just the economics or whatever, you know, recent immigrants or poor parents or whatever. They come, some of the kids that Alex's had [in his class], their parents were on drugs and doing this and that. And it's real foreign to me you know. And right now, at his age level, grade level, I don't think it's gonna affect him but these kids, when I see these, in this neighborhood and see these you know, these kids in junior high and they shouldn't be out there, they should be at home, inside or whatever, so I'm a little worried about that.

Here Mr. Hargrove was talking about a number of contexts at once, including not only the school, other children's families, and communities, but his own neighborhood.[6] All these places were linked for him as places where other people did things in ways he did not necessarily understand or approve of. Though he never talked about race directly, all the people to whom he referred were people of color. They were people whom he viewed as bad influences, and his solution was to try to remove himself and his son from the contexts in which these people operated.

Although in this example Mr. Hargrove was alluding to certain contexts as racialized spaces he wanted to avoid, minutes later he highlighted the role of context in shaping and subtly distinguishing racial identifications: "To be honest with you, if I see some Latino kids at 1 A.M. in the evening, looking kinda tough, oh yeah, I'll go to the other side of the street. But, I mean, I'm just saying that, you know, I do think about it in those terms. You know, put the neighborhood and the race together and I'd be a little worried." Here Mr. Hargrove demonstrated the power of context to shape our racial readings. He explained the importance of geography in marking off whether a particular racialized body was likely to be dangerous or not. In this way contexts not only are racialized (racially coded) but can themselves function to racialize—to shape ascriptions within them.

Self-Identification

Context shapes not only how we think about others but also how and whether we think about our own racial identities. Ms. Wilson, a teacher at Metro2, explained how her experience in Hillside generally and at Metro2 in particular led her to consider her racial identity for the first time. She had grown up in an almost-all-white environment, and these first experiences of feeling like an outsider in the city and in the school led her to think about her own whiteness in new ways.

Yeah. For the first time in my life, it wasn't until I got to this school that I felt racism. . . . Last year when we were trying to hire a special ed teacher I recommended this woman who had just gotten her credentials who had subbed here for awhile while I was out with an injury, and without saying any names, I said, "I really think you should consider M, she's really really good with the kids," and the response from [the] hiring people at the time, I don't want to say any names, was, "she's so blond," it, to me, mind you they had had a couple of glasses of champagne, this was when we were out, and I thought to myself, "What am I?" you know, it really hurt, it hurt a lot.

Mrs. Jones-Washington, who grew up in a racially segregated black neighborhood, had a similar response to a change in context.

>   *Amanda:* Um, when do you think you knew that you were an African
>   American, and that that had some meaning?
> *Mrs. Jones-Washington:* I think I always knew but I can't, probably sixth grade or like
>   high school when, where I wasn't around peers that were
>   African American, I mean not as many, that's what I remem-
>   ber as the biggest issue. Just before that, it didn't seem to be
>   an issue.

A number of Latino parents also discussed being surrounded primarily by those who were "the same" (because they lived in socially isolated, segregated neighborhoods) as a reason race didn't come up much. Race did arise in relation to a larger context in which hostile laws were contested or in interactions with large public institutions outside the immediate neighborhood; but in daily, local interactions with other Latinos, it was almost a nonissue. Several parents whose children were among the few white students at West City also reflected on their children's "minority" experience as the key factor that had led to their children's awareness of their own whiteness.

In light of these contextual issues, it was no surprise that the majority of white parents, children, and teachers in predominantly white Foresthills did not think much about their own whiteness and were mostly unable to talk about race in relation to their own lives. When I asked parents whether they ever thought about their own racial identity, it was not unusual to have someone respond, "Well I just haven't been around it too much." In this case, race appeared to them to have meaning only in relation to others. Yet, parents' comments made clear that their own race and the race of those around them mattered as a signifier of who would, for instance, make a good neighbor. But they regarded looking for sameness, or choosing to be around people they were comfortable with and could relate to, as distinct from avoiding difference or excluding others.

Foresthills community members were especially likely to think about race in situations where they were one of few or where they had to engage with people across racial borders. As they crossed racial borders in different contexts (personal versus professional lives, home versus school, childhood versus adult life), people indicated, race mattered more or less depending on where they were. For example, I talked to one light-skinned Chicano mother in Foresthills who had been raised in a Latino neighborhood in Bayside, married a French-Canadian white man, and moved to the suburbs. She currently worked in an English as a Second Language program at a local middle school. She explained that her identity had more significance professionally in her work as an advocate for Latino children in a hostile institution than personally in her home life.

What her racial identity meant and how relevant it felt for her experientially thus varied across time and space.

For some children racial identity was different at home than at school—not only the specific category of identification but the content of what that identity meant.[7] For Sylvie, the biracial (black/white) student at Foresthills, her blackness felt different to her when she was staying with her African American father in the largely black town nearby than it did when she was with her white mom and sister at home in Sunny Valley or when she was "the black kid" at school. For some of the Latino children, the meaning of identity at home in either an all-Latino or all-white setting differed from the meaning at school, where they were surrounded by African American, lower-income Latino, or white children.

The Meaning of Race

Different environs also can lead to different understandings of what race means. As Forman (2001a) demonstrates, local school contexts shape children's understandings about race. Metro2 students tended to have much more complex understandings of the relationship between race and social structure. Metro2 students generally understood that race and racism affected peoples' lives and opportunity structures. In answering a question about why some people are rich and others poor, one Metro2 student responded, "Some people have families that got more money than other families so they just passed on the money when they died . . . [and] because maybe their race. Because maybe they don't get the job opportunities as another race." Metro2 students also tended to have some understanding of the impact of the past on the present. But although many white Metro2 students were able to recognize the impact of race beyond the school, they continued to perceive their school as an ideal community that was above or separate from an unfair world. They said that students "here" would never be mean to other students because of their race or color. "Because, the teachers have taught us well . . . equality . . . yeah . . . to be fair to everybody."

Others at Metro2, primarily the black and dark-skinned Latinos, described school as a place where racialized behavior was still very much in place, where they were still likely to confront racial antagonism in the schoolyard. For example, an African American fifth-grader and I had the following exchange:

Amanda: Why do you think that some kids don't like to play with other kids?
Vanessa: Maybe because they think that they're different in some way and maybe because they don't like them for some reason.
Amanda: Do you think that happens here?
Vanessa: Yeah.
Amanda: In what kind of ways?

Vanessa: In what kind of ways like, "oh, you're black, you can't play," or "you're Mexican, you can't play," or "you're Latino, you can't play." "No Latinos allowed" and stuff like that.

Amanda: Why do you think they feel that way?

Vanessa: Maybe because they think like that different colors are more important than other ones [because they think] one color is better than another color.

Amanda: Is it one group that mostly does it to other kids or is it everybody that does it?

Vanessa: Um, not to be racist or anything but I think that sometimes . . . most of the time it's white people, white kids.

At West City, understandings of race were more mixed, based not only on students' own race but also on their class status. Many of the working-class and the few middle-class black and Latino children had sophisticated understandings of the relationship between race, structure, and opportunity, while poor black and Latino children had more traditional explanations for social inequality. For example, Rodney (who lived in a large housing project) explained black poverty as result of laziness, while Darnell, the son of a nurse, suggested the following:

Darnell: White people are supposed to be real good, they're supposed to be the best people in the world.

Amanda: Well do you think that white people are the best people in the world?

Darnell: No.

Amanda: When you say "the best" do you mean like all uptight or actually the best?

Darnell: They're like on top of everything, they're perfect. They don't get any of their math problems wrong. They read on seventh-grade levels.

Amanda: Do you think that's true?

Darnell: Well for some white people, yeah. But they have a better start than we do.

Amanda: So you think white people read better because they have a better start in life, what do you mean by that?

Darnell: I mean like white people when they're younger their parents teach them how to read at like one year old. They start better and some black people don't care if they read or don't read. But my mom taught me to read when I was about five or six. She taught me to read and I read and I'm reading well. If like 50 percent of like every black person did that, then it would be a better place.

Amanda: Why do you think some parents don't teach their kids how to read when they're young?

Darnell: Because they probably live in a poor neighborhood and they're working two jobs and they don't have time.

Amanda: Do you think most black people work pretty hard?

Darnell: Yeah a lot of black people work very hard. Almost every black person works hard, they work hard whatever they do. Selling drugs, they probably work hard, nurses work hard.

Amanda: Why do you think more black people are poorer than white people?

Darnell: Because we started off wrong with like racism and stuff. If we didn't start off like that we would probably be at the same place where white people were.

Darnell understood the role of history, resources, and access in shaping outcomes. It was not, as he talked about it, an issue of hard work—black people (even drug dealers) worked hard—but a matter of opportunity.

Although white children at West City recognized that racism still existed and that it existed locally, in their own school, they were likely to see themselves as victims of it as much as blacks or Latinos. They had, for instance, heard black and Latino children called names, just as they themselves had been called "whitey" during recess. They did not have any way of differentiating these experiences or any frame for understanding their schoolyard experiences as different in nature from other forms of racism.

Finally, in Foresthills, as discussed in Chapter 2, with the exception of Sylvie and one Latino son of immigrants, most students were unable to talk about race. Many children did not know what race or racism was. As one student stated when I asked her what she would say if someone asked her what race she was, "I don't know. I don't [know] what race means." Moreover, those who did know what prejudice and racism were thought they were remnants of the past that were no longer relevant. Whiteness was quite clearly still normatively in the center as both white and nonwhite children talked about difference as not applying to whites.

Challenging Boundaries

A few school community members were actively engaged in challenging racial boundaries with the expressed interest of creating a more just world. Ms. Wilson, at Metro2, described one of her classroom practices, the "culture bag," as a way to get children to understand that they were all both similar and different:

> "Culture bag" is about unveiling the mysteries, it's about kids having the opportunity to see that kids in their classes that they may not have thought were like them are really like them in a lot of ways. That everybody has a baby blanket even though they're from totally different backgrounds or different colors. That everybody's got some favorite stuffed animal just about or some

family member that they love. I wanted them to see what was alike about them
and I wanted them to appreciate what was different about each other.

In observing a number of these "culture-bag" events, in which children brought
artifacts from their culture to share in class, I regularly heard students mur-
muring to themselves, "Oh I have one of those," visibly enthralled by something
they had not known about. In this way they were encouraged both to see continuities among themselves and to value differences. Also, their assumptions
were regularly tested as they shared who they were in a mostly unfiltered fashion. Thus, when Vanessa shared aspects of her Jamaican ethnic heritage, students became aware of her as more than black; they became aware of diversity
within the category black. Another time, the entire class was surprised as a student who most had assumed was white shared that he was part French, part
Irish, part Latino, and part African American. Thus automatic racial readings
based on visible physical features were made problematic if not challenged.

In other cases, adults talked about ways they challenged racialized assumptions in a variety of forums. Roy Burns, a white, working-class father from the
Midwest, talked about actively rejecting other whites' inclusion of him within a
category that automatically assumed racist sympathies:

> I'm white so I get, white people you know will come up and say, this happened
> to me recently, I'll tell you. I was getting like some glass cut over here, this
> glassmaker over here, and I'm standing outside and the man, the supervisor
> of the back, he may even be one of the owners, I don't know but he's out there,
> he gave the orders to do this and do that and we're standing outside maybe
> talking about the weather and this black woman came around the corner,
> walked past us and he said something extremely derogatory, "some of these
> fucking niggers, blah, blah, blah" . . . this and that and that sort of thing you
> know, I was like, I almost choked him, I mean, I said, "You did two things
> wrong, for one thing you assumed something about her, you don't even, do
> you know that woman? Do you know her name? Anything about her? You
> know nothing about her. The other thing—you assumed something about me.
> You assume because I look like you I feel about her the same way as you do.
> You're wrong and I don't like people making assumptions about me like that
> and you can take your business and shove it up your ass," and walked off. I
> got my money back, I wanted to rip his . . . you know, like that.

As Mr. Burns discussed throughout our interview, struggling with racism was
part of his responsibility as a progressive white person, and this struggle
included making sure his daughter understood that race still mattered in today's
world.

In another example, Mr. Morales, who is Latino, talked about his son Omar learning to stand up for his rights. His son had found out about the lawsuit against Denny's food chain for discriminating against blacks and Latinos. As Mr. Morales summarized it, "There was a group of people who took this restaurant chain to court and it was very prominent in all [the state]." One day, after Mr. Morales picked Omar up from the airport, they passed by a Denny's. Omar's response was to enthusiastically suggest they go there. "He said, 'Denny's! That's the restaurant! Why don't we go there?' We had talked about how no one should exclude you, and if someone does then we have to do something about it. So then we went there and I liked his attitude about how he didn't let himself be inhibited. 'Let's go, and we are going to buy something there and they are going to treat us well.'"

Conclusion

Race is continually at play inside and outside schools. It is present in the "hidden curriculum," in explicit historical lessons, in discipline practices, and in interpersonal relations; race is a part of what is happening in schools as much as it is anywhere else. It is one lens through which people read the world around them and make decisions on how to act, react, and interact. Using data from ethnographic research in three school communities, I've attempted to demonstrate how racialization processes work. These processes describe the ways racial identities are assigned to individuals and how racial categories are mapped onto groups. These ascriptive processes work primarily through interpersonal interactions in which we attempt to assess what we know about another person, first through the instantaneous reading or interpreting of available clues (e.g., visible cues such as skin color or facial features, auditory cues such as accent, spatial cues such as neighborhood), and second through rereading or reinterpreting initial assumptions as additional information becomes available. These processes operate in a largely relational manner: some people are determined to be "same" (or "like me") and others are determined to be "different."

At all steps, institutional processes and dynamics affect these racial interactions and interpretations. Both racial ascription and racial self-identification are contextual processes influenced by local meaning systems, rules, demographics, relationships, and structures. For example, as discussed in Chapter 3, blackness took on specific meanings at West City in relation not only to a larger culture but also to a specific set of practices within that school. At Metro2, white students' sophisticated understanding of the relationship between race and structure was not accidental but seemed at least partially related to a school context in which racism, power, and equity were an explicit part of the curriculum. Foresthills students' limited language for talking about race was understandable in the context of dominant local racial discourses of color blindness, which framed race as largely irrelevant.

 Racial ascriptions are also not solely about deciding what category an individual belongs to but also about the mapping of systems of meaning onto individuals. A person categorized as black, white, or Asian is being linked with a category already imbued with meanings. The sameness or difference ascertained is not a neutral measure like shoe size or ear shape but a central clue about who a person is. The moment of identification is also a moment of inclusion or exclusion; an understanding is not merely formed but in many cases is subtly or explicitly acted on. Inclusion or exclusion can take form in how one is treated in a particular context (e.g., the slightly cool treatment of a waitress or the particularly welcoming greeting from a new neighbor) or in concretely material processes of who gets access to what kind of resources (e.g., what mortgage rate a bank offers).

Everyday interactions, the moments in which the social category "race" takes shape and is given meaning in social interaction, are the means through which boundaries between groups are created, reproduced, and resisted. One is a member of a particular group at least in part because one is not a member of another. Systems of social inclusion and exclusion are organized (to some extent) around the resulting racial categories and the boundaries between them.[8] Racialization thus involves the assignment of bodies to racial categories and the association of symbols, attributes, qualities, and other meanings with those categories (which then are understood to belong to those bodies in a primordial or natural way). Racial categorizations are used to decide who is similar and different; opportunities and resources are then distributed along racial lines as people are included in or excluded from a range of institutions, activities, or opportunities because of their categorization.

Although racial categorization is not externally imposed in an uncomplicated or automatic way, the range of available racial categories and the meanings associated with them necessarily shape and limit the kinds of racial identifications that are possible. As Benjamin's failed efforts to reject identification (cited at the beginning of the chapter) illustrate, one cannot decide to opt out altogether. Yet collective action can alter the content or boundaries of categories (e.g., black efforts during the 1960s to redefine blackness—"black is beautiful"). And individual interventions are not meaningless; when, Benjamin, a multiracial (and visually racially ambiguous) child, resists identifications, he is at once illuminating the idiocy of a process that tries to find a singular and simple place for him and affirming the power of a process that works hard to pigeonhole him. What one is able to claim for oneself is clearly limited by context and the available categories. Though Tiger Woods created the racial/ethnic category Cablinasian to describe himself, the category was not widely (or even narrowly) accepted. His actions did, however, encourage an occasionally more complex reading of his person, which otherwise (and most often) is still read as black.

The state historically has played an important role in the creation and alteration of categories, usually in interaction with the groups involved (Almaguer and Jung 1999). For instance, efforts on the part of multiracial groups and Asian–Pacific Islanders among others have led to new census categories that allow for different or multiple racial designations (Wright 1994). These individual claims and state actions may be a sign of changes to come. However, their only moderate success may be an indicator of just how entrenched current racial categories are. At issue are not only the borders between categories— whether they exist, what shape they take, whether they are permeable or fixed—but also the content of the categories themselves. What does it mean to be white, black, Latino, Asian? Who decides what category a person belongs to? Are these categories mutually exclusive?

In practice, these questions have no single answer. What the boundaries are and how they work are not established and universally consistent social facts. Nor is the content and meaning of any racial category consistent across space, culture, or time. This indefiniteness lies at the heart of what it means to talk about race as a social construction. Though the idea that race is a social construction is widely accepted, the reality of race in daily life has received little attention.

The lack of fixed and permanent markers and the flexibility of meanings may not, however, signal the declining significance of race. Although I find evidence of confusion, indefiniteness, and disagreement about racial identities and their meaning, I find little evidence of any weakening of the racial-ascription process or of the power of race to shape opportunities and outcomes. Possibly the patterns I identify are a sign of new times. However, they may well be just a sign of new configurations, of adaptations in the making that will yield a slightly different but still powerful and entrenched racial system.

Six

Schooling and the Social Reproduction of Racial Inequality

The previous chapter looked at the racialization process as it played out in the three school communities. Along with understanding the role schools play in the production of racial ideas, however, it is essential to understand the role of schools in the reproduction of racial inequality. Racial inequality in education, specifically racial gaps in achievement, have been receiving new attention. The black-white gap in particular has become the subject of front-page articles in national newspapers, of books, and of discussion within educational policy circles. Many observers suggest that the problem begins within the black community, that it is an issue of values (do blacks care about education?), peer relations (do black peers discourage their friends from achieving?), or identity (do blacks reject school success because they think it is a "white" thing?). Others, however, argue that perhaps processes within school buildings lead to these differences (Ferguson 1998a, 1998b; Roscigno and Ainsworth-Darnell 1999). In this chapter I suggest a set of mechanisms both inside and outside school that lead many children of color to have fundamentally different schooling experiences than their white peers do, mechanisms that are separate from these children's values, desires, and identity struggles. Rather than being "the great equalizer," I argue, educational institutions play a key role in the reproduction of racial inequality.

One key for understanding racial stratification in educational experiences and outcomes is a conceptual frame first developed by Pierre Bourdieu to explore the social reproduction of class. Subsequently utilized by a whole cadre of scholars (DiMaggio 1982; Farkas 1996; Lamont and Lareau 1988; Roscigno and Ainsworth-Darnell 1999; Smrekar 1997), Bourdieu's theory built on a Marxian notion of economic capital to suggest that other forms of capital—cultural, social, and symbolic—are also means for accessing power and improving social status. *Capital* is essentially a resource that serves to advance one's position or status within a given context. Bourdieu discussed four types of capital: economic (money and property); social (connections, social networks); cultural (cultural knowledge, educational credentials); and symbolic (symbols of prestige and legitimacy). Each of the forms of capital (all distributed unequally in the population) help those who already have resources maintain or increase their status and power. Under the right conditions, each form of capital can be converted into the others in order to enhance or maintain positions in the social order (Connolly 1998: Swartz 1997). However, as Lareau and others have pointed out (Lareau 1989; Lareau and Horvat 1999; Lamont and Lareau 1988), having capital does not automatically translate into advantages or resources; in order to provide benefit, capital must be put to use and put to use effectively. For example, recent graduates may have a great deal of capital in the form of social networks, but if they do not tap into these networks in their job-search process, that capital will not prove useful in finding work.

These various kinds of resources, however, are not directly equivalent to capital. For example, all individuals, families, and communities have a wealth of cultural resources. However, only some of those resources are useful within specific social contexts. Only when cultural resources assist one in gaining access to additional resources within a particular place can they be considered capital. Thus, though all children and families have specific kinds of social connections and may even have access to symbols of prestige, these resources provide advantage only within particular settings. For example, cultural knowledge important for navigating a low-income neighborhood (e.g., knowing which corner stores accept food stamps, which blocks are safe after dark, how to play "the dozens") would provide little assistance in successfully negotiating a corporate law firm's holiday cocktail party. Moreover symbols of prestige at the cocktail party (e.g., specific styles and brands of clothes) would likely not function similarly in the low-income neighborhood. Some resources, then, that are critical in certain contexts become almost meaningless in others.

Though it is analytically useful to talk about these various forms of capital as distinct, in practice the boundaries are quite blurry. For example, parents may use economic capital to pay for their children's private schooling, which bestows important educational credentials (cultural capital) and often social connections (social capital), which the children may then use to get good jobs, which lead to future economic capital. In this chapter I often discuss forms of capital separately, but in practice each interacts with the others in complicated ways—access to one form often provides access to others. For instance, social connections can often provide access to those who have cultural knowledge important in a particular situation (e.g., knowing a doctor who can assist in securing the best medical care because of knowledge about local hospitals, specialists, and insurance policies and practices; or knowing a college professor at a local university who can help your child compose an admissions essay and can provide advice about how to structure an application and whom to ask for recommendations).

The notion of capital is important because it inherently challenges one of the dominant narratives for understanding educational success and failure—the ideology of meritocracy: people are understood to be successful solely because of their individual efforts and abilities; schools are understood to be places that reward effort and talent so that those who "deserve" to excel in fact do so (Apple 1982, 1990). Absent from this narrative are the vast inequities in types and quality of schooling experiences (Kozol 1991; Oakes 1985; Orfield and Yun 1999). In essence, the concept of capital fundamentally challenges the meritocratic ideology by uncovering the mechanisms that differently prepare children to come to school and differently reward them once they are there.

Using the theoretical lens of capital, I suggest a set of interactions in which the racialized social system is reproduced at least partly through processes of schooling. Possession of one or more forms of capital not only assists in (a) securing access to good schools but also helps (b) to maximize experiences within schools and therefore (c) to secure access to additional capital. At each step (initial access, maximizing experiences, and further acquisition of capital), race comes into play to the benefit of some and the detriment of others. Using this analytic tool, I address the following questions: What role does schooling play in the reproduction of racial inequality? How does race shape the distribution of economic, social, cultural, and symbolic capital? How do children come to have access to quite different educational experiences?

Economic Capital

Families at Foresthills, Metro2, and West City had very different financial resources available to them. With few exceptions, white families tended to be at the high end of each school communities' resource distribution, while students of color were at the low end. For example, few white students were eligible for free or reduced-price lunch, while a majority of black and Latino students were eligible. Only black and Latino students were currently living in public housing or receiving welfare support. Despite some variation within groups, whites clearly had more economic capital, and blacks and Latinos had far less.[1] Moreover, although there is some variation in socioeconomic status among Latino groups in the United States as a whole, they are generally not much better off and in some cases are worse off than African Americans. Almost all Latinos at the three schools studied here were Mexicans and Central Americans; overall these two groups have median family incomes close to those of blacks and poverty rates higher than blacks' (31 percent and 29.9 percent, respectively, as compared with 28.3 percent for blacks) (Marger 2000).

Although at West City, Foresthills, and Metro2 whites, as a group, generally had more economic resources than did blacks, Latinos, and most Asian groups, it is important to acknowledge that the white poor and working classes also struggle with economic deficits. It is also true, however, that they are still relatively better off than poor and working-class people of color. As Oliver and Shapiro (1995) have pointed out, in regard to wealth the white poor and working classes are collectively better off than even the black middle class. Moreover, and especially important when talking about schools, low-income whites are much less likely to be economically segregated than are low-income blacks or Latinos.

This uneven distribution of economic capital among racial groups has clear historical origins and major ramifications for life outcomes. For example, as Bobo, Kluegel, and Smith (1997: 17) discuss in relation to African Americans, blacks' "unique and fundamentally disadvantaged structural position in the U.S. economy and polity" is a "legacy of historic racial discrimination." This legacy is powerful; even if all direct, present-day racial discrimination against them were eliminated, "African Americans would [still continue to] be disadvantaged because of the cumulative and multidimensional nature of historic racial oppression in the United States" (17). Racial discrimination, however, has not been eliminated (Bonilla-Silva and Lewis 1999; Massey and Denton 1993; Oliver and Shapiro 1995), and so African Americans are systematically in a disadvantaged economic position because of both historic and present-day racism. Therefore, when we discuss the gaps in economic capital (class status) between groups and the impact of these gaps, we are talking about racially generated economic realities.

Black-white gaps in socioeconomic standing include not only differentials in unemployment rates but persistent income gaps, job segmentation and other forms of labor-market discrimination, and major gaps in wealth (Bobo, Kluegel, and Smith 1997; Bonilla-Silva and Lewis 1999; Collins 1997; Farley 1984; Feagin and Feagin 1996; Jaynes and Williams 1989; Landry 1987; Pinkney 2000). For example, in general, blacks earn about 60 percent as much as whites; even when controlling for differences in education and other characteristics, blacks still earn 10 to 15 percent less than whites (Bonilla-Silva and Lewis 1999). This gap is often referred to as the "black tax" or "the cost of being black."

Possibly even more important than these persistent income gaps are the gaps in wealth between similarly situated blacks and whites. As Oliver and

Shapiro (1995) powerfully demonstrate, blacks lag far behind whites in accumulation of wealth. Even low-income white households have far more resources than low- to middle-income black households. In fact, Starr (1992: 12, as quoted in Bobo, Kluegel, and Smith 1997: 18) reports that white households with annual incomes between $7,500 and $15,000 have "higher mean net worth and net financial assets than black households making $45,000 to $60,000." As a number of authors have argued, these differences in wealth, largely a legacy of historic discrimination, may be more important than income or other measures for understanding racial inequality (Conley 1999; Oliver and Shapiro 1995). Wealth stands as a measure not only of potential quality of life but also of the precariousness of family status (e.g., is there a reserve to draw on in case of emergency or unemployment?). More than providing just a safety net, wealth in its various forms (home equity, liquid assets) can also, for example, provide access to higher education or other supplemental educational opportunities.

Thus, although some authors have argued that the persistent social problems of blacks are more a result of class differences (the lack of resources) than of race per se (e.g., Conley 1999), clearly, these class disparities are fundamentally racial in nature. For example, Conley (1999) demonstrates that nothing about the nature of African Americans explains their higher levels of unemployment or higher school drop-out rates (i.e., once one controls for class status in the form of family wealth and assets, blacks are significantly less likely than whites to engage in socially deviant behavior/activities). Nonetheless, the racialized social location of blacks makes it more likely that they will be poor and without key economic resources. Thus, if blacks as a group are being held back in school more often than other groups for reasons related to their collective lack of wealth (Conley 1999), they are collectively without wealth in large part because they are black. In this way race matters as a socially produced reality rather than as a biological or cultural one.

In regard to educational access and school performance, economic capital matters in a number of ways. Economic capital can provide parents with options such as access to good schools—they may elect to send their children to private schools or may select housing in areas where schools are high performing. For instance, among the parents at the three schools studied here, white parents generally expressed a great deal of volition with regard to how they chose their current neighborhood, while most black and Latino parents talked about their constrained choices, about wanting to move but being stuck. As one black mother put it when I asked her whether she liked her neighborhood, "If I could find something better, I'd move away from here in the next five minutes." Another Latino family was looking to move but having trouble. The father explained, "It all comes down to the amount of money [you have] to allow you to have options where you want. Me, I can say that I want to move over there, but if I don't have the money I can't do that."

Although some white parents used their resources to buy a house in a carefully researched suburban neighborhood, Sunny Valley, where the schools had a successful record, other white families used their resources to maximize their child's experience within the urban public school system. White urban parents talked about using available money to provide their children with access to extracurricular activities or educational help and tutoring not obtainable through the public schools. In this way financial resources provided students with access to cultural capital that they would not otherwise have had. As one parent described it, "There was always the question of private schools, but we wanted to take that extra money and use it to get supplementary things, you know, like piano and girl sports, horse-riding lessons, just stuff." Parents talked about sending their children to special music programs, getting them involved in various athletic activities, and also hiring tutors for them. These issues came up as Ms. Wilson, the fifth-grade Metro2 teacher, talked about three students in her class (two white males and a Latina) who were struggling with reading: "Kids like David and Kenny are very low readers, but I'm not quite as worried about them because they're getting support. They have wonderful families who will resource for them. The other kids' families I'm not sure that their families will resource for them as well, you know, I worry about Yolanda." Both David's and Kenny's parents enrolled them in expensive supplemental reading programs. Home resources played a direct role in supplementing school instruction and thus in improving readings skills and achievement. As Ms. Wilson explained, these students, who had similar academic skills, were in the same school building, and had access to the same instruction, were not necessarily in the same position with regard to the outcomes of their schooling—some had access to extra resources and some did not.

Resources are also important in providing parents with the flexibility needed to make schools work for their children. As Mr. Valenzula, a Metro2 parent, said of working-class Latino parents, many have work obligations that limit the time they have to help their children:

I can say for Latino parents, one of the big obstacles in us being part of our kids' education is the type of work we do. Most of us . . . have low-wage jobs or you know, what do you call it, cleaning and restaurant and those jobs. So, in a way I feel really bad because our kids are the ones that are losing, and it's not their fault and it's not the parents' fault because the reason why the parents are not there for them is because they have these jobs that keep them from home when they're supposed to be home helping the kids out. They can't do nothing about that because they need those jobs for the families. So that's where I see the big problems.

Availability is not only about being around to assist a child in doing homework but also, for instance, about being able to miss work to appeal to the district, the school, or a teacher on behalf of a child or about being able to visit the school regularly to monitor the classroom.

These logistical issues surface in other ways also. Sadie Davis and other African American parents talked about having to factor in logistical criteria in choosing their children's schools. Mrs. Davis explained that she agreed to have her children bused to West City because of complications in finding affordable child care. There was a children's center in her neighborhood where she could get free after-school care, and as she put it, "West City was the school that [the children's center] had on the list that the kids could go to, that they'd be bused out to school and back." This was not a total solution to her problems, however, as it raised other transportation difficulties: "I still have to worry, especially if the child turns sick, about how I'm going to get to him."

Family economic resources, then, not only affect the nature of children's learning experiences but also can influence their access to schools geographically. Some parents, like Mrs. Davis, had to consider far more than quality of education in selecting a school. In a context of extensive desegregation and busing, parents had to worry about getting themselves to a distant school in case of emergency. I witnessed a number of incidents at West City in which sick or hurt children had to wait for hours until a parent could pick them up.[2] Moreover, these parents had a hard time getting to the school for performances or after-school events. For one important PTA meeting, the principal at West City arranged to drive across town to pick up some parents, but, even with this extraordinary effort, she could fit only so many in her car. Normally, the many black and Latino parents who lived across town and did not have cars would have to spend upward of an hour on the bus getting to West City and another hour returning home. Unfortunately, many teachers read their resulting nonattendance at functions as a lack of support for their children's education and for the school.

The issue of busing children an hour each way to schools in neighborhoods far from their own was a controversial one. There were clear costs to children who left early and got home late every day. Some families, however, were motivated to get their children out of low-income neighborhood schools. But as the story of one such parent illustrates, even when savvy low-income parents of color were determined to get their children into better schools, it was not easy.

Tanesha Clive's older child, Ivy, had originally been assigned to Eureka, the school directly across from the project where they lived. But Mrs. Clive looked into the school and found out how low its state test scores were. Plus, she did not want Ivy to be "stuck" in the neighborhood they lived in. "I wanted her to go out, to learn about different cultures . . . and just to be around different types of people, different types of children, and to explore and to let her know that there is something better than just living here." Mrs. Clive spent a great deal of time on the weekends and during school breaks giving her children access to social and cultural resources (taking her children on day trips around the city), trying to give them a sense of a world of opportunities. For her, gaining access also meant getting her children to a school in a "different environment." She went through a series of struggles with the district, first to get Ivy assigned to another school and then to get the bus to pick her up. Eventually, Mrs. Clive had to recruit other neighbors to transfer their children to West City so she could muster the minimum number the district required to add a stop to the bus route. "So I even went down to district headquarters and filled out [the other parents'] transfer papers." Even after getting her neighbors' children transferred, Mrs. Clive had to access other resources, specifically the social and cultural capital of her supervisor at work, in order to write a proposal that she then presented at the school board meeting. Encouraged by her boss, she eventually "had to threaten to sue."

Mrs. Clive's efforts to get her daughter into West City were motivated partly by the perceived relative academic quality of the schools (in fact West City did have marginally better test scores than Eureka) and partly by West City's location (its neighborhood was relatively safer and the residents had greater wealth and resources). Ironically, few of the white children from the neighborhood surrounding West City attended the school. (In the class of more than thirty students I worked most closely with, only three children—all white—lived within walking distance of the school—more than in most classes.) Paradoxically, considering Mrs. Clive's struggle to get access to West City, several white, middle-class families whose kids attended the alternative school Metro2 lived close to West City and had originally been assigned to West City for kindergarten. They never seriously considered sending their kids there and fought to get them into Metro2.

These struggles did not end with elementary school. Mrs. Clive was at that moment again trying to recruit enough neighborhood parents so the school district would provide bus service to the middle school she liked. "That's what I'm working on now. . . . I want people to know that this is a Hillside public school. No one [around my neighborhood] knows about this school because there are 473 children go there and only 11 of them are African Americans. . . . Only 11 out of 473 and I am just like '*no.*' Everyone should be able to have that opportunity to send their child to a really good school and I don't think that it should be based on the neighborhood or the zip code that you live in." Based on her own experience attending Hillside schools in the 1970s and 1980s and on her current observations, Mrs. Clive understood herself to be struggling against an assignment process that was racially coded. For example, when I interviewed her, she related how, as a child, she had been driven past a nice-looking public high school on the way to visit her brother in the juvenile detention center, and she recalled wondering why only white kids got to go to that school. Though, as an adult, she put this understanding to use in getting her own children access to better schools, her story demonstrates that even when low-income parents determinedly struggle, drawing on the social capital they have (in this case drawing on her white, college-educated boss's cultural capital), the road is difficult.

The district busing politics with which Mrs. Clive engaged had changed more than twenty years previously as part of the settlement from a lawsuit brought because of the disastrous, districtwide underachievement of African American students. Part of the settlement involved both a revamping of neighborhood schools in the Lancaster Valley area and institution of a complex busing plan to take children from low-income minority communities to schools all over the city. As with busing plans in other parts of the country, students were generally not bused in to attend schools in the poorer neighborhoods—the busing was unidirectional (Orfield and Eaton 1996). As Mr. Ortiz, the teacher at West City, described it:

> But [the busing is] not even fair either because the Asian population or white families, they go to their neighborhood schools. They're not bused. And every time that they talk about being bused, they come together very quickly and get organized very quickly and go down to the Board of Education and . . . as far as I'm concerned there are some issues of power. See, as long as you keep people disenfranchised, as long as you nickel and dime them, they can't get together. And the powers that be like that. I mean, I think that's just like regular, that's just basic organizational tactics. You just keep them divided and just give them little bits and pieces.

In fact, some Asian and white children were bused, mostly voluntarily, to alternative schools, but the patterns Mr. Ortiz noted were real. Power had a big impact on general patterns of busing. Also, as both Mr. Ortiz and Mrs. Clive explained in different ways, minority children were often bused to schools that were only moderately better than the ones near home. Ms. Sullivan, another teacher at West City, also questioned the busing situation:

I think the bus situation is weird. I think they should find out ways to make those [neighborhood] schools really, really good and that they should have teachers that, they don't have to be of that race, but they should certainly be schooled in the customs of that race where they're teaching. Make those the best schools and pay teachers more, give them a day off or something. Give them Friday off and have that be like electives or make it a four-day week or something. Give some incentives so that the best teachers will go to those schools. It seems more odd to make [students] travel so many minutes from their house just so that the education is equal.

As Ms. Sullivan suggested, busing is necessary only if children cannot get a good education within the schools in their own neighborhood. Resources are important not only at the level of individual families but also at the level of the community. Many of the central struggles of low-income blacks (and Latinos) today result from their living in areas of concentrated poverty; in these settings strong public institutions are largely absent. As Massey and Denton (1993) and others have documented, this concentration of poverty is not just about class. The white poor are much more likely than the minority poor to live in mixed-class neighborhoods, less likely to be densely concentrated in small geographical areas, and thus less likely to be segregated in high-poverty schools (Wilson 1987). As Orfield et al. (1997: 11–12) demonstrate, "A student in a segregated minority school is 16.3 times more likely to be in a concentrated poverty school than a student in a segregated white school." Moreover, although only about 6 percent of schools nationally that are 80 percent or more white have student populations that are 50 percent or more poor, more than 82 percent of schools that are 80 percent or more black and Latino have student bodies that are 50 to 100 percent poor (Orfield et al. 1997: 12).[3] In a number of ways, then, macrosocial patterns of housing segregation combine with group-level differences in economic capital to leave some communities able to deploy many more resources on behalf of their children than others. In terms of both individual families and communities, economic resources clearly have an impact on the nature and quality of a child's school experiences. Key for school outcomes, however, are not just economic resources but social, cultural, and symbolic capital as well.

Social Capital

Social capital involves resources garnered through social connections and networks and has long been acknowledged by scholars such as James Coleman (1988), Angela Valenzuela (1999), and Ricardo Stanton-Salazar (2001) to be an important factor in school outcomes. However, I want to argue that social capital is important not only in relation to peer networks within schools, as much of this work has focused on, but also with regard to parents' informational networks, which assist in improving educational experiences and opportunities. Because social networks are often racially segregated (Sigelman et al. 1996), important information about how to maximize a child's educational experience (how to get access to particular teachers or schools, how to work the system to one's advantage) is not equally available to all groups. One mechanism involved here is housing segregation. As Massey and Denton (1993) and others have shown, residential segregation is still rampant throughout the country and is increasing in some areas. This dynamic leads not only to segregated social networks among parents and families but also to racially segregated schools. Much evidence indicated that race played a role in the housing choices of parents at the three schools—in a complicated nexus with school-choice processes. Race played a role in determining which neighborhoods people found suitable and which schools parents wanted their children to attend. Race mattered for housing choices and for school-selection processes both within and across districts. In the end, both processes have a big impact on school racial composition and thus on school outcomes (Orfield and Eaton 1996; Orfield and Gordon 2001).

Within the city itself, parents had several means of intervening in the matter of where their children attended school, the success of which depended on having access to various kinds of capital. First, those who could afford it could opt out of public school altogether and send their children to private school. Second, and dependent not only on economic capital but also on social capital, was the option of strategically purchasing a house in a neighborhood with a strong local school. This option required having resources to purchase such a home as well as the information necessary to know how to make such a purchase and where the good schools were. The third means, which involved a complex mix of economic, social, and cultural resources, was to apply through the optional enrollment process to enter one of the cities' public alternative schools; this is the option I discuss here.

Every year within the Hillside school district, an alternative enrollment process allowed parents to petition to have their children admitted to schools other than their assigned neighborhood schools. The process was complex enough that books had been written to explain it. On the face of it, parents needed just to fill out their basic information on a form and to list their top four school choices. However, getting admitted to a school required a great deal of more strategic information, such as knowing in which order to list the schools based on which you were likely to get into. For example, integration policies in the district were such that if Latino students applied to a school where Latinos already constituted a majority, their chances of getting in were not as good as they would be if they selected a school where a smaller percentage of current students were Latino. Because of these factors, one popular guidebook included not only statistics on which schools were near "ethnic capacity" but also a table showing the acceptance rate for each school, along with information about how to shop around, how to file appeals, and other strategies for "getting the public school you want."

During the year I was conducting research, the superintendent proposed a modification in this process that would have set aside some of the seats in most alternative schools for students living in the neighborhoods surrounding the schools. Intended to give the schools more of a neighborhood base, the plan became extremely controversial and was the subject of heated public meetings throughout the city for months. A newspaper opinion piece titled "Hillside Schools Can't Ignore White Kids" captures part of the controversy.[4] As the author wrote, "The rules will mean substantially fewer seats for students who are white" because the alternative-school neighborhood zones were largely non-white. She argued that white parents shouldn't be blamed for fleeing the district nor should they be asked "to roll up their sleeves and fix [their neighborhood schools]." The author continued, "It isn't racist to want a good school for your child," and reminded the district that far more white families applied to district kindergartens than the 13 percent whose children matriculated each year; if the district wanted white families to stay in the district, she suggested they rethink this proposal. She argued that this issue was not socioeconomic but racial: "White families often look to see if there are other white families in the school so they won't feel isolated. They have strong preferences for styles of teaching and curriculum. These reflect specific cultural points of view." I quote this article in detail because it captures the racial dynamics of the district in an unusually honest and succinct way. In my conversations not only with white parents at West City and Metro2 but with white parents "shopping" through the schools for the following year, race came up over and over again in implicit and explicit ways.

Mrs. Keyser, the mother of a fourth-grader at Metro2, described her and her husband's decision to apply to send their daughter to an alternative school as full of mixed emotions. The neighborhood school she was assigned to was Boone. "I looked at it and I was sort of, and it's that whole pull, you know, and Roy would've probably sent her, he wanted [her] to go to the neighborhood school, but I said, 'Well Metro2 is also close.'" Although her husband believed that everybody should just go to their neighborhood school, she felt uncomfortable with Boone. As she explained it, Boone had no neighborhood children of their kind.

> When our daughter was a little tiny baby we talked with other [white, middle-class neighborhood parents] about [going to Boone], and every generation of kids have tried to work with them but everybody just bailed out . . . I wanted to be in public schools but I didn't want to be "the only one" at the neighborhood school. . . . When I visited the classes, some of them were fine. I think it was more the atmosphere on the playground, the dynamic on the playground was more the issue. And I felt that the camaraderie with parents would be what was missing. I guess I thought partly about myself and my engagement [in the school].

As she explained it, all the white families she knew used Boone only as the morning bus stop to send their children to several different alternative schools—that is, if they didn't instead decide to send them to private school. She was not unaware of the result of white families deserting the neighborhood schools or unconcerned about it: "You know it's sort of the thing of the racial mix and how to make the races more equitable." However, she was quite happy with Metro2.

Mrs. Keyser was one of the few parents I spoke to who managed to get their children admitted to Metro2 on the first try. Most had to appeal several times. Others utilized other aspects of the enrollment process to their benefit. In deciding admissions for the coming year, the district at that time used a computer program that gave priority to siblings of students already enrolled in the school; to students living within specific neighborhoods that were largely low-income and minority; to those residing in public housing or who were Section 8 residents;[5] and to African American and Latino students. Given this system, social capital was key to parents' ability to get their children into the schools they wanted. Informational networks helped them plan early. For example, some parents I interviewed had factored this process into housing choices and had moved into middle-class areas on the edges of the designated neighborhoods. Others strategically chose their child's racial/ethnic designation based on admissions priorities. For example, when I interviewed Sally Hall, a white mother of a Metro2 fourth-grader, she explained that though her ex-husband was Nicaraguan, their daughter identified as white. However, on her official school forms, Mrs. Hall had checked off "Chinese" because she recognized it would help her get into Metro2, which already had high numbers of white and Latino students. Because Mrs. Hall's ex-husband's great-grandfather was Chinese, the choice was not entirely a misstatement. I also knew of a few families (and heard from parents and teachers about several more) who had explicitly lied (e.g., white families selecting "African American").

To make the system work for them, parents used information from other parents they knew (e.g., whom to talk to, which schools had openings, how to plan ahead). White, middle-class parents expressed a sense of entitlement and control: they were clear about which schools their children were or were not going to attend. This sense of authority extended to their children. When the fifth-grade students first learned of their middle-school assignments, several white students laughed and said that they were "never" going to that school.[6] As Ms. Wilson explained to me, "They [the assignments] don't mean much in regards to these kids; their parents are so powerful, they'll never end up in those schools." In contrast, Latino and black students assigned to many of those same schools reported those assignments as fact rather than folly. In my interviews with parents about their school choices, many white parents talked about their assigned school as "not an option," while Latino and black parents talked about lacking options, about being discouraged from pursuing other placements or from trying to switch schools.

West City and Metro2 were grappling with the racial politics of school-choice processes during the year I was there. West City had just undergone a name change and had been designated an alternative school. Although the student body was still made up primarily of students assigned through the previous attendance-zone process, the principal, Ms. Grant, worried a great deal about what was going to happen to the school in the following years. Given the school's location, on the edge of four different white, middle-class neighborhoods, she noted that "the potential for [West City] to soon be like every other alternative school is really high; . . . there's a ton of people [living] around here that can't get into Oakpark." (Oakpark was the popular alternative school nearby.)

In the weeks during which parents were encouraged to visit schools and "shop around," Ms. Grant had scheduled tours twice a week in the afternoon. As she described the process of parents coming through, she stated:

> It's very stressful. It's really very stressful. Some because you know you're on display, which is always stressful. But some because you know that, you just want to tell 'em, "Go somewhere else." [laughs] When they start asking you how their special child, who's had you know, who's a proven genius factor, and who has had a privileged life, how he is gonna fare in a classroom where not everybody's even been to school, and they're gonna pick up all this kind of "language," and it's like, "Okay, if that's your worry, go find another private school." But you can't tell 'em that. You know. And they ask, "How do you pitch to the top 25th percent instead of the bottom 25th percent"—and this is kindergarten mind you. I mean we don't look at 'em quite in the level of established quartiles.

Just that day I had spoken with a mother who was visiting the school. When I asked whether she was considering her neighborhood school, she stated that she wasn't really: "Well, we're not gonna go there because they don't have the diversity, you know, in *reverse*." When I asked her what that meant, she replied, "Well there—basically there's not enough white kids." As she explained it, the school was less than 10 percent white. She did not think she would feel "comfortable" there and also interpreted the racial demographics to mean that it "wasn't a very good school." Here she was quite explicitly using race as one proxy for school quality. As Ms. Grant explained when I told her this story later in the day, "Well that's why a lot of them are in the alternative circuit. Because it's perceived as more the purview of white upper-middle-class people, who, you know, can pick and choose."

Ms. Grant was committed to keeping the school diverse. As she explained, without that diversity, the school would have a hard time living up to its commitment to civil rights, "other than maybe to teach white, privileged kids about the other half and how they might live." To maintain diversity, she was engaged in recruiting in the Barnsworth projects as well as making sure current parents filled out the paperwork for siblings and asking them to network with friends. As the period for filling out the alternative enrollment request forms was ending, she was not yet sure of the impact the changes would have for the following year. However, she had not given up on getting a diverse kindergarten class:

> We have no idea of who's actually [turned their enrollment forms in] yet because they can turn their forms in anywhere. We have quite a few siblings. And the siblings are fairly diverse. But the people who showed up for the orientations and the tours were all yuppie white neighborhood people. So, I don't know who's actually [turned their forms in yet] and who hasn't, and what their diversity level is or not. One of the second-grade students lives in the Barnsworth projects, and I had been meaning to call his mother 'cause she's really really proud of the school, she loves the school, she's African American. She thinks we've done wonders with her kid. So I called her and I asked her if she knew of any kids, or siblings, or others that weren't registered, and she said, "Well Thomas has a four-year-old brother that's gonna be five, and she hasn't registered him, and . . . " The enrollment period has already passed. She said she knew at least eight or nine kids in the same situation. So tonight at four o'clock, we made a little invitation. She works for the Community Center at the projects and she's gonna host this little kindergarten orientation over there, and I called the district office and got permission to fill out [enrollment forms], and backdate 'em.

As this narrative demonstrates, parents who lack the social capital necessary to navigate through district policies often lose out by default. Thus, even though siblings have first priority for admissions, if parents do not fill out the paperwork in time, they lose priority. In this case Ms. Grant called in some favors to extend the deadline by a few days because she had not been aware how many current parents had not filled out paperwork for their younger children for the following year. Despite all her efforts, the demographics of West City were changing. In fact, the percentage of white kindergartners nearly tripled, increasing from 7 percent to 17 percent to over 20 percent in the two years after the school officially got alternative status.

Metro2 had been struggling with these issues for years. Its ideal enrollment would have included many more Spanish-speaking Latino students than were currently enrolled. This gap between ideal and real enrollment, several teachers and administrators explained, was a result of the enrollment process: middle-class families with resources and the know-how to negotiate complex power structures managed to take the best advantage of the system and were thus overrepresented at schools like Metro2. Thus children from the immediate neighborhood made up only 20 to 25 percent of the student body. The student body as a whole was 39 percent Latino, but approximately half those students were from middle-class households, sometimes with biracial parents or with parents whose families had been in the United States for generations (or both). The school had made systematic efforts in recent years to reach out to the parents of Latino children in the Title 1 preschool located nearby. These neighborhood children were the students in the school who spoke Spanish as a first language, who were either recent immigrants themselves or children of recent immigrants (from Mexico and Central America), and who qualified for free or reduced-price lunch. Though these students did not do as well at Metro2 as their white and middle-class peers, there is reason to believe that they fared much better than did their peers who attended traditional schools (Christian 1996). Thus, within the largely low-income Latino neighborhood surrounding Metro2 sat a high-functioning dual-language school that would have benefited the local, at-risk children in multiple ways but to which few of them could get access.[7]

As these examples demonstrate, social capital creates options, choices, and increased chances for good schooling. Racial politics, however, not only influence which students end up in which school but also affect the experiences of students once they are inside particular school buildings. In the next section I look more closely at cultural capital as it affects the educational experiences and outcomes of different groups within schools and classrooms.

Cultural Capital

Cultural capital has been defined in various ways. Drawing from Bourdieu, Swartz (1997) specified three kinds: cultivated and learned dispositions that are internalized during socialization and that "constitute schemes of appreciation and understanding" (76)—these allow one to consume or appreciate the meaning of certain kinds of cultural goods (e.g., music, art) and lead to dividends in school; objectified forms that provide one with the cultural ability to use different objects (paint brush, scientific instruments); and institutionalized forms, including the educational credentialing system, which allocates status and is fundamental to reproducing the social-class structure. Lamont and Lareau (1988) defined cultural capital as high-status cultural signals. These include attitudes (such as the belief that knowing what constitutes a good wine is important), formal knowledge (such as knowing how to consume and evaluate wine), preferences (such having a sense of how conspicuous wine consumption should be in order to be tasteful), and possession of goods (such as a wine cellar). In other arenas, cultural capital includes being at ease with abstract thinking, knowing the appropriate range of conversational topics in specific settings, using middle-class speech patterns, and possessing cultural knowledge.

I am using *cultural capital* here, however, not just in the limited definition, as that knowledge held valuable in high-class cultural circles, but instead, more broadly, as those sets of knowledge and skills valuable in a particular field or social setting (Bourdieu 1977a, 1977b; Bourdieu and Passeron 1990; DiMaggio 1982). For example, although parading knowledge about opera or wine might well signal one's insider status in some settings, in others it would render one an instant outsider. Generally then, I understand cultural capital to include having a general facility for interacting appropriately in various contexts, a knowledge of and an ability to use the rules of engagement in particular settings, general cultural knowledge relevant for and held in esteem in a particular situation,[8] and certain kinds of possessions or credentials.[9]

All students have acquired in their home and neighborhood lives important cultural resources, which serve as valuable assets in those settings. Problems arise when the students enter new fields—for example, school—where these skills and knowledge sets are not rewarded. When, in these different settings, other forms of cultural resources are the currency of exchange, students not only have trouble accessing resources but may be penalized for trying to put other understandings to work. Although all groups have cultural resources that are valuable within their local community contexts, only certain resources are legitimate in school settings and function as cultural capital there. Those resources help students successfully navigate the terrain, provide them with important knowledge, and help them appear to be the correct kind of student. As discussed in Chapters 3 and 4, cultural capital is a key part of everyday school interactions and provides students who have it with multiple benefits. Bourdieu even suggested that cultural capital is more important to school success than are other more commonly thought-of factors such as individual intelligence or effort (Bourdieu 1986; Bourdieu and Passeron 1990).

In previous chapters I documented exchanges between teachers and students in which cultural resources were differently legitimized and rewarded. For example, in the curriculum these exchanges occurred in the form of assumptions about prior knowledge and experience. During the year I was working in the schools, numerous children were rewarded for having information that had not been taught (e.g., in the USA Bingo game at Metro2). In these cases experiences outside school provided direct advantages within classrooms.

Another major pattern, and the one I spend more time discussing here, was the culturally driven expectations about acceptable forms of interaction. In daily classroom and school interactions, a student's culturally embodied performances were read as being either engaged or disruptive, appropriate or troublemaking. For example, during a math game at West City, children variously expressed their satisfaction with getting the right answer. When Malik stood up, spun around, and raised both arms in the air in a "raise-the-roof" motion, he was promptly sent from the classroom. His form of celebration was understood as inappropriate, and the response was to exclude him from the rest of the lesson.

Thus cultural resources that serve a student well in one setting (e.g., home, community) do not always provide advantages or protection in another setting (school) and can even be deleterious. For example, the rules that govern life at home sometimes clash with rules at school. In the yard one day, an African American fourth-grader told me about waiting with her grandmother at the bus stop the day before and being confronted by a man with a knife. She was prepared to fight him to protect her grandmother before a police car drove by, scaring him off. She and I were talking at that moment because she had been benched just that day for getting in a fight. The teacher had counseled her to turn her back and walk away if another student harassed her, to get a teacher if someone hit her. Although few would question a rule against fighting in school, it is also easy to understand why this child had a hard time going back and forth between a context in which she had to be prepared to stand up for herself and not let anyone "get over" on her and one in which (as she understood it) she was expected to do exactly the opposite.

Rodney, an African American fifth-grader, raised these issues with me when he tried to explain the differences between black people and white people:

Rodney: Because black people have their way and white people have their way.
Amanda: What do you mean?
Rodney: Black, kind of like black people whereas [sic] not to let things go or only sometimes let things go.
Amanda: What do you mean, don't let things go?
Rodney: Like if somebody punch them, they don't let it go. They hit them back.
Amanda: And white people do let it go?
Rodney: Mmmhmmm, yeah, at least sometimes.

Rodney had already at a young age recognized differential patterns in handling conflict. He had learned them from his interactions with peers and adults at West City. He, however, read these styles as merely different, while teachers seem to be reading them as right or wrong.

In another example, groups of African American boys would sometimes engage in large play fights they called "beat-downs." Their rationale for playing the game was eerily similar to the rationale eighth-graders in another city gave for playing a comparable game: "If you get jacked out there on the street, you got to know how to cover up. Otherwise, you're gonna get seriously hurt" (Noguera 1996: 12). As one fifth-grade boy at West City told me, "You gotta, you know, know how to take a beating or get away or whatever." Again, though beat-downs was not necessarily a game the school should have condoned, teachers needed to take into account students' interpretations of their behavior and their motivations for it. It is unreasonable to assume that five-, eight-, or ten-year-olds will simply leave their home lives on the bus each day when they disembark. Yet these moments in which a student's cultural resources are delegitimized can quickly become moments of social exclusion (Lareau and Horvat 1999)—dramatically so when the student is kicked out of the classroom.

In longitudinal ethnographic work, Corsaro (1996: 453) tracked transitions from home and preschool to formal schooling. He found that "culturally meaningful activities" in the home, community, and preschool do not always have "desirable priming effects" for transitions to formal schooling—particularly when that transition involves going from an African American community and preschool to a predominantly white school. For example, in tracking one African American girl facing just this transition in her move to kindergarten and first grade, Corsaro found that although she had been relatively successful academically in preschool, she began to have a series of social and academic problems. Strategies and styles that had served her well in her home and in the local Head Start program "contributed to unanticipated (and often misunderstood) problems in kindergarten or first grade" (453). Moreover, Corsaro states, "a cycle can develop" where these differences in cultural styles "are misinterpreted, leading children to limit further interaction and to also [translate] these differences into personal characteristics or traits that are then linked to race" (446). In this way, differences are read as deficiencies not only in teacher evaluations but also in peer interactions. They can thus affect racial attitudes (e.g., with Ms. Harrison's first-graders).

As outlined in Chapter 3, I had a series of conversation with staff at West City about why African American boys were so often in trouble. Though they made up less than 20 percent of the student body, they accounted for an overwhelming majority of the disciplinary referrals.[10] Typically they were, like Malik, sent from their classroom to another room or to the student advisors. When we talked about it, the principal of West City discussed the role of styles of interaction on such disciplinary outcomes:

> I would say that if someone's gonna get sent out, it's typically an African American male. First of all it's typical racism. Throughout. Most of these kids live in Lancaster Valley or the Barnsworth projects. There's a more aggressive problem-solving style at home. They yell at each other. Mom's yellin' at the kid, the kid's yellin' back. I've seen a lot of that. Then I also think that the tolerance for little boys who work things out physically is pretty low. Especially when they're African Americans. It's a societal problem, it's an educational problem, it's a teacher problem. It's part of the reason why it's not good to have all-white staff. I mean, you know you can be trained to understand, you can talk about multiple intelligences, but um . . . you know when it comes to Mr. Jordan [the African American student advisor] versus Ms. Guzman [the Latina student advisor] disciplining Malik or Darnell or Edward, it's gonna be Mr. Jordan. You know. And that's why I think it's real important that there be African American teachers and staff members, and that there be Latino—not just people like Peggy, who speak Spanish, but Latino teachers and paraprofessionals, and that they are actively engaged and involved with the kids. Culturally, and disciplinewise and academically. That isn't to say that other teachers can't deal with other kids. I mean there's a great book out called *Other People's Children* [Delpit 1995] that argues that it is the role of all teachers to teach all children no matter what color they are.

As Ms. Grant suggests, a complex process is operating here in which particular, largely racially specific, cultural norms dominate the school context and lead to intolerance of the behavior of certain children who follow other cultural norms. This dynamic involves more than race. As Alexander, Entwisle, and Thompson (1987: 665) suggest, "Teachers' own social origins exercise a strong influence on how they react to the status attributes of their students."

When I talked to Ms. Harrison, one of the few black staff members at West City, about these patterns, she explained that she faced them too—her own blackness did not make her immune to racism and its pervasive messages about black male deviance. Ms. Harrison recognized that many aspects of elementary schools are alien if not hostile to these boys. She struggled with making sure she did not, as she talked about it, turn her problem into the boys' problem by punishing them for her own limitations. When issues came up with particular African American male students, she was especially careful to look at the structure of the school (e.g., institutional policies and practices) and her own behavior in trying to understand what was going on. In this way she did not read problems as inherent within particular children but as instructional, pedagogical, or institutional issues that were at least in part her responsibility to change.

As Ms. Grant herself noted, drawing on Delpit's (1995) work, all teachers should be able to teach all children. But teaching all children successfully requires some reflection on the cultural rules that dominate classroom contexts and the ways those rules do or do not reflect the cultural resources and understandings that different children bring to school with them. It is not practical to expect children to know the rules of engagement intuitively. As Delpit (1995) suggests, to equalize the playing field, such cultural tools must be explicitly taught.

Cultural capital also has an impact on school performance. When I asked Ms. Wilson, the Metro2 teacher, about the differential performance of racial/cultural groups within her classroom, she explained it as a result of the "home environment:"

> A lot of it has to do with culture. A lot of the high-achieving kids that we're talking about come from highly achieving white families that were educated and went on to further their college or whatever, versus maybe some of the more biracial families, they'll have some influence of that, some sort of support around that in the home and then it could be that you know, families that are primarily Spanish speaking have recently immigrated here and have sort of been in a struggle their whole lives and haven't been maybe through as much school themselves. I find that a lot of the Latino kids' parents in this class, their parents didn't go on to school past high school, if even to high school, so there's that, and maybe they just don't know how to support the kids. They don't have the language skills, they don't have the academic skills, or whatever, maybe they're working, maybe both parents are working versus one may be home.

Ms. Wilson highlights much of the kind and amount of cultural capital that students have available to them—parents' education, language skills, and academic skills. Though she begins by talking about environment and culture, Ms. Wilson is referring not to beliefs or values in the traditional sense but to the availability of cultural resources that are important for school success. She does not refer to ability or potential.

A Latina mother from West City highlighted many of these same issues in relating her struggles to help her daughter with school. Despite her desire to help her children, she did not always have the skills or knowledge to do so. "It seems difficult for me. They say that wanting it is making it, but sometimes I just don't know, sometimes it's very difficult. . . . I understand a little bit and I can talk a little bit, but not enough to help them do their homework and all that. I can help the little one because they are not very big things, but Gloria needs a little bit more." Clearly, lack of value for education is not the problem. As she states, "wanting it" doesn't automatically lead to "making it." Just recently she had borrowed English-language tutorial videotapes so she could help her daughters more, but as she was working two jobs at that time, it was hard to devote much time to studying.

Cultural capital also affects the success parents have in their interactions with schools. As Lareau and Horvat (1999) discuss, parents' own histories with formal schooling can lead them to approach school interactions in quite different ways. Thus, though parents may try to intervene on behalf of their children (putting their cultural resources to work), only some manage to be successful. in their interactions with staff, who have their own expectations for how parents should behave. Ms. Grant, Mr. Ortiz, and Ms. Guzman from West City described the school's interactions with one black mother, Ms. Rashaad. The mother of Malcolm, a black third-grader, Ms. Rashaad had come in a number of times to protest the treatment of her son. Though the school year began with staff members wondering where Ms. Rashaad was and why she wasn't more involved with her son's education, they soon wanted her out of the way and less involved. Ms. Rashaad was convinced that Malcolm was being treated poorly at least in part because he was black. Her involvement, which included telling her son to watch out for racist teachers, was not considered to be "supportive" of the school or of her son's possibility for success. Staff eventually avoided dealing with her and, in doing so, often avoided doing much with regard to Malcolm's school engagement. Ms. Grant relayed a story of her own discomfort in dealing with Ms. Rashaad. "It took me a while to, to feel comfortable, feeling like [her coming in and yelling] was okay. I mean she went off at Mr. Jordan, 'He's not to come near my child, under no circumstances.' I said, 'Okay, I'll mediate between the two of you'—what a fool I was. I had to leave the two of them with the door closed. And eventually they just [worked] it out enough to the point where, a form of respect came in where they can work together." In fact, however, neither she nor Malcolm's teacher ever had much success with Ms. Rashaad. In some cases, school personnel like Ms. Grant might even be open to engaging with Ms. Rashaad about her charges of racism—but not in the particular style she had chosen. In this particular situation, a cultural clash between school personnel and a parent hindered possibilities to collaborate on Malcolm's behalf.

Thus, many interactions among staff, between personnel and parents, between teachers and students, and among children involve the bringing together of people with differences in cultural styles, preferences, tastes, and strategies. Certain kinds of cultural styles are institutionalized and then become those that tend to pay off within schools, serving as cultural capital. Daily unsuccessful or inequitable exchanges eventually contribute to unequal educational outcomes. Within the same school buildings, students' educational experiences are stratified in part because of their different cultural resources. (As I argue in the next section, sometimes stratification results not from differences in social, cultural, or economic resources but from differences in color.)

At times, however, it is not enough even to have the requisite cultural capital and to attempt to put it to use; similarly shared resources are not always rewarded equally. As Farkas (1996), Lareau and Horvat (1999), and Roscigno and Ainsworth-Darnell (1999) have all found in separate analyses, race is a mediating factor in one's ability to turn cultural resources into cultural capital in schools. For example, Roscigno and Ainsworth-Darnell (1999) demonstrate that cultural resources don't automatically become capital. Rather they are mediated by gatekeepers (e.g., teachers), who differentially reward or legitimize resources, and by institutions (e.g., schools), which can relegate people to less desirable positions (e.g., tracks) where their resources are harder to maximize (in vocational tracks, for example, academic cultural capital may carry less weight than in a college-preparatory track). They argue that researchers have paid too little attention, for example, to studies of teachers' expectations for and evaluations of students' efforts and to studies of institutional regulation that have found race and class bias. For instance, Farkas (1996) found that teachers' evaluations of student skills and orientations differed across racial, class, and gender groups, with repercussions for the grades students received. As Roscigno and Ainsworth-Darnell (1999: 161) put it: "It is unclear whether black students are rewarded in the same manner as their white counterparts. If cultural capital is predicated, in part, on the social position of its possessor and consequential micropolitical processes, the subordinate racial status of blacks may limit their ability to convert cultural capital and educational resources into academic success." Thus not only do gaps exist in access to cultural capital, but groups are differently rewarded for the resources they have.

Symbolic Capital

In late 1997 the school board in a small town in Southern California decided to name its new high school the Martin Luther King Jr. High School. Almost immediately a number of white parents protested the district's choice, eventually bringing legal action. As reported in a local newspaper, these parents worried that "King's name could jeopardize their children's college acceptance chances" as college admissions officers would think it was a black school (Acosta 1998). Though these parents eventually lost their battle, their concerns highlight the precise way in which race can serve as a form of symbolic capital. In both its more abstract forms (e.g., the name of a school) and its embodied forms, race can function as a resource for some because it serves as a conveyer of meaning, implying legitimacy and high status (or lack thereof).

As Swartz (1997: 83) summarized Bourdieu's position, symbolic capital relates to symbolic systems that, as means for making sense of the world, perform the multiple functions of "cognition, communication and social differentiation."[11] These symbolic systems can function as codes that convey deep structural meanings shared by those in a particular culture or context, and therefore they operate as instruments of communication and knowledge. Thus, for example, a number of authors have talked about the use of racial code words (e.g., "welfare queen") to refer to a whole set of social relationships or narratives whose significance would be unintelligible to an outsider (Bonilla-Silva 1997; Gilens 1995, 1996; Omi and Winant 1994). Symbolic systems also function as instruments of domination in that they provide ways of distinguishing between groups and ranking them. They also provide a means for legitimizing that ranking and thus for getting the dominated to accept the hierarchies of social distinction (Swartz 1997). Race can be thought of as a symbolic or signifying system that serves as an instrument of communication and knowledge (it tells us about people before we even know them) and as an instrument of domination that sorts and ranks groups. As Swartz (1997: 84) suggests, "The fundamental logic of symbolic processes and systems . . . is one of establishing differences and distinctions in the form of binary oppositions[;] . . . symbolic systems, from this perspective, are classifications systems built upon the fundamental logic of inclusion and exclusion." As discussed in the previous chapter, these processes of differentiation, domination, and exclusion are closely linked in the way race functions in people's daily lives.

One form of symbolic capital—racial categorization or skin color—is accrued directly through the effect it has on the way people are treated. As Connolly (1998: 21) states, "It is clearly the case that white skin, for instance, can represent symbolic capital in certain contexts. Some teachers may be influenced (whether directly or indirectly) by a set of racist beliefs which encourages them to think of white children as being more intelligent and well behaved than black children. In this sense, having white skin represents a form of symbolic capital which brings with it better treatment and more educational opportunities." Because of racist assumptions and stereotypes, race functions at a conscious or subconscious level to shape interactions. For example, black skin might function as symbolic capital if the goal is to get picked for a schoolyard basketball game but not necessarily if the goal is to get picked for a study group (Lewis, Chesler, and Forman 2000). As I discussed in the previous chapter, racial categories such as white or black carry with them a host of meanings. Thus it was useful for a white mother (Ms. Hivert) to claim she was Puerto Rican when she was trying to explain why she was working in a garment factory. Ascribed race automatically tells us something about people, can immediately provide them with legitimacy or cause their status to be questioned. As one mother put it, "That's the first thing you notice, someone's skin color, that's the way it is. And [being white] helps."

White parents almost unanimously talked about benefiting from their whiteness. Although some politically progressive white parents talked about whiteness as a privilege that they had not in any way earned and that they hoped to subvert, others talked about feeling "lucky" or "glad" they were white. Though several suburban parents alluded to "reverse racism" affecting their children's lives, they acknowledged that in most settings being white could only help.

Symbolic capital operates in schools in many complicated ways. Parents of color related a number of their own or their children's schooling experiences where assumptions were made about them because of their race. Ms. Sullivan, a teacher at West City, seemed to allude to such racialized presumptions in her explanation of teachers' perceptions of Latinos: "The unspoken assumption is that they do better [than African American kids], I mean, they're better students at least, a lot of them have their families intact, mother and father on site. Most of them do better and I think teachers expect them to do [better], they're the ones who pull your scores up, once they get English down, you know." Though Ms. Sullivan was factually wrong—achievement levels were basically the same for both groups—she was accurate in that assumptions about Latino family stability, relative to assumptions about black family dysfunction, led teachers to believe that Latinos were likely to do better in school. Thus, in West City, Latinos were in some ways better situated than the other large group in the school, blacks. So on multiple levels, interactions between teachers and students included more than just the surface minutiae—they were rife with larger ideas and assumptions. In this way, race worked as symbolic capital for certain students.

As discussed in the previous chapter, minority parents were aware of this dynamic. Given their own educational experiences, they understood that race would have some impact on their child's schooling. A Latino father related some of his own memories:

> Looking back you know, Latinos and blacks get discriminated from left and right and you just have to deal with it, you know you go around it or try to deal. . . . You know, how kids get treated when something happens. When you get in trouble, how was the issue dealt with if you're black or Latino, versus if you're white or you know, you've seen the difference. And then if you're in a classroom and you don't like the classroom and you want to be changed to another class, like you can tell the difference, which preferences and all that was there.

From generation to generation, race has remained a regular part of everyday school interactions. Aretha Jones-Washington's own history with racism in schools had had a big role in her decision to send her son Darnell to a relatively new black-run middle school in her neighborhood rather than to the high-scoring, highly sought-after but predominantly white school to which he had first been admitted. Given a long history of struggling with school personnel around racial issues (both with regard to her son and during her own school years), she had decided that the social benefits of his not having to deal with racism in school everyday outweighed the potential academic costs of going to the new black school. In fact, she had decided that he was more likely to do well in a setting where he did not have to deal with the social and emotional toll of being one of few black students. In this case, a black middle-class family that was able to deploy some social and cultural resources in the school-choice process had to factor race into their final decision. Specifically, this mother recognized that in different settings her son's race would have different symbolic meaning—in one setting leading to various possible disadvantages, while leading to more neutral or even positive outcomes in another.

Symbolic capital also matters in finding a place to live, in walking down the street, in eating in a restaurant, in getting a job (Bonilla-Silva and Lewis 1999; Bobo, Kluegel, and Smith 1997; Essed 1991; Feagin and Sikes 1994; Oliver and Shapiro 1995; Yinger 1995). Race came into housing choices in different ways for white parents and parents of color in the study. As several minority families discussed, their housing choices had to incorporate factors aside from just money. Where one can "afford" to live can be about more than finances. Several black and Latino parents talked about looking at housing in the mostly white neighborhood near West City but encountering, as Mrs. Oliva, a Latina mother, put it, "a very racial kind of thing happening there." Thus these families had to take local racial climates into account when making housing choices—particularly with regard to whether they could "afford" to have their children exposed to racial hostility (Essed 1997). Though they wanted to leave their current neighborhoods, both to gain access to better schooling and to find safer environs, their options were constrained along a number of dimensions. For almost all the parents interviewed, the presence or absence of resources was primary in enabling them to realize their desires for their children's education or in hindering the realization of their goals.

Race also played a role in many white families' choices about where to live or send their children to school (or both). Findings by Farley and others have indicated how racial stereotypes continue to play a key role in whites' housing choices and thus in persistent housing segregation patterns across class lines (Farley et al. 1994; Farley et al. 1978; Massey and Denton 1993). In the Foresthills community, parents explicitly talked about moving to the suburbs in the context of their children's schooling; throughout their discourse, race was a regular part of the subtext. Though most of them spoke in code words and euphemisms (e.g., not wanting to be in a "rough" neighborhood), race was clearly one of several factors that influenced their decision about where to live. In a diverse metropolis, electing to live in an almost entirely white town is not racially neutral.

As a result of their decision to live in Sunny Valley, Foresthills parents had almost-all-white community social networks. These parents also reported that even their wider networks of friends, co-workers, and acquaintances—from whom they drew in order to learn about the "best" schools, the tricks to getting accepted by various schools or to getting assigned to specific teachers, and the processes of appeal—were all fairly segregated. Moreover, even most of those white families in Hillside who lived in minority neighborhoods for financial reasons, like Alex's family in Chapter 3, were in the neighborhood but not of it. They knew few of their neighbors, did not let their children play outside after school, and had little interaction with those around them. In various ways, white parents at the three schools fit general patterns of white abandonment of urban areas and specifically of urban public school systems.

Several measures are available for assessing white abandonment of the urban public school system—movement out of the city, movement into urban private schools, and movement from neighborhood public schools into select, alternative public schools. The general trend of movement out of the city altogether was represented by many Sunny Valley parents. This was the trend in Hillside as a whole between the 1960s and the 1990s; for example, the percentage of the Hillside population that was white declined between 1970 and 1990 from 71 to 54. The largest outpouring took place between the 1970–71 and 1971–72 school years, just after the first citywide desegregation plan was implemented. Within one year, 24 percent of the district's white students had left the public schools.

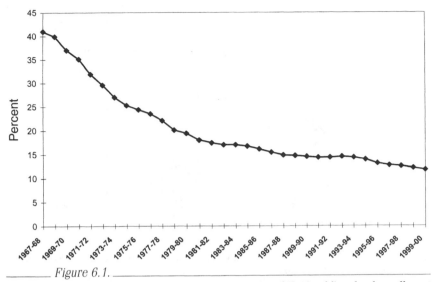

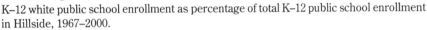

_____ *Figure 6.1.* _____

K–12 white public school enrollment as percentage of total K–12 public school enrollment in Hillside, 1967–2000.

In addition, many whites who remain in cities move their children out of the public school system into private schools. Although in the late 1960s whites constituted over 40 percent of Hillside's public school enrollment, by 1996 that number had dropped below 15 percent (see Figure 6.1). As Figure 6.2 shows, the percentage of students attending public schools dropped much more quickly than the total percentage of whites in the city. Some of this decline was related to the movement of whites out of the city, but although less than 30 percent of white Hillside students attended private school in 1960, almost 50 percent did so by 1990 (see Figure 6.3). In 1990, white students were two to three times more likely than any other group to attend private school (see Figure 6.4).

Finally, white students are often overrepresented in a city's high-achieving alternative schools. In Hillside, except at the alternative schools in the low-income Lancaster Valley area (which had an Afrocentric focus), white student enrollments at alternative schools were two to three times white students' general representation in the district. A number of white parents said the decision to keep their children in public schools was contingent on their getting admitted to an alternative school. Foremost in this selection process were issues of school quality, but according to a number of indicators race may be a key variable not only in decisions about whether a school is suitable but in shaping who has access to the information necessary to gain entry to these schools.

In an analysis of the school-choice process in a large metropolitan area,

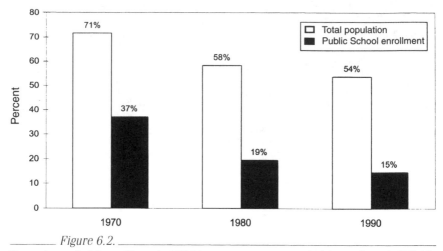

———— *Figure 6.2.* ————

Percentage of white residents in Hillside versus percentage of white students in Hillside public schools, 1970, 1980, 1990.

Saporito and Lareau (1999) found that white parents use race as a criterion in selecting among available schools and demonstrate an aversion to schools that are predominantly minority. They suggest that "choices unfold in a multi-stage process in which some alternatives are eliminated from serious consideration based upon socially salient characteristics" (418). Thus white families elimi-

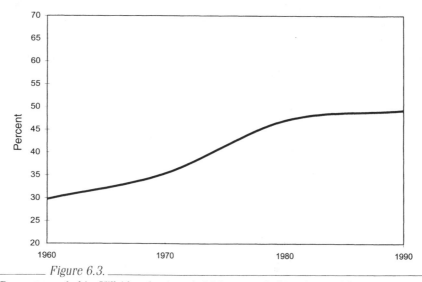

———— *Figure 6.3.* ————

Percentage of white Hillside school-aged children enrolled in private schools, 1960–1990.

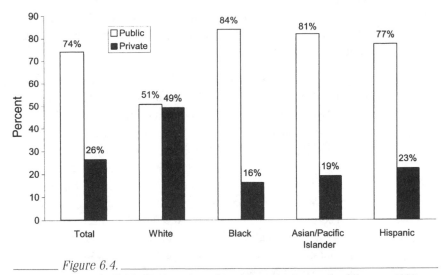

——— *Figure 6.4.* ———
Percentage of Hillside K–12 students in public and private school by race, 1990.

nated certain schools from consideration based on race and then utilized other criteria to decide among the remaining schools. Similar to these findings, race was a significant factor in Hillside parents' school-choice processes. Whether race was used as a proxy for school success, as a gauge of potential comfort level for both parent and child, or as some other measure, it affected how many families evaluated the potential fit, or appropriateness, of a particular school for their child. Race functioned as a symbolic system that collectively benefited some schools and communities and disadvantaged others. As Orfield et al. (1997) and others have outlined in discussions of school segregation, these patterns have significant effects on school outcomes as resources continue to be pooled along racial lines.

Race also factored into the school preferences of parents of color but in quite different ways. Parents of color talked about having to think strategically about race in evaluating whether a school was likely to work well for their children; like Darnell's mother, they were most often concerned with minimizing the likelihood of racism. For example, both Latino and black parents described looking at the race of those who ran the school when evaluating middle-school options. They had a firsthand awareness of these issues because their everyday lives (both inside and outside school) involved negotiating issues of race and symbolic capital.

Mr. Jackson, an African American Metro2 father, related many stories of having to negotiate the symbolic meanings of race; for example, his legitimacy in the workplace was regularly questioned because he was black. Importantly, as he pointed out, one's experience walking down the street as well as one's right to the presumption of innocence are racially inflected:

Mr. Jackson: Last Friday I was going to the market, and these two young Latino boys were walking across the street, it was dusk—it wasn't dark yet but it wasn't daylight. And they were just walking across the street just, basically minding their own business. And this police car—you know the van—rolled up slow behind. And this one cop he's leaning out the window and he, you know the handcuffs that they use? He dangled them out the window and was staring at them. And they [the cops] slowed down. . . . Whether you want to think about [race] or not, somebody's gonna keep you on [the defensive]. Now these kids weren't doing anything particularly loud, they weren't drunk, they crossed at a light, you know not doing a thing. They were just walking down the street—going from point A to point B.

Amanda: How did they respond?

Mr. Jackson: Well they—you know I think they were shocked, you know. And then they, and then they, they kind of talked amongst themselves. But it affected me. So I knew it affected them. So, see, you can never get away from who you are.

As Mr. Jackson indicated, this was a collective experience, one he shared with the two youths crossing the street, even though none of the attention was directed at him. It was a reminder that his skin color mattered all the time. These kinds of events inevitably shock and create stress. Conversely, skin color can serve as symbolic capital to whites in a protective way; it can shield them from these same types of everyday mental, emotional, and even physical stress.[12]

Even those within minority communities have the possibility of gaining access to some of the symbolic capital of whiteness, depending on their skin color or ability to "pass." As Mrs. Clive put it:

It's just this thing that people with fair, with lighter-tone skin is kinda placed on a different line, you know. I can remember, [my children's] dad is really light and he has green eyes and if you were to see him, you probably would have thought that he was something but not an African American, and I can remember someone telling him, "Gee you're gonna get far in life" and he was just like "Why?" "Because you look white." And I was like, "no that is not true, it's the qualities that you possess that get you where you want to be." But basically it do work out that way, I've seen it happen. I guess if I would have never seen things like that happen I would totally disagree because I am just a firm believer that it's the qualities that we possess that gets us where we want to be in life and not the color of our skin. But I've seen it.

As she said, if she had not seen it she would not believe it. It was a reality that continued to enrage her daily. Even with this knowledge, though, she made it clear to her children over and over again that hard work was the only answer. She just recognized that she would often have to work twice as hard to get what she wanted (e.g., access to better schooling for her children).

Symbolic capital includes the ability to have your status go unquestioned, to have your right to be in a particular place assumed—to get the benefit of the doubt. These kinds of benefits are often invisible to those who have them. Only through examining the experiences of those who do not do they become apparent. Mrs. Jones-Washington's experience with colleagues at a restaurant highlights this benefit well.

Mrs. Jones-Washington: So, a couple of us had lunch, and it was a restaurant where they didn't come and serve you, you had to get your stuff at the counter and then you can go, either sit inside or you could sit outside, so two of us had lunch and two of us didn't, so the two that didn't walk to the counter to get their lunch and the other two of us went to sit down and I pulled out my lunch and then the waitress said, "This is the worst thing I've ever seen." She was pointing at me and she goes, "This is terrible, you have to leave!" And I was thinking, "Well, maybe I should ask first" or whatever, but they weren't talking to the other women that were with me. They're Spanish speaking but they look white. So then the owner comes to me and said, "You have to get out now!" They're not saying anything to [the other woman who brought her lunch].

Amanda: She's sitting there with her lunch?

Mrs. Jones-Washington: Yeah, so I was kicked out and then my friends would get outraged, they were so upset, you know, it's like "how could they do that," "that's blatant racism and we have to write letters," "we have to talk to this person and that person" and I said, "Why are they surprised at this," and they were saying, "Why aren't you reacting to this, why aren't you angry," I'm like, "I can't spend my energy on that because I deal with stuff like that all the time," you know, like going into the store and somebody following you around or having to pro-

> duce an extra set of ID. It's just every day and I cannot
> spend all my energy on that, there are days that I have a
> lower tolerance for it than other days.

Symbolic capital manifests itself at exactly that moment when a waitress walks up to a table and intuitively assumes the legitimacy of certain people and questions the right of others. As Mrs. Jones-Washington said, racism is an "everyday" experience; in that way symbolic capital provides real benefits when understood in relation to the experiences of those who do not regularly have access to it.

Moreover, as Mrs. Jones-Washington and other parents of color understood and discussed, their children were learning to navigate through this same world, a world in which their legitimacy would often be questioned. The racist ideas that pervade our culture inevitably invade our schools. There is no reason to expect that somehow teachers, administrators, or students will be immune to their influence. As the earlier examples demonstrate, children do not walk in with a blank slate. Neither their behavior nor their treatment are pre-scripted and determined, but neither are children free to make the world anew, to create a space in which only their individual talents and merits matter. It is impossible to live outside the system of racial narratives (Hall 1984, 1990).

Symbolic capital did not guarantee that all white children in the schools succeeded or were treated well at all times. It did mean, however, that some children (and adults) more often received the benefit of the doubt, a second chance, a few extra seconds to answer a question. The concept of symbolic capital captures the way racist ideas lead us almost unconsciously to assume we know something about people before they open their mouths. It illuminates the way race shapes our evaluations, our expectations, and our interpretations. It is not merely a matter of the "symbolic" order of things however. In the way it shapes life opportunities and outcomes, symbolic capital not only can have a significant influence over the quality of one's life but can sometimes make the difference between life and death.[13] For many children of color, it is one more way in which they are shortchanged on a daily basis.

Conclusion

In this chapter I have argued that economic, social, cultural, and symbolic capital are not distributed equally among racial groups in the United States. Though not uniquely available to particular groups, these forms of capital are for historic and contemporary reasons more widely available to some than to others. Importantly, each not only is a resource in securing access to good educational experiences but helps students to succeed and achieve. In these ways, capital plays a key role in the reproduction of racial inequality. Having access to it in certain forms facilitates getting access to it in other forms. Clearly one cannot simply or directly "cash in" social or cultural capital at the bank to pay the rent, but both provide advantages in securing a good education— still the surest path to future economic stability. Despite the prevalent assumption that our school system is open, equitable, and fair, in many ways the system is not nearly so meritocratic. Students do not all have an equal chance for success or even a fair shot at it. Despite some dynamic tension, educational options and opportunities are largely constrained before the child even enters the classroom.

This is not to suggest that we live within a closed system in which the alleged opportunities do not exist. There is much evidence to the contrary. In the past few decades, affirmative action has opened up many opportunities for middle-class people of color. Jobs once secured primarily through social networks are now more widely publicized and thus more widely available. Some schools, such as Metro2, regularly challenge and question their own practices in an effort to ensure that students' individual qualities count as much their parents' resources if not more. Fair-housing laws and other antidiscriminatory policies have chipped away at some forms of prejudicial treatment. Moreover, the furor around unfair law enforcement has focused a harsh light on the automatic assumption of black criminality. There are cracks in the walls.

However, past inequality is also still reproduced more often than it is challenged. In many ways schools continue to play a key role not only in the reproduction of racial inequality in the United States today but as justification for not doing more about it. In the face of persistent evidence of vast racial inequities, many continue to assert that equal opportunities exist for all in the availability of universal schooling. Differences in outcomes are explained as the result of either individual failure or group-level deficiency. I have tried to demonstrate that the imbalance is not the result of these individual or collective factors; rather, it is the larger systemic, structural, and institutional processes that produce racial inequality both in school outcomes and beyond.

Seven

Schools as Race-Making Institutions

Foresthills, West City, and Metro2 were very different educational institutions. They had different demographics, dynamics, and cultures. Yet, in each place, racial processes were at work. Each was what Thompson (1975) and Wacquant (2002) have labeled a "race-making institution." As Wacquant eluci- dates, "They do not simply process an ethnoracial division that would somehow exist outside of and independently from them. Rather each *produces* (or co-pro- duces) this division (anew) out of inherited demarcations and disparities of group power" (54). Schools play a role in the production of race as a social cat- egory both through implicit and explicit lessons and through school practices. Children at Foresthills, West City, and Metro2 learned what it meant to be white, black, Asian, or Latino within the contexts of those institutions. They were becoming what teachers assumed they already were—racial subjects. Race is not merely a fixed characteristic of children that they bring to school and then take away intact but something they learn about through school lessons and through interactions with peers and teachers. Moreover, schools do not merely produce children as racial subjects—they produce racial disparities in life outcomes. Children were not only learning racial lessons but were receiv- ing different educational opportunities. Racial inequalities then are, at least in part, products of racialized institutional and interactional practices within the education system.

Educational research that ignores these racialization processes and that treats race simply as a variable reifies racial categories and misses the role schools play in the production and reproduction of race, racial identities, and racial inequality. Race is never a finished product; it functions as a dynamic, artificial, and powerful category that applies to us—and that we react to—in new and old ways on a daily basis. Racial ascriptions, racial identities, and even racial categories are, as outlined in Chapter 5, continually constructed, reconstructed, struggled over, and resisted. Racial identities and racial categories, then, are less stable than much of our sociological discussion and analysis implies. I have heeded Almaguer and Jung's exhortation to study "how racial lines . . . are being re-drawn contemporarily" (1999: 213). However, as I have tried to emphasize throughout this book, that same drawing and redrawing involves not merely ideas and identities but also power and resources. The color line is unstable, but its power to shape life chances is not abating. Long histories of racial oppression leave us with unequal resources; continuing discrimination and institutional racism perpetuate and exacerbate these old racial hierarchies and help create new ones. Too often schools, which might ameliorate some of these inequities, instead reinforce them.

This work is not only about educational systems but also about dominant understandings of race. If we take seriously the fact that race is a social construction, we must pay attention to how racialization processes work—that is, how race is produced and perpetuated on an everyday basis. Building on the theoretical literature (Omi and Winant 1994; Bonilla-Silva 1997), I describe empirically what racial-formation processes look like, including the daily racialization of our bodies and the daily renegotiation of racial boundaries.

Methodologically, this work demonstrates that it is important to study not only what people say about race and racial issues but also what they do in particular contexts. Historically, survey research has been useful for charting transformations in racial attitudes. It has not, however, been as useful for understanding the meaning of race in people's experiences. What do they think about their own racial subjectivities? How does race shape their daily lives? In the post–civil rights era, as racial ideas have undergone transformation, qualitative and ethnographic work has become even more important. Although survey research shows a growing liberalization in racial attitudes, interview research and particularly this kind of ethnographic research has shown that such attitudes are more complex than can be captured in closed-ended survey items (Bonilla-Silva and Forman 2000). For example, as demonstrated in Chapter 2, whites who might agree in a survey with abstract principles such as the legality of interracial marriage offer quite different and contradictory responses in interviews about the suitability of intermarriage for their own children. In-depth research in specific local settings can enrich our knowledge about people's racial understandings and the ways these perceptions get put to use in daily life.

This work is meant as a story of hope as well as pain. It illuminates many troublesome and disheartening realities; it also shows how these realities are made and remade daily. These conditions are not immutable but are quite vulnerable to change (Sewell 1992). In fact they change all the time. However, saying that they are mutable does not mean they are easily transformed. Recognizing the difficulties involved in challenging racial inequities is necessary before anything can be done about them. To quote Durkheim (1973: 7), "If the enterprise is possible and necessary, if sooner or later it had to be undertaken, . . . it is well to realize [that it will be difficult], for only if we do not delude ourselves concerning these difficulties will it be possible to triumph over them." Change, however, does not inevitably mean movement toward equality. As others have argued, change can mean the creation of sophisticated adaptations in defense of the status quo (Bobo, Kluegel, and Smith 1997; Bonilla-Silva 1997, 2001; Forman 2001a; Gould 1999). These authors have described new forms of racism that are adaptations to new circumstances. The color-blind ideology described in Chapter 2 provides one telling example of evolving and adapting racial ideas—they are different but are not necessarily emancipative. Still, as the case of Metro2 shows, if we are searching for openings through which to intervene, they are there.

Schools potentially have a special role in both challenging and reproducing the contemporary racial formation. In an otherwise segregated world, they are one place where groups who often have little contact come together. They are the place where we learn about ourselves beyond the context of our immediate family, where children have an opportunity to learn about and, one hopes, to value difference. They offer lessons about history and the present social world. They provide access to resources and build on and reward the resources children have. But they also play a role in providing excuses and justifications for not making systematic efforts to redress inequalities. As the narrative goes, "everyone has a chance"—universal schooling. However, that chance is nowhere an equal one. In fact, for many it does not serve as much of a chance at all.

Yet schools, for many of us who spend time in them and write about them, remain places of hope—they offer the possibility for new realities. Focusing on schools encourages us to emphasize the becoming and the emerging—the inevitability that racial understandings and racial rules must all be learned, that race does not exist inert and separate from us, and thus that racial lessons might be learned differently. Examining schools challenges us not merely to document what is but to begin to imagine how it might be better. As Greene (1988: 3–4) argues, if we are interested in human freedom, in all people having the ability to live just and dignified lives, we must build our capacity to "surpass the given":

We are free[, John] Dewey said, "not because of what we statically are, but in so far as we are becoming different from what we have been." To become different, of course is not simply to will oneself to change. There is the question of being able to accomplish what one chooses to do. It is not only a matter of the capacity to choose; it is a matter of the power to act to attain one's purposes. We shall be concerned with intelligent choosing and, yes, humane choosing, as we shall be with the kinds of conditions necessary for empowering persons to act on what they choose.

However, the power to choose, the power to act on one's choices, is not evenly distributed in the population. Racism often means that some have more options than others, more choices, and more resources with which to realize their hopes. This is both the gift and the trap of our educational system. Only through education (in traditional or nontraditional settings), through the acquisition of knowledge and skills, will people acquire the ability to challenge "what is." Moreover, often through learning and education we come to see "what is" and to recognize it as a problem. As Greene (1988: 5) states, people must become "conscious of lacks" if they are to move forward. "[People] do not reach out for fulfillment if they do not feel impeded somehow, and if they are not enabled to *name* the obstacles that stand in their way. . . . As has been said, a rock is an obstacle only to the one who wants to climb the hill." One major obstacle to the transformation of our education system is the set of racial narratives that suggest that problems originate from individual or cultural deficiency. Such accounts reinforce a looking inward. Blaming the powerless for their failure, protecting institutions from blame, these narratives provide answers that are too simple and that mask, rather than reveal, the obstacles to our success. Both in our theory about schools and in our schools themselves, we need to confront racial realities rather than ignoring them. Only then can our educational system become one where children like Malik, Gloria, Alex, and Ivy learn to make intelligent and humane choices, learn what is necessary to be able to act on those choices, and—when they are stymied—learn to name the obstacles that stand in their way.

All the teachers and school personnel I met work hard. They, like most of us, want to do the right thing. They, for many of the right reasons, wish race did not matter in their classrooms. They want schools to be places that are liberating and empowering. They want to live in a color-blind world. And, in fact, in some small ways, this color-blind ideal is perhaps a sign of progress from earlier times of explicit Jim Crow–style racism. However, in reality we do not live in a color-blind world. We cannot begin to "surpass the given," to challenge the racism that pervades our social world, until we recognize it and confront it. In her book *Why Are All the Black Kids Sitting Together in the Cafeteria?* Tatum (1997: 11–12) offers a useful metaphor:

> I sometimes visualize the ongoing cycle of racism as a moving walkway at the airport. Active racist behavior is equivalent to walking fast on the conveyor belt. The person engaged in active racist behavior has identified with the ideology of White supremacy and is moving with it. Passive racist behavior is equivalent to standing still on the walkway. No overt effort is being made, but the conveyor belt moves the bystanders along to the same destination as those who are actively walking. Some of the bystanders may feel the motion of the conveyor belt, see the active racist ahead of them, and choose to turn around, unwilling to go to the same destination as the White supremacists. But unless they are walking actively in the opposite direction at a speed faster than the conveyor belt—unless they are actively antiracist—they will find themselves carried along with the others.

Only in the active taking up of the struggle—the turning around on the walkway and moving actively in the opposite direction—will change occur. If we merely close our eyes and try by sheer force of imagination to will ourselves into a color-blind world, we will just end up blind to the effects of race and color in the world around us—carried along the moving walkway. When we fail to intercede, to do something different, we allow (if not enable) racist outcomes to be reproduced unchecked. Far too many school personnel, with all the best intentions, remain bystanders, standing passively on the walkway. Their passive racist behavior, similar to what Forman (2001b; forthcoming) has labeled "racial apathy," is far from neutral in its effect. It functions as support for the status quo, fostering the reproduction of racial inequalities. Intervention can take the form of both large and small efforts. At times, it may involve challenging existing racial narratives; Metro2's curriculum provides a good example in the way it encourages children to have critical and complex understandings of the world they live in. At other times intervention may take the form of direct action, such as Ms. Grant's efforts to recruit families of color to her school, Roy Burns's challenging of racist remarks, and young Omar's plea to go to Denny's and demand service.

These efforts alone are not enough. With institutional racism, the kinds of systemic issues discussed here were not created by and will not be overcome by the actions of one or even several individuals. More broad-scale, truly redistributive policies are necessary before we can even begin to imagine a world where race has less of an impact on life chances. As discussed in Chapter 6, racially based economic disparities play a critical role in educational outcomes. Schools also play a crucial role in reproducing and justifying these racial inequalities. But it is hard to imagine moving toward redistributive policies in a context where color-blind and meritocratic ideologies dominate. Such accounts individualize success and failure and erase history as they tell us we all deserve what we have—good or bad—when, in fact, as Darnell so aptly put it, hard work is not the issue. Lots of people work hard. At issue is the basic opportunity to have hard work rewarded equitably and to be able to act on one's choices. And the first step may be to fundamentally challenge available explanations for current social realities. This work was meant as such an intervention.

One of the largest remaining barriers to both the transformation of educational institutions and the destruction of racial inequality is the dominance in the United States of limited definitions of equality. Apple (1988) has termed this the support of negative rather than positive freedom. He distinguishes freedom from inhibition in the free-market sense (i.e., what Bobo, Kluegel, and Smith (1997) call "laissez-faire racism") from freedom to have access to the resources necessary to live a dignified life. For example, unlike most industrialized nations, which fund schools nationally, the United States has historically funded schools locally, with many resulting disparities (Kozol 1991). As state lawsuits contesting this funding scheme have demonstrated, support for universal education has repeatedly come up against the even stronger force of parental desire for advantages for their own children (Hadderman 1999). As James Coleman (as quoted in Kahlenberg 2001: 64) put it, "The history of education since the industrial revolution shows a continual struggle between two forces: the desire by members of society to have educational opportunity for all children, and the desire of each family to provide the best education it can afford for its own students." The second of these competing forces has been the historic winner in the United States. School outcomes then are not so much a result of student effort as of family resources.

Coleman (as quoted in Kahlenberg 2001: 61) set the challenge: "Schools are successful only insofar as they reduce the dependence of a child's opportunities upon his social origins. . . . This is a task far more ambitious than has ever been attempted by any society: not just to offer, in a passive way, equal access to educational resources, but to provide an educational environment that will free a child's potentialities for learning from the inequalities imposed upon him by the accident of birth into one or another home and social environment." If we judge our schools by how well they meet this challenge, then they are failing miserably. As survey data have repeatedly shown, this situation is not likely to change as long as we continue to support only abstract principles of racial equality without committing to the implementation of such principles (Schuman et al. 1997).

Many current school-reform efforts are based on limited understandings of racial equality and, as a result, are likely to exacerbate inequality rather than lessen it. Zero-tolerance policies have had a particularly devastating effect on students of color, intensifying already disproportionate discipline rates for African American males in particular. These policies, a response to highly publicized incidents of school violence, take an individualized approach to school safety, suggesting schools need only identify and eliminate the "bad element." Studies have shown these policies to be ineffective in addressing the original goals of improved student safety (Henault 2001; Skiba and Peterson 1999). As Skiba and Leone (2001) report, "After over ten years of implementation around the country . . . there is little to no convincing evidence that zero tolerance has improved either student behavior or overall school safety." Unlike programs such as the small-schools movement that reduce educational anonymity and increase community, zero-tolerance policies are purely punitive measures (Perry 1999). As Noguera (1995) has argued, if we want to understand the persistent violence in schools today and how we might reduce it, we have to look to structural and institutional factors such as school communities and the relationships and atmosphere in them. Problems include large, anonymous schools, where teachers lack any knowledge of who their students are, and the legacy of social control, which often leads to inhumane reactions to school problems (Hyman and Snook 2000).

Voucher programs have emerged as another popular reform effort (Johnson, Della Piana, and Burlingame 2000; Kennedy 2001; McEwan 2000; Meeks, Meeks, and Warren 2000). Hailed by some as the solution to educational inequality, these programs are based on the premise that free-market competition will stimulate school improvement (Ridenour, Lasley, and Bainbridge 2001). Although little evidence has been provided that supports such outcomes, vouchers do promise to assist a few—but at the expense of the many. As critics have pointed out, at best vouchers aid a small percentage of low-income, minority students (along with many white, middle-class students already attending private schools), with most students remaining in underfunded and undersupported public schools. Given the country's limited number of private schools (e.g., in California, private schools can serve less than 1 percent of the state's students), voucher programs cannot work as a broad-scale solution to the inadequacy of educational programs serving low-income and minority children (Johnson, Della Piana, and Burlingame 2000; Lindjord 2001).

The premise of high-stakes testing efforts, another current reform movement, is that increasing accountability through testing will force teachers and students to improve. But, by holding schools and children to higher standards without providing the resources necessary to meet those standards, they punish students who have received a poor education, and fuel drop-out rates (Lopez 2000; Mizell 2001). Moreover, as Darnell's and Malik's reactions to testing at

West City show, we should regard test results with suspicion. Standardized test results are never direct reflections of student aptitude. Sometimes they are measures of student anxiety, alienation, and distrust. Vast racial disparities in scores have occurred in a number of states that have implemented high-stakes tests (Brennan et al. 2001; Mizell 2001). This result is not a measure of the individual students' failure; rather it is a measure of the collective failure of the entire school system, which provides unequal educational opportunities. Racial categories have no connection to innate talents; racial disparities in testing should instead be understood as evidence of institutional failure, of collective disadvantage and discrimination.

All these reforms appear ineffective for improving school performance, school safety, or educational outcomes, but all seem likely to be effective at exacerbating existing inequalities. Like many reform efforts of the past, each individualizes school success and failure and does not deal with major disparities in school resources. They all leave the current educational system largely intact—layering on top of it mechanisms that weed out already top-performing students and leave the rest behind, if not out of school altogether. Instead, all students need to be provided with high-quality instruction in well-funded schools. The Applied Research Center, a public-policy research institute in Oakland, California, has called for SMART schools: *s*mall classes and schools; *m*oney for quality education for all students, especially those with the greatest need; *a*uthentic assessment and high standards instead of standardized, high-stakes tests; *r*acial and economic equity in educational policies, opportunities, and outcomes; and *t*op-notch teaching and rigorous curriculum (Johnson, Della Piana, and Burlingame 2000). Along with efforts to increase the cultural relevance of educational experiences, to implement humane disciplinary policies, and to introduce critical multiculturalism into the curriculum, these kinds of efforts hold much promise as a means to improve educational experiences and outcomes for all students (Ayers, Dohrn, and Ayers 2001; Delpit 1995; Foster 1997; Ladson-Billings 1994; Noguera 1995).

However, one of the other lessons of this book is that school reforms alone will not be enough to address racially unequal school outcomes. If our goal is racial justice broadly, school reforms need to be undertaken in conjunction with larger struggles. As long as racial injustice persists and as long as racial ideologies continue to justify these inequalities and suggest that disadvantaged groups are to blame for their failure, it is hard to imagine these kinds of progressive changes happening.

One step in the right direction would be a transformation in the way we understand what race means. To understand the relevance of race in various realms of social life requires that we begin to think about race fundamentally differently than we have—both in research and in daily living. When we try to understand racial patterns in disciplinary outcomes, for instance, or racial disparities in test scores, the way we interpret those patterns depends on our understandings of what race is and how it works. Racial data do not make any sense outside our racial theory (Zuberi 2001). Anthropologists and biologists have long recognized that race is not a biological category; this understanding does not seem to have stopped race from being treated as if it were an indicator of innate characteristics. At the same time, not enough attention is paid to race as a social category that has a substantial impact on people's lives. For example, black children living in inner cities have alarming rates of asthma because of the high level of environmental pollutants in their neighborhoods. This is not a genetic issue, but a social one. The long-term cure here would not be a steady stream of individually prescribed inhalers and medications but actions to eliminate the pollutants and to prevent the continued dumping of such toxins into poor neighborhoods filled with disenfranchised people of color (Bryant 1995; Bullard 2000; Cole and Foster 2000; Pulido 2000).

In schools, race cannot tell us about our students' innate proclivities to learn, to work hard, or to play sports. It cannot provide information about whether their parents care about schooling or believe in hard work. It can give us information only about the students' social location. It can, however, caution us to question our assumptions, to remember our cultural specificity, to take care in thinking we know too much. It can also challenge us to be extra careful, particularly diligent, to have especially high expectations for those students for whom education is one of few channels to success and who have few social and financial safety nets at home. It can remind us that all students—white, black, Asian, Latino, or Native American—need access to critical multicultural educational experiences that are honest and that confront the world they live in rather than providing false narratives. Thus, it is quite appropriate and in fact desirable to encourage in our students an aspiration for a world in which color doesn't matter—but only as part of a larger curriculum that helps them understand that race continues to matter and that only through our collective hard work will it come to matter less.

Appendix

Research Methods:
Stories from the Field

In the beginning of their book *Journeys through Ethnography,* Lareau and Shultz (1996: 2) lament the scarcity of texts that show "how research actually gets done." They argue that field researchers historically have engaged in a mix of what DeVault (1997) describes as "discretion and disclosure." Either overly general or "filled with platitudes" (Lareau and Shultz 1996: 2), such work has often failed to reveal difficulties confronted or bumps in the road (Weis and Fine 2000). Researchers have feared that disclosure of obstacles and problems might prevent their work from being taken seriously. In fact, those who have engaged with field research know that it does not come without difficulties. Only through honest discussion of the actions taken, choices made, and problems confronted in the course of an investigation can we assess the quality of the data and the analysis produced. And such openness allows us to learn from past projects—allows others to avoid repeating our mistakes. Just as survey researchers must report their response rates and answer questions about the validity of their findings when such rates are low, qualitative and field researchers must report fully on procedures involved in the collection and analysis of their data. The process must become less shrouded in mystery so that the usually careful, often rigorous, and generally sound methods involved may be seen.

The Setting

This research was limited to studying a small number of schools in one geographical region. Although many identify California as a unique place, it was a useful location for this work for a number of reasons. First, the state has been experiencing major demographic transformations in the last few decades, trans-formations that will affect the country as a whole over the coming years. Sec-ond, these demographic changes have brought racial issues to the forefront of many residents' minds. Third or, in some cases, as a consequence, race has played a large role in popular, political, and legal struggles in the state since the early 1990s (e.g., Proposition 209, Proposition 187, the Rodney King verdict, the 1992 Los Angeles rebellion, the O. J. Simpson trials), with whites and racial minority groups taking largely disparate positions. As Winant (1995: 587) argues, "California . . . pioneers in racial matters. Presently it is at the forefront of the race-baiting and scapegoating that seem to sweep across the country every few decades. The state has led the national assault on immigrants' rights, and appears poised to do the same for affirmative action." Fourth, not only is California leading the nation in social, economic, and political trends, it also is doing so in the nation's most diverse context. Unlike in many other parts of the country, California's racial dynamics are not a black-white affair.[1] In the rest of the nation this kind of diversity is likely to typify racial encounters in the com-ing decades; California offers a unique setting in which to begin to study such dynamics today.

Southern California and the city of Hillside itself offer a compelling setting because of their great racial diversity and relative racial integration.[2] Because of Hillside's small size, its many racial groups are not as geographically separate from one another as they are in other major cities. In addition, the schools are racially diverse. Thus, Hillside and the metropolitan area surrounding it are the site of extensive interracial interaction.

School Selection

One central aspect of interpretive work is the process of theoretical sampling. In this project, the process took place on multiple levels, the first of which was the selection of schools to study. Inevitably in the study of schools, the selection process has two components—one driven by theoretical issues, the other by practical issues. As Chapter 1 discusses, from the beginning I wanted to incorporate three schools: a fairly typical and diverse urban school, a fairly typical and homogenous suburban school, and a school that structurally and culturally was a bicultural or nonwhite space.

Looking first for a fairly typical urban school, I eliminated schools with spe-cial programs that made them unique or unusual (such as language immersion or K–8 populations). I then looked for places that had as their largest compo-nents the two largest minority groups in the United States, blacks and Latinos.[3] A dozen schools matched these criteria. I eliminated schools where large tran-sitions were likely at the beginning of the school year. For example, several schools were under review for reconstitution because of their consistently low test scores, and several others had either a temporary principal or a principal known to be leaving at the end of the year. The result was a final list of five schools, each of which I visited. All the principals I spoke with in this initial stage were open to the project. One of the criteria I used to narrow the selection further was that the school had to be relatively successful and not at an extreme in either academic performance or social conflict. Two schools in my final five were in the lowest quartile on all test scores, and one of these two was also almost entirely internally segregated because of bilingual programs. In another school, because of scheduled staffing fluctuations in the coming year, it was not going to be possible to get a fourth/fifth-grade teacher to sign on to the project.[4] Thus I narrowed the choice to two and revisited those schools to have more in-depth conversations with the principals. In the end I selected West City elementary because it met all the criteria laid out and because, in my meetings with her, the West City principal seemed interested in having me there rather than just being tolerant of my presence. As anyone who has conducted research in schools knows, the support of local leadership is important. In this case I was not worried that her interest would bias my results, as her concern about the issues involved would, if anything, lead to underestimates of problems. In other words, if one of the issues under investigation was relations between racial groups, it would be logical to expect that, all other things being relatively equal, those relations would be better in institutions in which people in leadership positions were committed to promoting positive relations. Selecting a school this way would likely lead to an overestimate of willingness to talk and an underestimate of problems.[5]

Most national data demonstrate that white students continue to attend schools that are almost entirely white. I therefore wanted to include a predominantly white school that would closely mirror the experiences of most whites in the United States today. I initially thought that gaining access to a suburban school for this type of research might be difficult, but in the end it was quite easy. I began by using school district data to find suburban areas that were 80 percent or more white. I eliminated very wealthy areas or areas that seemed no longer to have any relationship to Hillside (either because they were themselves becoming separate cities or because they were more closely affiliated with another city). Along one major commuting corridor, many of the towns were clearly identified as suburbs of Hillside, all were over 80 percent white, and several were relatively middle-class.[6] I targeted two districts in particular and called principals of several elementary schools in each district. All the principals were open to the study. I eventually selected Foresthills because it fit all the important criteria and I had some familiarity with the district.

In selecting the alternative setting, I found four possible schools. All four were described as Afrocentric or as having strong multicultural programs. All had large minority student enrollments and large minority representation among the staff. When I visited these schools, I looked at the material culture, public discourse, curricular focus, and demographic composition. I finally decided on Metro2, a school with a Spanish-immersion program and large Latino student and staff populations; it was located in a large Latino neighborhood and had a strong commitment to Spanish instruction and multicultural curricula. This choice was going to challenge my almost nonexistent Spanish, but the principal was encouraging and suggested it would not be a problem if I was going to base myself in the fourth/fifth-grade classroom where English was the language of instruction. In the next section I describe how my lack of Spanish played out in day-to-day interactions.

Metro2 also provided a useful comparison with the other schools in relation to one of my research questions, the social construction of whiteness. Although whites were a numerical minority among the student body at West City, the staff was almost all white, the school was situated in an almost all-white neighborhood, and the school's structure and culture did not seem to directly mirror the school's multicultural goals. Metro2, however, appeared to be more of a "nonwhite" space culturally and demographically, even though it was also one of the city's alternative schools in which there were significant numbers of white students (30 percent). How would whiteness play out in a setting where it was not necessarily culturally dominant? As one goal of the project was to examine the role of whiteness in these schools, it seemed particularly advantageous to have the contrasts on several dimensions (demographics, school culture) that these two schools provided.

Data Collection

Ethnographic methods incorporate multiple strategies for data collection; in this study I used participant observation, formal and informal interviewing, and collection of site documents and other examples of material culture. As Denzin (1978, 1989) and others point out, this kind of triangulation of sources is an effective way to bolster validity. The combination of these various data-collection methods, along with the comparison of sites, did provide a way of looking at issues of whiteness and racial-identity formation across several axes of difference. Moreover, interviewing both whites and nonwhites allowed me to contrast the experiences of the groups and also to attempt to untangle the relational quality of identity formation. Although this research design makes it difficult to secure a representative sample of any group, data-collection strategies did yield a large sample of incidents, interactions, and casual and formal statements from which to draw.

Participant Observation

I began the school year in West City and Metro2 schools, spending two to three days a week in each school along with attending back-to-school night, PTA meetings, staff meetings, and other special events. At the end of the first semester, I shifted from Metro2 to Foresthills. Though I still visited Metro2 at least twice a month and continued to attend after-school events and meetings, I spent most of my time after January in Foresthills and West City. In my days in school, I was located primarily in a fourth/fifth-grade combined class in each school, though I periodically visited other classrooms and spent a lot of time in public spaces. I observed the variety of practices (curricular, pedagogical, organizational) operating in each school, described the material culture of the school, and charted the nature and extent of intraracial and interracial interactions between teachers and students, among peers, and between school personnel and parents. I observed in classrooms, in the cafeteria, on the playground, in the faculty lunchroom, in the main office, during staff and PTA meetings, during after-school events, and in the hallway. In all, I spent more than a thousand hours in the schools and wrote more than fifteen hundred pages of fieldnotes on my observations.

In each location my role was slightly different, but in each school I was a participant as well as an observer. My contract with the schools was twofold: to feed the findings back to the school once the analysis was done and to help in various ways while I was there. Primarily I helped out in the classrooms where I was based. This work varied from room to room but included, among other things, watching the classroom when the teacher needed to step out, circulating and helping students who were confused about classroom work, and cleaning up after art activities. Generally, I was another adult in the room, an extra pair of hands. All the teachers I worked with knew I had some elementary teaching experience, and all were short on help. Managing the balance between maintaining good relations with teachers and having good relations with children was never simple, but I got regular feedback from both groups that indicated I was mostly successful.[7] Making myself additionally available in the school to assist in unusual circumstances (e.g., covering a classroom for an hour in the morning for a teacher whose car broke down on the way to school) went far to gain the trust and respect of adults.

My role in each school was a product of my interactions with each institution's distinct organizational structure and culture. In Metro2, with few exceptions, I functioned as a participant only in the classroom and was not much involved, other than as an observer, in the rest of the school. In explaining who I was to their parents, students described me as "a sort-of teacher," "she helps us in the class" "she's like a student-teacher but also like a big kid." There were lots of adults around the building, and though students treated them with respect, relations tended to be less hierarchical and more democratic (e.g., all adults were addressed by their first names), and thus it made sense to students that I might be there and help out but not necessarily be a teacher. Parents understood from Ms. Wilson, the teacher I worked with at Metro2, that I was in the class every day helping out, and they were always friendly to me as someone who was providing assistance in their children's classroom.[8]

In West City I had a somewhat different role. It quickly became clear that it would be unfeasible to participate in that school community and not function more as a traditional adult than I had at Metro2. For example, respect from both children and adults was based on not allowing children to break basic school rules in my presence. If I allowed children to run past me down the hallway without asking them to slow down, they would assume either that I did not care or that I was unable to assert authority (a justification for lack of respect). In this way I found that for children at West City to see me as someone who was "on their side" or sympathetic to their point of view did not mean entering their world by subverting my adult position. Rather it meant having genuine conversations about their lives, listening to them carefully when they spoke, helping them when they were confused, and expressing care. Although I never took charge when other adults were around, I did, for instance, help keep students focused during assemblies, cajoled them into the morning circle, and told them to slow down in the hallway. Like other adults in the school, I was addressed by a courtesy title (Miss) and my last name.[9] However, although I was always recognized as an adult and as someone who wouldn't let students run in the hallway or play in the bathroom, I was not like other adults in the school. I fulfilled adult tasks quite differently from other school personnel (often with humor and occasionally by telling the students we were all going to get into trouble if they didn't act right). I also spent a great deal of time in the school-yard talking and playing with students in all grades. Although I was clearly identified as being a teacher (there were few other adult roles available), when students referred to me as a teacher, they often added modifiers that set me off as having an in-between status. They said things like "You're different than the other teachers" or "You could never be a real teacher, you're too nice."

At Foresthills, as at Metro2, my participatory role was limited to the classroom. Though I was introduced at a staff meeting and my role was made clear, for the entire time I was there many of the adults thought I was one of the student teachers assigned to the school every spring. Most of the teachers at Foresthills were older (the average age was fifty-three) and had been at the school for a number of years; thus being "youngish" and a newcomer caused me to stand out in pronounced ways. Although early on I felt like a member of the community at both West City and Metro2, I always felt like an outsider at Foresthills. Because of district policy, even after several months at the school I still had to wear a visitor tag. Adults were tolerant and moderately friendly but generally uninterested in why I was there. Structurally and culturally, Foresthills teachers and classrooms functioned separately from and independently of one another. Thus, more than in the other schools, I was seen to belong to one teacher's classroom, and it was difficult to forge connections with anyone (students or adults) beyond the class.[10] Students again seemed to recognize me as having some kind of in-between status; I was one of the few adults around who had close familiarity with the pop-culture icons they worshipped—for example, I could draw their favorite South Park characters. I was often asked which Spice Girl I liked best, whether I knew who Bob Marley or Ice Cube was, what it was like to live in the city, whether I had seen a new video, or whether I was rooting for the Bulls in the play-offs. In this way I crossed not only age boundaries but also gender boundaries and was generally perceived as intriguing and, as one student put it, "cool," if not different and a little weird.

Interviews

I waited until I had been in each school for several months and knew the setting and the people well before I made attempts to interview anyone other than the principal or the teacher in whose classroom I was working. Still, it was difficult to get staff at either Metro2 or Foresthills to agree to be interviewed. In almost all cases, teachers claimed they did not have enough time to do even the most important things for their classes (along with trying to lead lives outside of school), much less have extra time for interviews. Though the standard response was "Ask me again next week," next week never seemed to be any less hectic. Several times scheduled interviews were canceled because pressing issues had come up. Eventually I switched strategies and managed to have shorter, more informal conversations with the key staff at each school.[11] Though these conversations were informative, they never could cover everything. This was one price of doing research at three different locations. During the spring term, I was in the schools every day doing participant observation and scheduling interviews in the evenings with parents from all the schools. I had to juggle these interviews so they did not conflict with after-school events parents or I (or both of us) planned to attend. In addition I was spending several hours most evenings typing up fieldnotes. Given this schedule, finding time and energy to pursue reticent teachers week after week proved to be more than I could manage. If the reticence had been based in the topic of my work, I might have been more concerned. However most of the difficulty had to do with the fact that the teachers were overworked. At Metro2 several teachers who had expressed interest in the interviews canceled several times at the last minute because of unanticipated meetings or minor crises. At Foresthills I was more likely to receive a request to "just talk during lunchtime." Carrying out interviews was less of a problem at West City because of my different role there. I not only knew the entire staff better but was seen as a member of the school community in a different way. For example, people were regularly amazed that I did all I did in the school without "getting paid" for it and thus seemed to feel that they should make an effort to find an hour for me. Thus, although I managed to conduct at least informal, unstructured interviews with a number of teachers and staff at all the schools, I did not conduct as many formal interviews with as many staff members as I had originally planned. In the end, however, I felt satisfied with these multiple strategies; I managed to get multiple perspectives on both pressing questions and mundane issues and was able to have multiple informal conversations with those staff members whom I didn't interview formally.

I waited until I was in the fourth month of the project to begin scheduling interviews systematically with staff and parents and waited until further into the spring to interview students. In regard both to the content of the interviews and to securing permission, it was important to know the students and the schools well; scheduling the interviews this way gave me time to learn the lay of the land. The intensive nature of the work yielded important advantages: parents were aware of me as a regular member of their children's classrooms; I had a great deal of observational data to bring into the interviews; and I had time to build genuine and real relationships with students and parents who might not otherwise have known what to make of me. Thus, for instance, my overall response rate to interview requests was over 90 percent—only one parent I asked turned me down.[12]

I used several broad criteria to select my sample of interviewees. Overall my target was to interview 30 percent of the parents and children in each class, including a roughly representative number of parents of children from the different racial groups represented in each classroom (see Table A.1 for demographics of the final formal-interview sample).[13] Within this approach I oversampled parents of children who were racially located on the margins. Thus, I made a particular effort to interview parents whose children were biracial, along with parents of children who were "one of few" at their school.[14] In sampling Latino parents, I wanted to interview those who were relatively acculturated and also those who were recent immigrants.[15]

Though my original goal was to interview both mothers and fathers, getting access to fathers proved difficult for several reasons.[16] First, particularly at Foresthills, when I called a household and explained who I was, if a father

_____ Table A.1. _____
Number of formal interviews, by school and race/ethnicity

		West City	Metro2	Foresthills	Total
School Staff[a]		*9*	*4*	*4*	*17*
	White	4	2	3	9
	Black	3	0	0	3
	Latino	2	2	1	5
Parents		*14*	*16*	*9*	*39*
	White	4	8	7	19
	Black	4	2	0	6
	Latino	6	6	1	13
	Asian	0	0	1	1
Students		*12*	*10*	*8*	*30*
	White	2	3	3	8
	Black	6	1	1	8
	Latino	4	1	1	6
	Asian	0	0	1	1
	Mixed race	0	5[b]	2[c]	7

_____

[a]Many additional interviews with staff (including most of those conducted at Metro2 and Foresthills) were conducted informally.
[b]Four Latino/white and one Latino/African American.
[c]Both Asian/white.

answered the phone, I was immediately referred to the mother, the parent who dealt with anything related to the children or school. Second, because mothers more often than fathers participated actively in school, they were the parents with whom I had contact. Third, when parents were separated or divorced, the mothers more often had custody. Although it would have been optimal to speak to both parents, if I was going to speak to only one, mothers were in most cases the better option. I do not mean to suggest that fathers do not have a strong influence on their children, but it was preferable in the context of this study to speak to the guardian who spent more time with the children and who knew their schools better.[17] This pattern on its own says much about the persistence of gendered family responsibilities.

I can speculate about several biases this pattern could impose on the findings. In the suburban context, where I had virtually no contact with fathers, almost all the mothers referred to themselves as the more "liberal" parent or household member when it came to racial matters.[18] Several said that their husbands occasionally used racial epithets, while others described their husbands as less "open" or "tolerant." Thus, for these families, it seems clear that the results underestimate levels of negative racial attitudes. In the interviews with parents of biracial children, in every case but one I interviewed only the mother.[19] All these couples included one white parent and one parent who was a person of color (African American, Latino, or Asian American). However, the gender of the parent of color varied; thus, in these six cases, three of the mothers I interviewed were white and three were Asian or Latina. I did not find large differences in these mothers' discussions of their children and their own racial understandings. For example, in almost every case these mothers believed their child's primary identification was with the race of the "darker" parent.[20]

Conducting interviews with children could be the subject of a book in itself. One key reason I had selected the upper elementary grades as my base in the schools was evidence from past research that students in this age range have racial understandings close to those of adults: that is, their developmental understandings of social characteristics are similar to those of the culture that surrounds them (e.g., they do not tend to ascribe characteristics to humans that they ascribe to other living beings like animals) (Aboud 1988; Holmes 1995; Hirschfeld 1996; Katz 1982). Moreover, though these students have more developed understandings of race and racial categorizations than younger children, they have not yet been pressed into making many of the choices that middle school and high school demand in regard to peer culture.

In practice, students had a wide range of understandings of themselves and others. In trying to get a feel for appropriate questions to ask, I drew on past research as well as on my observations of students' classroom and peer interactions. I then tested many of my proposed questions in informal conversations in the schoolyard. For example, I often witnessed the casualness with which students inquired about each other's identities. One day in the yard a fifth-grade student asked a fourth-grader with whom he was playing ball, "What are you?" When the child asked the older boy what he meant, he replied, "Like, you know, like, what are you, Spanish, black, Indian." The younger student responded, "Black and Creole." "Then why do you speak Spanish?" The younger student replied, "Because of my auntie," while he spun around and tried to steal the ball, effectively ending the conversation. Observing these kinds of exchanges alleviated some anxiety I had about talking with students about these issues, as it became clear that they talked with each other about race in many different ways all the time. In another example I witnessed, a substitute teacher used the word *race* in describing a current event. When a fourth-grader leaned back and asked me what "race" meant, it became clear that I would have to be careful about the language I used in the interviews with the children.

To select the sample of students, I used a scheme similar to the one I used to select parents. I aimed for a general distribution across the racial groups present, while also oversampling those who occupied ambiguous racial locations or who themselves expressed some ambivalence about their racial identity.

Documents

Finally, I collected hundreds of key school documents and evidence of the material culture at each of the schools. I collected any paper documents distributed to teachers, parents, or students on the days I was in school. I also made an effort to collect all official school documentation, reports, weekly newsletters to families, letters to parents, pictures of the school building and classrooms, programs from school performances, and other documents distributed during the period I was at the schools.

Analysis

Initial analysis of the data began during the data-collection process. I periodically scanned for themes and wrote memos about patterns or themes that seemed to be emerging. This practice enabled several important processes. First, it led me to conduct member checks in the field to determine whether the themes and patterns I was seeing matched the world as at least some of my informants saw it.[21] Second, it facilitated the pursuit of additional data sources (multiple interviews; observations in different settings, schools, classrooms; and additional district documents) to test the validity of emerging themes (i.e., triangulation). Thus, for example, this early analysis affected my sampling strategies in that I made sure to speak to those who would potentially have either confirming or contradictory information. It also shaped final drafts of interview guides as I made sure to build in questions or probes about unanticipated issues that had come up in the field.

To demonstrate one example of this process, during one of my first days at Foresthills a white teacher talked about a fourth-grade girl playing the "race card." The teacher explained that the nine-year-old African American girl had been claiming that racial issues were coming up in her relations to other children in the class (none of whom were black). The teacher explained to me that these were really fourth-grade girl issues and that she had pulled in another teacher, the only African American teacher in the school, to explain the source of these issues to the child. The coherence of this narrative and of the motivations it attributed to the black fourth-grader were somewhat startling at the time. I wondered whether counternarratives existed. What was the child's understanding? How about her parents? How did white students understand these relations? What was going on with the students in their peer networks and relations? This narrative of the alleged irrelevance of race in the local context did not match the apparent relevance of race in the way school personnel talked about current events or in the actual demographic make-up of the surrounding neighborhoods. Was this an "enlightened" space in which race really didn't matter? If not, what role and purposes did the denial of its relevance serve? Because of the structure of the project, these were not questions I had to speculate about answers for once the data collection was over but ones I could pursue in the field as part of the developing research process. Thus, I made sure to interview the few Foresthills students who were on the racial margins, along with their parents, about this matter. In interviews with these children and adults as well as with their white peers, I probed when subjects offered color-blind discourse and noted where this construction of events contradicted articulations of color consciousness in their expressed beliefs and behavior. In my classroom observations, I regularly explored possible challenges to color-blind narratives, paying special attention, for example, during social studies classes to how both current events and history were discussed in texts and talked about. Even more, I compared observations among sites. Were there common racial narratives, discourses, and understandings of race? Did discourses function in the same way? Were alternative narratives available in other places?

Analysis after leaving the field proceeded at multiple levels. I coded all data sources within sites (e.g., all fieldnotes, interviews, and documents from a particular school) and coded categories of data across sites (e.g., interviews with white parents from all three settings). Themes emerged along both dimensions. I regularly compared the data and themes from the different schools (e.g., whether the racial logic in one setting was the same as or different from that in another and why). And I also compared data within and among groups (Were white parents' claims about the significance of race similar? Were they collectively different from those that black parents offered?).

To perform these analyses, I utilized qualitative-analysis software that allowed me to initially code segments of text in multiple ways. For example, a particular quote or event might be tagged with anywhere from one to five or more codes. I was thus able to generate lists of quotations associated with each particular code. I also compared the coding schemes generated in analysis of observational fieldnotes with those generated in analysis of interviews. I then grouped codes into metacategories, or "code families." For example, codes were generated that involved racial-boundary formation or negotiation. Through these processes, specific themes emerged—such themes as the nature of racial discourse in different settings; the processes of boundary formation and maintenance; and the nature, content, and processes of racial identification and ascription.

Conclusion

The current moment in academic research has led to new and increased attention to the construction of meaning and narratives in social life. Although structures, institutions, and struggles over material resources are still a central focus of my work (including this research), this project has been influenced by these recent trends in its attempts to theorize a more dialectical relationship between culture and structure and in its attention to the contextualized making of meaning. However, I do not believe recognizing the implications of social-constructivist assumptions necessarily implies that those constructions are any less "real," any less material, than if I were to suggest, for example, that racial categories were transhistorical or fixed. The "realness" of such social categories depends not so much on their naturalness or permanence as on their ability to be naturalized (to appear to be natural) and on the perception of them as permanent. Recognizing the situated-ness of knowledge (both ours and our subjects') and the socially constructed nature of our categories does not, therefore, prevent social analysts from studying and trying to describe the world as it is lived in by social actors. As Hasso (1998: 15) poignantly writes, our goal should be to describe and analyze precisely that "bounded reality" as people themselves perceive it and as it thus guides their perceptions and behavior. "Despite the difficulty of 'objectively' representing social facts and individual meanings, people in similar contexts often share values and experiences that lead them to construe social phenomena, including language, similarly. My goal, then, is to describe the 'bounded reality' that people consider their world, provide individual and collective interpretations of this world, assess the plausibility of different accounts and make an attempt at limited causal arguments within this reality."

The issue then is not whether racial categories are "real" but whether they originate as human constructions rather than as natural laws or permanent features of social existence. In this way things can be "socially real" even if not part of the laws of nature. This sort of understanding is important not only because it most closely matches the world as we live it but also because it frees us to imagine a future where things might be otherwise.

Notes

One Examining the Color Line in Schools

1. For examples, see Conley 1999 and Mickelson 1990.

2. Social-reproduction theorists examine the role of schools in maintaining inequalities and reproducing the current social order. People writing in this tradition have tended to fall into one of two categories: social-reproduction theorists (who are concerned with economic and cultural production) and social-production theorists (who are concerned primarily with cultural production) (Lubeck 1989; MacLeod 1995; DeMarrais and LeCompte 1995). Social-reproduction theorists, like Bowles and Gintis (1976), argue that social relations in schools are determined by the economic order and that schools train students for future work roles. Theorists of cultural production focus more closely on social processes as they take place in schools and outline how subordinated groups contest and resist their domination (Bernstein 1971; Bourdieu and Passeron 1990; Giroux 1983; MacLeod 1995; Rosen 1980; Willis 1977). Research on social reproduction in education has focused primarily on class reproduction, giving little attention to the reproduction of race or gender. There has been some limited work on race (Figueroa 1991; Troyna 1987; Troyna and Hatcher 1992) and some work that either is a gendered study of class (e.g., Valli 1986) or examines the production of gendered bodies in school settings (Mac an Ghaill 1994; Thorne 1993). Other work has looked at racial and gender inequalities in school achievement, in treatment in schools, or in the curriculum. These studies have generally paid attention to the impact of race and gender relations in schools and have contributed significantly to understanding the role of schools in the creation of social hierarchies, but they have not investigated how schools themselves reproduce racial and gender categories. Although some British research has examined the impact of race on children's school experiences (Figueroa 1991; Gillborn 1990; Milner 1983; Sewell 1997; Stone 1981; Troyna and Hatcher 1992), fewer studies have looked at the role of schooling in the development of racial understanding. Other work in the United States has looked at the development of racial identities in schools (Davidson 1996;

Olsen 1997; Peshkin 1991) but has focused exclusively on adolescents or narrowly on the impact of identity on school engagement (Davidson 1996; Flores-Gonzalez 1999; Pinderhughes 1997). With a few key exceptions (Ferguson 2000; Forman 2001a; Lacey 1970; McQuillan 1998; Perry 2002; Rosen 1980, 1977; Rosenfeld 1971; Van Ausdale and Feagin 2000), little existing research attempts to understand race as both a product of schooling and a part of the process of schooling. Moreover, little of this work examines both racial meaning and racial inequality or the interaction between racial ideologies and discourses and racial inequities more generally. In short, little research attempts to understand how race is reproduced through schooling processes and educational institutions.

3. For more on this concept, see Bourdieu 1977a, 1977b, 1986, and Bourdieu and Passeron 1990.

4. For more on schools as meritocratic institutions, see Apple 1982 and 1990. Meritocratic ideologies are also similar to what MacLeod (1995) refers to as the "achievement ideology."

5. These identifications are assumed as well as imposed. Jenkins (1996) talks about this as a dialectical process between internal identification and external identification.

6. Ethnographic or participant-observation research involves entering a social setting and getting to know the people who move within it well by participating in the daily routines of that setting. This research strategy permits the study of relations as they happen and develop. This kind of research is crucial for capturing the complexities of racial matters, including the consistencies or inconsistencies between what people say and what they do (Dennis 1998). Ethnographic work allows for capturing social action in a form close to the way it is understood by the actors themselves and for studying social action in its most complete form. See the Appendix for more details about the research process. All names of localities, schools, and individuals in this book have been changed. Pseudonyms were assigned to protect confidentiality. In some cases additional details about individual respondents were changed in order to ensure their anonymity.

7. In this study, I build on existing theories of racialization and identification to understand processes of racial ascription and identification, the ways racial categorizations are understood and put to use, and how they affect access to educational opportunities and resources. The uniqueness of the cases under study is not significant because the interest is in deepening or extending our understanding of how social processes function and relate to one another.

8. Here I am defining the school community as all those involved in the school, including staff, students, and parents.

9. I did make an effort to visit classes conducted in Spanish to see whether students' participation patterns differed, and I factored those differences into my analyses.

10. As Lincoln and Guba (1985) discuss, member checks involve reviewing research findings with informants or inhabitants of the research site to test the validity of the findings.

11. These realities generated various ethical dilemmas during the research process. For instance, at West City I was troubled by the lack of a substantial academic curriculum and thus the prospect of the fifth graders' heading off to middle school lacking important concepts. Early in the year, I was having an ethical crisis about sitting in a classroom and watching students learn little of the traditional academic curriculum. When

I called one of my advisors in a panic, I was advised to "climb down off my white horse" and follow through on the job of trying to understand. My early instinct to act was based in part on my arrogance, my assumption that I could immediately do something to change the situation, and in part on indignation about the educational opportunities children I was growing attached to were not being afforded. Though the tension never totally abated, I came to understand the complexity of the situation. However, these early instincts were useful to hold on to. Almost inevitably after enough time in a place, one becomes accustomed to the situation—even if at first it seems unjust and outrageous. Going through this process afforded me deeper insight into the process many of these children experienced as they sat through school day after day. Tolerable and enjoyable are not the same thing—over time the outrageous became normal, as I, like them, became numb and discouraged.

Two   There Is No Race in the Schoolyard:
Color-Blind Ideology at Foresthills

1. For some of the best of this research, see Patchen 1982; Peshkin 1991; Schofield 1982; and Wells and Crain 1997.
2. Source: California Association of Realtors. This figure is slightly above the county median of $197,000.
3. Although class sizes in the upper grades were large (more than thirty), statewide legislation had lowered class sizes in the early grades (K–3) to twenty.
4. For more on this criticism, see Wills 1994, 1996.
5. When asked similar questions, students at the two urban schools talked about inheritance, opportunities to go to college, and discrimination.
6. For other examples of such denial in schools see Schofield 1986 and Rist 1974.
7. For example, the suburban vote has had a deep impact on political platforms and electoral outcomes; the urban/suburban split has turned the tide in many elections (see Kinder and Mendelberg 1995; Kinder and Sanders 1996; Lipsitz 1998).
8. This quite common impression about the relative levels of drug use among urban and suburban children has been challenged as data have shown higher levels of drug use in suburbs than in cities (Clawson and Khang 1996; Davis and Thomas 1997; L. Harris 1999; Radin 1997).
9. Schofield (1982), Wells and Crain (1997), and others have found similar discrepancies between what they call a "color-blind perspective" and the clear salience of race in the schools they studied. Though their findings are similar, I am here trying to argue that color blindness is not merely a "perspective" but a set of narratives and understandings that are pervasive throughout the culture and that have a broad impact both inside and beyond schooling. Drawing on theoretical writing on color-blind ideology pushes us to think about the interests served by color-blind discourse rather than seeing it merely as a deficiency in how educators understand what is taking place in their school.
10. Crenshaw (1997: 100) provides an example of the way color-blind ideology works in her discussion of how O. J. Simpson was portrayed at the beginning of his criminal trial: "Mainstream commentators, perhaps in a preemptive response to possible concerns about whether Simpson could receive a fair trial, were quick to comment that Simpson was not thought of (by whites) as an African American, but as simply a *race-*

neutral celebrity. Yet such 'assurances' unwittingly revealed an underlying racial logic in which blackness remained as a suspect category that Simpson had been fortunate to escape. Implicitly, a defendant who *was* thought of as black might well have reason to worry."

11. Several scholars have discussed the use of racial code language as a way of talking about race and racial issues without appearing racist (Apple 1988; Omi and Winant 1994; Bonilla-Silva 1997). Terms such as *welfare, gangs, inner city, busing, crime* all are examples of strategic rhetoric used to talk about race without naming it or any particular minority group.

12. Sleeter and Grant (1988) talk about several other forms of multicultural education— single-group studies (e.g., Afrocentrism) focusing on one group at a time; efforts that emphasize cultural pluralism, including diverse staffing, unbiased and inclusive curricula, and affirmation of languages other than English; and finally a few efforts that both combine multiculturalism with a commitment to challenging inequality and promote diversity—but these are much less common than the forms named above.

13. See Carby 1992; Giroux 1998a, 1998b; McCarthy 1988; and Olneck 1993.

14. More research is clearly needed in this area to identify precisely what critical multiculturalism can and does look like when implemented in classrooms. Up to now, much of the writing on this topic has remained at the theoretical level.

15. For a discussion of national trends in white youths' racial attitudes, see Forman 2001b.

Three   Struggling with Dangerous Subjects: Race at West City Elementary

1. The city of Hillside uses the following racial/ethnic categories for collecting data on students: African American, Spanish surname, other white, Chinese, Japanese, Filipino, Korean, American Indian, and other nonwhite. When parents initially register their children, they must select one of these categories. In practice, "other nonwhite" is used in a number of different ways: for example, for a child who is biracial, for a child who does not fit into the existing categories (e.g., Samoan), and sometimes strategically to facilitate getting a child into a particular school. See Chapter 6 for more on this practice.

2. When I was speaking to administrators at district headquarters about possible places to conduct my research, they would occasionally remark that a principal was "one of their best." Several of these comments were made in regard to Ms. Grant.

3. I often wondered whether the norms that the adults in the school used to judge the acceptability of the behavior of other personnel or the acceptability of the curriculum would have been different if they had been talking about their own children. It is hard to argue that children do not need to understand basic premises about functioning in school, but that they could go so long without knowing and that acquiring this skill could be seen as a fair trade-off for not learning math seems possible only with a population of students from whom little is expected.

4. As Schofield (1982), Peshkin (1991), and others have reported, boys were much more likely to cross racial boundaries than were girls. This practice had to do with the kinds of activities they were involved in. Boys were much more likely to engage in large-group sports that required a specific number of players and not much intimacy.

Girls were involved primarily in smaller and more intimate play involving only two or three people at a time.

5. See Bonilla-Silva 1997, Edsall and Edsall 1991, Gilens 1996, or Omi and Winant 1994 for more on the use of racial code words.
6. For more on this categorization of families, see Lareau and Horvat 1999.
7. For more on this point, see Traub 2000.
8. For more on the blaming of children and families, see Payne's (1991) discussion of James Comer's school-reform model.
9. See Moraga and Anzaldúa 1981.
10. For further discussion of race and gendered patterns, see Grant 1984 and Weis and Fine 1993.
11. Darnell and I had a number of talks about what he wanted for his future and the need to at some point pick up his pencil and try.

Four   Breaking the Silence: Race, Culture, Language, and Power at Metro2

1. For more on the structure of dual-language programs, see Christian 1996.
2. Title I is a compensatory education program funded by the federal government to assist low-income and "at-risk" children to achieve in school.
3. This fact is not lost on the students, who, as I discuss later, generally viewed racial boundaries as less fixed and more permeable than did their peers in the other schools. For example, one day a fourth-grade girl stopped me to show me her journal. Writing about her background, she discussed how "very mixed" she was. She was, as she wrote, "Chinese, El Salvadorean, Peruvian, American, Spanish, and Mexican. My dad is Chinese, El Salvadorean and Mexican and my mom is also a mix of things."
4. This center was available not only to Metro2 students. School buses for a number of other elementary schools picked up and dropped off students at the school every day. More than one Metro2 parent I spoke to utilized the full time of available care. The parents I interviewed all said they were pleased with the program, as their children seemed happy to have the extra time at school. Students I spoke to enjoyed extra time to play with friends and visit with teachers.
5. For a discussion of macro patterns of housing and school segregation, see Massey and Denton 1993, Orfield and Eaton 1996, Orfield et al. 1997, and Valdes 1997.
6. The Unz Initiative, or Proposition 227, was a referendum outlawing most forms of bilingual education in the state. It was funded and driven primarily by Ron Unz, a billionaire businessman from Southern California.
7. Sheltered-language teaching is used to facilitate comprehension for those with limited language skills in the language of instruction (in this case Spanish). The instructor uses strategies such as visual cues to signal meaning. Often, low-level language is used so that non-native speakers can follow along.
8. Anglophone means literally a person who speaks English. At the school Anglophone was a referent for the English-speaking segment of the school, which was also predominantly white and middle-class.
9. Proposition 187 was known as the "Save Our State" initiative and was intended to "prevent illegal aliens in the United States from receiving benefits of public services in the State of California" (Suárez-Orozco 1995). Included as one goal was the exclusion of

hundreds of thousands of undocumented immigrant children from public schools. There was never a clear plan of implementation, but talk implied that direct-service workers such as teachers would be used to identify "illegals." Though the law is still being contested in court and much of it has been found to be unconstitutional, it caused a great deal of anxiety and turmoil at the time of its passage in 1996.

10. For a thoughtful discussion of the politics and power involved in the current discussion of Spanish-language education, see Aparicio 1998.

11. Proposition 209 outlawed all affirmative action programs in public institutions in the state.

12. In this case my hesitancy to talk more openly to students about my participation in the rally had to do both with my lack of forethought about how to talk to nine- and ten-year-olds about it in a way that would be meaningful to them and also with my concern about expressing my perspectives on racial issues openly to the class so early in my time in the field.

13. Members of the Consent Decree office visit city schools at least yearly to make sure the schools are abiding by regulations and to check what they are doing to meet integration goals.

14. Other literature on dual-language programs reports mixed findings on the social integration of students. As at Metro2, most found cooperative relationships in the classroom (Cazabon, Lambert, and Hall 1993). The few studies that looked beyond the classroom also found social separation that broke down along race/color lines (Freeman 1996).

15. Cindy had been struggling for some time in the school and was recently diagnosed with an auditory-processing learning disability. Based on recommendations from several teachers, her mother was seriously considering moving her to a regular classroom, where she wouldn't have to struggle with two languages.

16. I am excluding the two learning disabled students (one white and one Latino) from Table 4.1. They were both in the low group.

17. For example, in Omi and Winant's (1994) *Racial Formation in the United States*, they cite the case of Suzie Phillips, who discovered as an adult that her birth certificate listed her as black. Having lived her life as a white person, she asked the court to issue a new, corrected certificate. The court refused, citing her distant African ancestry. Though the ruling was not without any impact, it likely did not affect how she was "read" in everyday interactions with others.

18. Similarly, "Asians" as a group do not share a language, a country of origin, a history outside the United States, or a culture (Chan 1991).

Five   Learning and Living Racial Boundaries:
        Constructing and Negotiating Racial Identity in School

1. These judgments are what social psychologists such as Rob Sellers and Jennifer Crocker refer to as "Public Regard." See Sellers et al. 1998 and Luhtanen and Crocker 1992.

2. For more on this process, see Reskin 2002.

3. Batista Valley is a suburb outside Hillside just a few miles from Sunny Valley.

4. Mrs. Bonilla was interviewed by a research assistant in Spanish.

5. During this interview, conducted in Spanish, Mrs. Bonilla referred to blacks in the diminutive as "negritos."

6. As discussed in Chapter 3, Mr. Hargrove's family lived in a primarily Latino neighborhood that was beginning to undergo gentrification.

7. Harris and Sim (2000) discuss this issue in relation to students' self-identifications on a survey instrument. Students did not all claim the same racial identities in school as they did at home.

8. As Hall (1980, 1986a) describes it, when the signifying system of race is joined with power, it becomes an organized system of inclusion and exclusion that shapes social life and profoundly affects both identity and life chances. Systems of inclusion and exclusion are also organized around other social categories (e.g., gender).

Six Schooling and the Social Reproduction of Racial Inequality

1. I do not discuss Asians here because they were not represented in large numbers at any of the schools. Clearly the social and economic standing of Asian Americans ranges widely in the United States today, with some groups (e.g., southeast Asians) near the bottom of the distribution and other groups (e.g., Japanese, Asian Indians) near the top.

2. A frequent complicating factor was the absence of a home phone.

3. For more on this disparity, see Orfield and Gordon 2001 and Orfield et al. 1997.

4. Op-ed piece from major local newspaper.

5. Section 8 is an alternative program for low-income families that gives them vouchers to use in the private housing market rather than providing discounted rent in public housing.

6. Social capital also came in the form of school friendship networks, which provided students with information about schools and how to get into them.

7. A number of Latino parents of West City students had tried unsuccessfully over the years to get their children into Metro2.

8. For example, Ms. Wilson often engaged in long conversations with several boys in her class about professional baseball. Although baseball would not be considered high culture in the traditional sense, in this setting understanding baseball was much more useful than extensive familiarity with classical music.

9. For more on these issues, see Bourdieu 1977a, Lamont and Lareau 1988, Lareau and Horvat 1999, MacLeod 1995, Roscigno and Ainsworth-Darnell 1999, and Swartz 1997.

10. For an insightful and in-depth discussion of these issues, see Ferguson (2000).

11. For more on Bourdieu's view of symbolic capital, see Bourdieu and Passeron 1990.

12. As Williams and others have documented, racism directly affects both mental and physical health. See, for example, Takeuchi, Williams, and Adair 1991, Williams and Collins 1995, and Williams et al. 1997.

13. For example, racial profiling and the resulting police shootings of African Americans in cities across the country or the spate of racial violence in the late 1990s that led to the deaths of African Americans, Asian Americans, and others.

Appendix A Research Methods: Stories from the Field

1. For example, see work by Saito (1998) and others (Horton 1995; Pardo 1998) on the multiracial politics in Monterey Park, California.

2. Below the state level, all geographical names are pseudonyms, which I have introduced to help protect the confidentiality of the research sites.

3. I looked also at a number of schools in which Asians were one of the largest subpopulations, and, by not choosing one of these, I clearly lost some important information. However, it was impossible to select all patterns of variation, so I chose to focus on blacks and Latinos.

4. In order to ensure that I could get to know one group of students and their parents well, I based myself primarily in one classroom in each school. I selected fourth/fifth-grade classrooms not only because these students were developmentally most likely to have clear understandings of race and their own racial identities but because they were also young enough that some of these ideas were still in flux. Also, given my intention to interview the students during the year, it was important to select a grade where students would be most likely to be able to articulate their ideas and engage in conversation about somewhat abstract concepts. I wanted to do this all, however, in elementary schools, where families still have a significant presence and where students of different racial/ethnic groups continue to occupy the same classrooms and social circles.

5. This is not so much an issue of the representativeness of the school as an attempt to anticipate possible bias in the data caused by selection criteria.

6. By "relatively" I mean in relation to many other towns surrounding Hillside that are very high-income. The cost of living in this metropolitan area is one of the highest in the country, so even towns I refer to as relatively middle-class have median household incomes far above the national average. However, the towns I targeted have few country clubs, luxury homes, or high-priced cars. In the Sunny Valley community, where Foresthills school is located, many parents have union jobs, work in middle management, are teachers, or constitute dual-income households.

7. Negotiations went on constantly to determine the work I would be available for. For example, in Metro2 the teacher began organizing center work (in which students were broken into small groups and rotated through different centers, two of which the teacher and I staffed) during the days I was at the school. In this way she could take advantage of having two adults with experience teaching in the room to give students extra time for supervised reading in small groups. Her attempt to utilize me in creative ways was "data" about her pedagogical orientation. It also gave me a chance to assess students' skills and knowledge in small-group settings and to evaluate peer relations in this context, and it provided data on grouping patterns. It did not, however, allow me to observe whole-group process or to observe the interactions of students outside my group. Though the arrangement had advantages and seemed feasible as a periodic use of my time, I had to negotiate with the teacher about how often she would involve me in this work. She was receptive to my concerns and cut back, scheduling centers once a month or less.

8. Early in my time at each school, I sent a letter home to parents introducing myself and explaining the project. The letter included a slip for them to sign giving me permission to include their children in the study. In the end, I received only one no, from a family at West City. At the time these parents were having a struggle with social services, and I was not surprised by their hesitancy.

9. This mode of addressing adults was so firmly established that, even after the year was over, when I told several students with whom I had established strong relationships that they could address me by my first name outside of school, they could not bring themselves to do it. Our compromise was for them to address me simply as "Lewis" rather than as "Miss Lewis."

10. These relations were not research problems but in effect provided additional data about the school's structure and culture.

11. These conversations often took place during yard duty, in the teacher workroom while making copies, in the lunchroom, or at an after-school event.

12. This Foresthills parent was a single mother who was managing two jobs at the time and did not want to give up any of the little time she had with her children outside of work.

13. At one point during the school year I had a long, tense, and interesting conversation with one mother who happened also to be an academic. She wanted to know how I was deciding what racial/ethnic category students fit into in this representative sample. I explained that one of the central topics of my study was how these processes of categorization unfold. Obviously, this was an issue primarily with regard to students whose racial identification was not immediately clear. In most cases I automatically selected those students, as I intended to target those at the margins or borders of racial categories. As I explained to her, in these cases I did not decide where they "fit" but only that I wanted to talk with them and their parents about how they understood their location in existing racial schemas. Seemingly satisfied with my responses, she became more friendly as the conversation continued and consented to be interviewed.

14. By "one of few" I mean cases where a class had only one or two students of a particular race. Thus, for instance, I interviewed parents of both the black students in the class at Metro2 and the (white) parent of the one black (biracial black/white) student at Foresthills.

15. I hired an undergraduate student from a local university as a research assistant to interview Spanish-speaking parents. The interviewer was a Mexican national who had lived in the Hillside metropolitan area for several years just before and while attending college. She had also taken a number of ethnic-studies courses in college and had excellent skills and knowledge for the position. She conducted, transcribed, and translated the eight interviews she did. I later had another Spanish speaker check several of the English translations against the original tapes; she verified the accuracy and quality of the translations. All the parents my assistant contacted agreed to be interviewed. Though she had less information than I did about the schools and students to use as probes during the interviews, we spent a great deal of time before and between interviews strategizing about probes she could use. The interviews generally demonstrate a strong rapport between her and the parents.

16. I eventually did interview six fathers; three of them participated in joint interviews with their spouses.

17. In most cases, students' custodial guardians were a heterosexual couple.

18. This finding is consistent with most national survey data, which regularly find gender to be a significant predictor, with women having less negative racial attitudes.

19. I interviewed both members of one couple in which the mother was Chicana and the father African American.

20. The one exception was the white mother of a white/Latina daughter. The mother offered several explanations for her identification of her daughter as white. Not only was the child blond and similar in coloring to her mother, but her father was "not a big influence in her life," and, the mother believed, "the mother is more important for these things." It is left for us to surmise whether this identification would have been possible had her daughter been dark or Mestizo in appearance.

21. Here I say "some" because one of my findings is that there were competing narratives about what was transpiring in the schools. Sometimes member checks involved talking to several informants about a particular pattern I was seeing to verify that it existed (e.g., enrollment or discipline patterns). Other times member checks involved talking to various key people to verify patterns in differing accounts of the patterns themselves.

Bibliography

Aboud, Frances. 1988. *Children and Prejudice*. New York: Blackwell.

Abrams, Charles. 1955. *Forbidden Neighbors: A Study of Prejudice in Housing*. New York: Harper.

Acosta, Mark. 1998. "King's Name for School Draws Fire: Some Parents Fear Bias by Colleges, Others Want to Honor Citrus Heritage." *Press-Enterprise* (Riverside, Calif.), 3 January, p. B1.

Alarcon, Norma. 1981. "Chicana's Feminist Literature: A Re-Vision Through Malintzin/or Malintzin: Putting Flesh Back on the Object." In *This Bridge Called My Back: Writings by Radical Women of Color*, 2d ed., edited by Cherríe A. Moraga and Gloria Anzaldúa. New York: Kitchen Table Press.

Alexander, Karl L., Doris R. Entwisle, and Maxine S. Thompson. 1987. "School Performance, Status Relations, and the Structure of Sentiment: Bringing the Teacher Back In." *American Sociological Review* 52: 665–682.

Almaguer, Tomas. 1999. "Honorary Whites." Talk given at the Center for Research on Social Organization, University of Michigan, Ann Arbor, Fall.

Almaguer, Tomas, and Moon-Kie Jung. 1999. "The Enduring Ambiguities of Race in the United States." In *Sociology for the Twenty-First Century*, edited by J. L. Abu-Lughod. Chicago: University of Chicago Press.

Aparicio, Frances R. 1998. "Whose Spanish, Whose Language, Whose Power? An Ethnographic Inquiry into Differential Bilingualism." *U.S. Latino Cultural Studies* 12: 5–26.

Apple, Michael. 1982. *Education and Power*. Boston: Routledge.

———. 1988. "Redefining Equality: Authoritarian Populism and the Conservative Restoration." *Teachers College Record* 90: 167–184.

———. 1990. *Ideology and Curriculum*. 2d ed. New York: Routledge.

Au, Kathryn, and Cathie Jordan. 1981. "Teaching Reading to Hawaiian Children: Finding a Culturally Appropriate Solution." In *Culture and the Bilingual Classroom*, edited by H. Trueba and K. Au Rawley, Mass.: Newbury House.

Ayers, William, Bernardine Dohrn, and Rick Ayers. 2001. *Zero Tolerance: Resisting the Drive for Punishment in Our Schools.* New York: New Press.

Bernstein, Basil. 1971. *Class, Codes and Control.* London: Routledge.

Blumer, Herbert. 1958. "Race Prejudice as a Sense of Group Position." *Pacific Sociological Review* 1: 3–7.

Bobo, Lawrence, James R. Kluegel, and Ryan A. Smith. 1997. "Laissez Faire Racism: The Crystallization of a 'Kinder, Gentler' Anti-Black Ideology." In *Racial Attitudes in the 1990s: Continuity and Change,* edited by S. Tuch and J. Martin. Westport, Conn.: Praeger.

Bonilla-Silva, Eduardo. 1997. "Rethinking Racism: Toward a Structural Interpretation." *American Sociological Review* 62: 465–480.

———. 2001. *White Supremacy and Racism in the Post–Civil Rights Era.* Boulder, Colo.: Lynne Rienner Publishers.

Bonilla-Silva, Eduardo, and Tyrone A. Forman. 2000. "'I Am Not a Racist but . . .': Mapping College Students Racial Ideology in the USA." *Discourse and Society* 11: 50–85.

Bonilla-Silva, Eduardo, and Karen Glover. Forthcoming. "'We Are All Americans': The Latinoamericanization of Race Relations in the USA." In *The Changing Terrain of Race and Ethnicity,* edited by M. Krysan and A. Lewis. New York: Russell Sage Foundation.

Bonilla-Silva, Eduardo, and Amanda Lewis. 1999. "The New Racism: Racial Structure in the United States, 1960s–1990s." In *Race, Ethnicity, and Nationality in the United States,* edited by P. Wong. Boulder, Colo.: Westview Press.

Bourdieu, Pierre. 1977a. "Cultural Reproduction and Social Reproduction." In *Power and Ideology in Education,* edited by Jerome Karabel and A. H. Halsey. New York: Oxford University Press.

———. 1977b. *Outline of a Theory of Practice.* New York: Cambridge University Press.

———. 1986. "The Forms of Capital." In *Handbook of Theory and Research for the Sociology of Education,* edited by J. G. Richardson. New York: Greenwood Press.

Bourdieu, Pierre, and Jean-Claude Passeron. 1990. *Reproduction in Education, Society and Culture.* London: Sage.

Bowles, Samuel, and Herbert Gintis. 1976. *Schooling in Capitalist America: Educational Reform and the Contradictions of Economic Life.* New York: Basic Books.

Brennan, Robert T., Jimmy Kim, Melodie Wenz-Gross, and Gary N. Siperstein. 2001. "The Relative Equitability of High-Stakes Testing versus Teacher-Assigned Grades: An Analysis of the Massachusetts Comprehensive Assessment System (MCAS)." *Harvard Educational Review* 71: 173–216.

Bryant, Bunyan. 1995. *Environmental Justice: Issues, Policies, and Solutions.* Washington, D.C.: Island Press.

Bullard, Robert D. 2000. *Dumping in Dixie: Race, Class, and Environmental Quality.* Boulder, Colo.: Westview Press

Bulmer, Martin, and John Solomos. 1998. "Introduction: Re-thinking Ethnic and Racial Studies." *Ethnic and Racial Studies* 21: 819–837.

Butchart, Ronald E., and Barbara McEwan. 1998. *Classroom Discipline in American Schools: Problems and Possibilities for Democratic Education.* Albany: State University of New York Press.

Carby, Hazel. 1992. "The Multicultural Wars." In *Black Popular Culture,* edited by M. Wallace and G. Dent. Seattle: Seattle Day Press.

Carter, Stephen. 1997. "Is White a Race? Expressions of White Racial Identity." In *Off White: Readings on Race, Power and Society*, edited by M. Fine, L. Weis, L. Powell, and L. M. Wong. New York: Routledge.

Cazabon, Mary, Wallace Lambert, and G. Hall. 1993. *Two-Way Bilingual Education: A Progress Report on the Amigos Program*. Santa Cruz, Calif.: National Center for Research on Cultural Diversity and Second Language Learning.Cazden, Courtney B. 1988. *Classroom Discourse: The Language of Teaching and Learning*. Portsmouth, N.H.: Heinemann.

Cazden, Courtney B., Vera P. John, and Dell Hymes, eds. 1972. *Functions of Language in the Classroom*. Prospect Heights, Ill.: Waveland Press.

Chan, Sucheng. 1991. *Asian Americans: An Interpretive History*. Boston: Twayne.

Christian, Donna. 1996. "Two-Way Immersion Education: Students Learning through Two Languages." *Modern Language Journal* 80: 66–76.

Clawson, Linda, and Kathy Khang. 1996. "Juvenile Drug Arrests Increase at Faster Rate in Suburbs Than City: Factors Include Greater Police Vigilance, Affluence and Unmonitored Children." *Milwaukee Journal Sentinal*, 15 August, p. 1.

Cole, Luke, and Sheila Foster. 2000. *From the Ground Up: Environmental Racism and the Rise of the Environmental Justice Movement*. New York: New York University Press.

Coleman, James. 1988. "Social Capital in the Creation of Human Capital." *American Journal of Sociology* 94: S95–S120.

Collins, Patricia Hill. 1991. *Black Feminist Thought: Knowledge, Consciousness, and the Politics of Empowerment*. New York: Routledge.

Collins, Sharon. 1997. *Black Corporate Executives: The Making and Breaking of a Black Middle Class*. Philadelphia: Temple University Press.

Conley, Dalton. 1999. *Being Black, Living in the Red: Race, Wealth, and Social Policy in America*. Berkeley: University of California Press.

Connolly, Paul. 1998. *Racism, Gender Identities and Young Children: Social Relations in a Multi-ethnic, Inner-City Primary School*. New York: Routledge.

Corsaro, William A. 1996. "Transitions in Early Childhood: The Promise of Comparative, Longitudinal Ethnography." In *Ethnography and Human Development: Context and Meaning in Social Inquiry*, edited by R. Jessor, A. Colby, and R. A. Shweder. Chicago: University of Chicago Press.

Crenshaw, Kimberlé W. 1997. "Color-Blind Dreams and Racial Nightmares: Reconfiguring Racism in the Post–Civil Rights Era." In *Birth of a Nation'hood*, edited by T. Morrison and C. B. Lacour. New York: Pantheon Books.

Crichlow, Warren, Susan Goodwin, Gaya Shakes, and Ellen Swartz. 1990. "Multicultural Ways of Knowing: Implications for Practice." *Journal of Education* 172: 101–117.

Davidson, Ann Locke. 1996. *Making and Molding Identity in Schools: Student Narratives on Race, Gender, and Academic Engagement*. Albany: State University of New York Press.

Davis, F. James. 1991. *Who Is Black?: One Nation's Definition*. University Park: Pennsylvania State University Press.

Davis, Patricia, and Pierre Thomas. 1997. "In Affluent Suburbs, Young Users and Sellers Abound: 12,000 in Fairfax Were Treated in Last 4 Years." *Washington Post*, 14 December, p. A1.

Delpit, Lisa. 1988. "The Silenced Dialogue: Power and Pedagogy in Educating Other People's Children." In *Facing Racism in Education*, edited by Nitza Hidalgo, Ceasar McDowell, and Emilie Siddle. Cambridge, Mass.: Harvard Educational Review.

————. 1995. *Other People's Children: Cultural Conflict in the Classroom.* New York: New Press.

DeMarrais, Kathleen Bennet, and Margaret D. LeCompte. 1995. *The Way Schools Work: A Sociological Analysis of Education.* White Plains, N.Y.: Longman.

Dennis, Rutledge. 1988. "The Use of Participant Observation in Race Relations Research." *Race and Ethnic Relations* 5: 25–46.

Denzin, Norman K. 1978. *Sociological Methods: A Sourcebook.* New York: McGraw-Hill.

————. 1989. *The Research Act: A Theoretical Introduction to Sociological Methods.* Englewood Cliffs, N.J.: Prentice-Hall.

Derman-Sparks, Louise. 1989. *Anti-bias Curriculum: Tools for Empowering Young Children.* Washington, D.C.: National Association for the Education of Young Children. ED 305 135.

————. 1993–1994. "Empowering Children to Create a Caring Culture in a World of Differences." *Childhood Education* 70: 66–71.

DeVault, Marjorie L. 1997. "Personal Writing in Social Research: Issues of Production and Interpretation." In *Reflexivity and Voice,* edited by R. Hertz. Thousand Oaks, Calif.: Sage.

DiMaggio, Paul. 1982. "Cultural Capital and School Success: The Impact of Status Culture Participation on the Grades of U.S. High School Students." *American Sociological Review* 47: 189–201.

DiMaggio, Paul, and John Mohr. 1985. "Cultural Capital, Educational Attainment, and Marital Selection." *American Journal of Sociology* 90: 1231–1261.

Drake, St. Clair, and Horace R. Cayton. 1962. *Black Metropolis: A Study of Negro Life in a Northern City.* New York: Harper & Row.

Durkheim, Emile. 1973. *Moral Education: A Study in the Theory and Application of the Sociology of Education.* New York: Free Press.

Edsall, Thomas Byrne, and Mary D. Edsall. 1991. *Chain Reaction: The Impact of Race, Rights, and Taxes on American Politics.* New York: Norton.

Erikson, Frederick, and Jeffrey Shultz. 1982. *The Counselor as Gatekeeper: Social Interaction in Interviews.* New York: Academic Press.

Essed, Philomena. 1991. *Understanding Everyday Racism: An Interdisciplinary Theory.* Newbury Park, Calif.: Sage.

————. 1997. "Racial Intimidation: Sociopolitical Implications of the Usage of Racist Slurs." In *The Language and Politics of Exclusion,* edited by S. H. Riggins. Thousand Oaks, Calif.: Sage.

Falcón, Angelo. 1995. "Puerto Ricans and the Politics of Racial Identity." In *Racial and Ethnic Identity: Psychological Development and Creative Expression,* edited by H. Harris, H. Blue, and E. Griffith. New York: Routledge.

Farkas, George. 1996. *Human Capital or Cultural Capital? Ethnicity and Poverty Groups in an Urban School District.* New York: Aldine de Gruyter.

Farley, Reynolds. 1984. *Blacks and Whites : Narrowing the Gap?* Cambridge, Mass.: Harvard University Press.

————. 1985. "Three Steps Forward and Two Back? Recent Changes in the Social and Economic Status of Blacks." In *Ethnicity and Race in the U.S.A.: Toward the Twenty-First Century,* edited by R. D. Alba. Boston: Routledge.

————. 1995. *State of the Union: America in the 1990s.* New York: Russell Sage Foundation.

Farley, Reynolds, and Walter Allen. 1989. *The Color Line and the Quality of Life in America.* New York: Oxford University Press.

Farley, Reynolds, Howard Schuman, Suzanne Bianchi, Diane Colasanto, and Shirley Hatchett. 1978. "Chocolate City and Vanilla Suburbs: Will the Trend toward Racially Separate Communities Continue?" *Social Science Research* 7: 319–344.

Farley, Reynolds, Charlotte Steeh, Maria Krysan, Tara Jackson, and Keith Reeves. 1994. "Stereotypes and Segregation: Neighborhoods in the Detroit Area." *American Journal of Sociology* 100: 750–780.

Feagin, Joe R., and Clairece B. Feagin. 1996. *Racial and Ethnic Relations.* 5th ed. Upper Saddle River, N.J.: Prentice-Hall.

Feagin, Joe [R.], and Melvin Sikes. 1994. *Living with Racism.* Boston: Beacon Press.

Feagin, Joe R., and Hernan Vera. 1995. *White Racism: The Basics.* New York: Routledge.

Ferguson, Ann A. 2000. *Bad Boys: Public Schools in the Making of Black Masculinity.* Ann Arbor: University of Michigan Press.

Ferguson, Ronald F. 1998a. "Can Schools Narrow the Black-White Test Score Gap?" In *The Black-White Test Score Gap,* edited by C. Jencks and M. Phillips. Washington, D.C.: Brookings Insititution Press.

———. 1998b. "Teachers' Perceptions and Expectations and the Black-White Test Score Gap." In *The Black-White Test Score Gap,* edited by C. Jencks and M. Phillips. Washington, D.C.: Brookings Institution Press.

Figueroa, Peter. 1991. *Education and the Social Construction of "Race."* New York: Routledge.

Fish, Stanley. 1993. "Reverse Racism or How the Pot Got to Call the Kettle Black." *Atlantic Monthly* 272: 128–130.

Flores-Gonzalez, Nilda. 1999. "Puerto Rican High Achievers: An Example of Ethnic and Academic Identity Compatibility." *Anthropology & Education Quarterly* 30: 343–362.

Forman, Tyrone. 2001a. "Social Change, Social Context and White Youth's Racial Attitudes." Ph.D. diss., Department of Sociology, University of Michigan, Ann Arbor.

———. 2001b. "Social Determinants of White Youth's Racial Attitudes." *Sociological Studies of Children and Youth* 8: 173–207.

———. Forthcoming. "Color-Blind Racism and Racial Indifference: The Role of Racial Apathy in Facilitating Enduring Inequalities." In *The Changing Terrain of Race and Ethnicity,* edited by M. Krysan and A. Lewis. New York: Russell Sage Foundation.

Foster, Michele. 1997. *Black Teachers on Teaching.* New York: New Press.

Frankenberg, Ruth. 1993. *White Women, Race Matters: The Social Construction of Whiteness.* Minneapolis: University of Minnesota Press.

Freeman, Rebecca D. 1996. "Dual-Language Planning at Oyster Bilingual School: 'It's Much More Than Language.'" *Tesol Quarterly* 30: 557–582.

Gallagher, Charles. 1997. "White Racial Formation: Into the Twenty-First Century." In *Critical White Studies: Looking beyond the Mirror,* edited by R. Delgado and S. Stefancic. Philadelphia: Temple University Press.

———. 2000. "Misperceiving Race: Why Blacks and Whites Distort Group Size." Unpublished manuscript, Department of Sociology, Georgia State University.

Gilens, Martin. 1995. "Racial Attitudes and Opposition to Welfare." *Journal of Politics* 57: 994–1014.

———. 1996. "'Race Coding' and White Opposition to Welfare." *American Political Science Review* 90: 593–604.

Gillborn, David. 1990. *"Race," Ethnicity and Education: Teaching and Learning in Multiethnic Schools*. London: Unwin Hyman.

Gilroy, Paul. 1998. "Race Ends Here." *Ethnic and Racial Studies* 21: 838–847.

Giroux, Henry A. 1983. *Theory and Resistance in Education: A Pedagogy for the Opposition*. South Hadley, Mass.: Bergin & Garvey.

———. 1988. *Teachers as Intellectuals: Toward a Critical Pedagogy of Learning*. Granby, Mass.: Bergin & Garvey.

———. 1991. *Postmodernism, Feminism, and Cultural Politics: Redrawing Educational Boundaries*. Albany: State University of New York Press.

———. 1998a. "The Politics of Insurgent Multiculturalism in the Era of the Los Angeles Uprising." In *Critical Social Issues in American Education: Transformation in a Postmodern World*, edited by H. S. Shapiro and D. E. Purpel. Mahwah, N.J.: Erlbaum.

———. 1998b. "Youth, Memory Work, and the Racial Politics of Whiteness." In *White Reign: Deploying Whiteness in America*, edited by J. L. Kincheloe, S. Steinberg, N. Rodriguez, and R Chennault. New York: St. Martin's Press.

Gitlin, Todd. 1995. *Twilight of Our Common Dreams: Why America Is Wracked by Culture Wars*. New York: Metropolitan Books.

Glenn, Evelyn Nakano. 1992. "From Servitude to Service Work: Historical Continuities in the Racial Division of Paid Reproductive Labor." *Signs* 18: 1–43.

Gonzalez, Francisca E. 1998. "Formations of Mexicananess: Trenzas de Identidades Multiples: Growing up Mexicana: Braids of Multiple Identities." *Qualitative Studies in Education* 2: 81–102.

Gould, Mark. 1999. "Race and Theory: Culture, Poverty, and Adaptation to Discrimination in Wilson and Ogbu." *Sociological Theory* 17: 171–200.

Gramsci, Antonio. 1971. *Selections from the Prison Notebooks*. New York: International Publications.

Grant, Linda. 1984. "Black Females' 'Place' in Desegregated Classrooms." *Sociology of Education* 57(2): 98–111.

Greene, Maxine. 1988. *The Dialectic of Freedom*. New York: Teachers College Press.

Hadderman, Margaret. 1999. "Equity and Adequacy in Educational Finance." *ERIC Digest* 129. Retrieved from http://eric.uoregon.edu/publications/digests/digest129.html

Hall, Stuart. 1980. "Race, Articulation and Societies Structured in Dominance." In *Sociological Theories: Race and Colonialism*. Paris: UNESCO.

———. 1984. "The Narrative Construction of Reality." *Southern Review* 17: 3–17.

———. 1986a. "Gramsci's Relevance for the Study of Race and Ethnicity." *Journal of Communication Inquiry* (Special Issue) 10: 5–27.

———. 1986b. "On Postmodernism and Articulation: An Interview with Stuart Hall." *Journal of Communication Inquiry* (Special Issue) 10: 45–60.

———. 1990. "The Whites of Their Eyes: Racist Ideologies and the Media." In *The Media Reader*, edited by M. Alvarado and J. Thompson. London: British Film Institute.

Harris, Cheryl. 1993. "Whiteness as Property." *Harvard Law Review* 106: 1710–1791.

Harris, David R. 1997. *The Flight of Whites: A Multilevel Analysis of Why Whites Move*. Ann Arbor: University of Michigan Population Studies Center.

———. 1999. "All Suburbs Are Not Created Equal: A New Look at Racial Differences in Suburban Location." Research Report 99-440. Ann Arbor: University of Michigan Population Studies Center.

Harris, David R., and Jeremiah Joseph Sim. 2000. "Who Is Mixed Race? Patterns and Determinants of Adolescent Racial Identity." Research Report 00-452. Ann Arbor: University of Michigan Population Studies Center.

Harris, Lyle. 1999. "Their Turn." *Atlanta Journal and Constitution*, 28 October, p. 1C.

Hasso, Frances. 1998. "Paradoxes of Gender Politics." Ph.D. diss., Department of Sociology, University of Michigan, Ann Arbor.

Heath, Shirley Brice. 1983. *Ways with Words: Language, Life, and Work in Communities and Classrooms*. New York: Cambridge University Press.

Henault, Cherry. 2001. "Zero Tolerance in Schools." *Journal of Law & Education* 30: 547–553.

Hirschfeld, Lawrence. 1996. *Race in the Making: Cognition, Culture, and the Child's Construction of Human Kinds*. Cambridge, Mass.: MIT Press.

Hochschild, Jennifer L. 1995. *Facing Up to the American Dream: Race, Class, and the Soul of the Nation*. Princeton, N.J.: Princeton University Press.

Holmes, Robyn M. 1995. *How Young Children Perceive Race*. Thousand Oaks, Calif.: Sage.

Holt, Thomas C. 1995. "Marking: Race, Race-Making, and the Writing of History." *American Historical Review* 100: 1–20.

Hopkins, Ronnie. 1997. *Educating Black Males: Critical Lessons in Schooling, Community, and Power*. Albany: State University of New York Press.

Horton, John. 1995. *The Politics of Diversity: Immigration, Resistance, and Change in Monterey Park, California*. Philadelphia: Temple University Press.

Howard, Elizabeth R., and Donna Christian. 1997. *The Development of Bilingualism and Biliteracy in Two-Way Immersion Students*. Washington, D.C.: Center for Applied Linguistics.

Hyman, Irwin A., and Pamela A. Snook. 2000. "Dangerous Schools and What You Can Do about Them." *Phi Delta Kappan* 81: 489–498, 500–501.

Jackman, Mary R. 1994. *The Velvet Glove: Paternalism and Conflict in Gender, Class and Race Relations*. Berkeley: University of California Press.

Jackson, Kenneth T. 1985. *Crabgrass Frontier: The Suburbanization of America*. New York: Oxford University Press.

Jaynes, Gerald D., and Robin M. Williams. 1989. *A Common Destiny: Blacks & American Society*. Washington, D.C.: National Academy Press.

Jenkins, Richard. 1996. *Social Identity*. New York: Routledge.

Johnson, Tammy, Jennifer Emiko Boyden, and William J. Pittz, eds. 2001. *Racial Profiling and Punishment in U.S. Public Schools*. Oakland, Calif.: Applied Research Center.

Johnson, Tammy, Libero Della Piana, and Phyllida Burlingame. 2000. *Vouchers: A Trap, Not a Choice*. Oakland, Calif.: Applied Research Center.

Jones-Correa, Michael, and David L. Leal. 1996. "Becominig 'Hispanic': Secondary Panethnic Identification among Latin American–Origin Populations in the United States." *Hispanic Journal of Behavioral Sciences* 18: 214–254.

Kahlenberg, Richard D. 2001. "Learning from James Coleman." *Public Interest* 144: 54–72.

Katz, Phyllis. 1982. "Development of Children's Racial Awareness and Intergroup Attitudes." In *Current Topics in Early Childhood Education*, edited by L. Katz. Norwood, N.J.: Ablex.

Kennedy, Sheila Suess. 2001. "Privatizing Education: The Politics of Vouchers." *Phi Delta Kappan* 82: 450–456.

Kinder, Donald R., and Tali Mendelberg. 1995. "Cracks in American Apartheid: The Political Impact of Prejudice among Desegregated Whites." *Journal of Politics* 57: 402–424.

Kinder, Donald R., and Lynn M. Sanders. 1996. *Divided by Color: Racial Politics and Democratic Ideals*. Chicago : University of Chicago Press.

Kozol, Jonathon. 1991. *Savage Inequalities*. New York: Harper.

Krysan, Maria, and Reynolds Farley. 2002. "The Residential Preferences of Blacks: Do They Explain Persistent Segregation?" *Social Forces* 80(3): 937–980.

Lacey, Colin. 1970. *Hightown Grammar: The School as a Social System*. Manchester, England: Manchester University Press.

Ladson-Billings, Gloria. 1994. *The Dreamkeepers: Successful Teachers of African American Children*. San Francisco: Jossey-Bass.

Lamont, Michele, and Annette Lareau. 1988. "Cultural Capital: Allusions, Gaps and Glissandos in Recent Theoretical Developments." *Sociological Theory* 6: 153–168.

Landry, Bart. 1987. *The New Black Middle Class*. Berkeley: University of California Press.

Lareau, Annette. 1989. *Home Advantage: Social Class and Parental Intervention in Elementary Education*. New York: Falmer Press.

Lareau, Annette, and Erin McNamara Horvat. 1999. "Moments of Social Inclusion and Exclusion: Race, Class, and Cultural Capital in Family-School Relationships." *Sociology of Education* 72: 37–53.

Lareau, Annette, and Jeffrey Shultz. 1996. *Journeys through Ethnography: Realistic Accounts of Fieldwork*. Boulder, Colo.: Westview Press.

Lewis, Amanda, Mark Chesler, and Tyrone Forman. 2000. "The Impact of 'Colorblind' Ideologies on Students of Color: Intergroup Relations at a Predominantly White University." *Journal of Negro Education* 69: 74–91.

Lincoln, Yvonna, and Egon Guba. 1985. *Naturalistic Inquiry*. Beverly Hills, Calif.: Sage.

Lindjord, Denise. 2001. "School Vouchers and Underprivileged Families: An Examination of the Controversy." *Journal of Early Education & Family Review* 8: 5–6.

Lipsitz, George. 1998. *The Possessive Investment in Whiteness: How White People Profit from Identity Politics*. Philadelphia: Temple University Press.

Logan, John R., and Harvey Molotch. 1987. *Urban Fortunes: The Political Economy of Place*. Berkeley: University of California Press.

Lopez, Nancy. 2000. "The Missing Link: Latinos and Educational Opportunity Programs." *Equity & Excellence in Education* 33: 53–58.

Lubeck, Sally. 1989. "Nested Contexts." In *Class, Race, and Gender in American Education*, edited by L. Weis. Albany: State University of New York Press.

Luhtanen, Riia, and Jennifer Crocker. 1992. "A Collective Self-Esteem Scale: Self-Evaluation of One's Social Identity." *Personality & Social Psychology Bulletin* 18(3): 302–318.

Mac an Ghaill, Martin. 1994. *The Making of Men: Masculinities, Sexualities, and Schooling*. Bristol, Pa.: Open University Press.

MacLeod, Jay. 1995. *Ain't No Makin' It: Leveled Aspirations in a Low-Income Neighborhood*. Boulder, Colo.: Westview Press.

Marger, Martin N. 2000. *Race and Ethnic Relations: American and Global Perspectives*. Belmont, Calif.: Wadsworth.

Massey, Douglas S., and Nancy A. Denton. 1993. *American Apartheid: Segregation and the Making of the Underclass*. Cambridge, Mass.: Harvard University Press.

McCarthy, Cameron. 1988. "Rethinking Liberal and Radical Perspectives on Racial Inequality in Schooling: Making the Case for Nonsynchrony." In *Facing Racism in Education,* edited by Nitza Hidalgo, Ceasar McDowell, and Emilie Siddle. Cambridge, Mass.: Harvard Educational Review.

———. 1990. "Multicultural Education, Minority Identities, Textbooks, and the Challenge of Curriculum Reform." *Journal of Education* 172: 118–129.

———. 1995. "Multicultural Policy Discourses on Racial Inequality in American Education." In *Anti-racism, Feminism and Critical Approaches to Education,* edited by R. Ng, P. Staton, and J. Scane. Westport, Conn.: Bergin & Garvey.

McCarthy, Cameron, and Warren Crichlow. 1993. *Race, Identity, and Representation in Education.* New York: Routledge.

McEwan, Patrick J. 2000. "The Potential Impact of Large-Scale Voucher Programs." *Review of Educational Research* 70: 103–149.

McQuillan, Patrick J. 1998. *Educational Opportunity in an Urban American High School: A Cultural Analysis.* Albany: State University of New York Press.

Meeks, Loretta F., Wendell A. Meeks, and Claudia A. Warren. 2000. "Racial Desegregation: Magnet Schools, Vouchers, Privatization, and Home Schooling." *Education & Urban Society* 33: 88–101.

Melville, Margarita B. 1988. "Hispanics: Race, Class, or Ethnicity?" *Journal of Ethnic Studies* 16: 67–88.

Merton, Robert. 1972. "Insiders and Outsiders: A Chapter in the Sociology of Knowledge." *American Journal of Sociology* 78: 9–47.

Mickelson, Roslyn Arlin. 1990. "The Attitude-Achievement Paradox among Black Adolescents." *Sociology of Education* 63: 44–61.

Milner, David. 1983. *Children and Race: Ten Years On.* London: Ward Lock Educational.

Mizell, Linda. 2001. "Horace Had It Right: The Stakes Are Still High for Students of Color." In *Racial Profiling and Punishment in U.S. Public Schools,* edited by Tammy Johnson, Jennifer Emiko Boyden, and William J. Pittz. Oakland, Calif.: Applied Research Center.

Moraga, Cherríe A., and Gloria Anzaldúa, eds. 1981. *This Bridge Called My Back: Writings by Radical Women of Color.* Watertown, Mass.: Persephone Press.

Nelson, Candace, and Marta Tienda. 1985. "The Structuring of Hispanic Ethnicity: Historical and Contemporary Perspectives." In *Ethnicity and Race in the U.S.A.: Toward the Twenty-First Century,* edited by R. D. Alba. Boston: Routledge.

Noguera, Pedro A. 1995. "Preventing and Producing Violence: A Critical Analysis of Responses to School Violence." *Harvard Educational Review* 65: 189–212.

———. 1996. "Confronting the Urban in Urban School Reform." *Urban Review* 28: 1–19.

Oakes, Jeannie. 1985. *Keeping Track: How Schools Structure Inequality.* New Haven, Conn.: Yale University Press.

Oliver, Melvin, and Thomas Shapiro. 1995. *Black Wealth, White Wealth.* New York: Routledge.

Olneck, Michael R. 1990. "The Recurring Dream: Symbolism and Ideology in Intercultural and Multicultural Education." *American Journal of Education* 98(2): 147–174.

———. 1993. "Terms of Inclusion: Has Multiculturalism Redefined Equality in American Education?" *American Journal of Education* 101: 234–261.

Olsen, Laurie. 1997. *Made in America: Immigrant Students in Our Public Schools.* New York: New Press.

Omi, Michael, and Howard Winant. 1994. *Racial Formation in the United States: From the 1960s to the 1990s.* New York: Routledge.

Orfield, Gary. 1993. "School Desegregation after Two Generations: Race, Schools and Opportunity in Urban Society." In *Race in America,* edited by H. Hill and J. E. Jones. Madison: University of Wisconsin Press.

Orfield, Gary, Mark D. Bachmeier, David R. James, and Tamela Eitle. 1997. "Deepening Segregation in American Public Schools: A Special Report from the Harvard Project on School Desegregation." *Equity & Excellence in Education* 30: 5–24.

Orfield, Gary, and Susan Eaton. 1996. *Dismantling Desegregation.* New York: New Press.

Orfield, Gary, and Nora Gordon. 2001. *Schools More Separate: Consequences of a Decade of Resegregation.* Cambridge, Mass.: The Civil Rights Project, Harvard University.

Orfield, Gary, and Frank Monfort. 1992. *Status of School Desegregation: The Next Generation.* Alexandria, Va.: National School Boards Association.

Orfield, Gary, and John T. Yun. 1999. *Resegregation in American Schools.* Cambridge, Mass.: The Civil Rights Project, Harvard University.

Pardo, Mary. 1998. *Mexican American Women Activists: Identity and Resistance in Two Los Angeles Communities.* Philadelphia: Temple University Press.

Patchen, Martin. 1982. *Black-White Contact in Schools: Its Social and Academic Effects.* West Lafayette, Ind.: Purdue University Press.

Payne, Charles M. 1984. *Getting What We Ask For: The Ambiguity of Success and Failure in Urban Education.* Westport, Conn.: Greenwood Press.

———. 1991. "The Comer Intervention Model and School Reform in Chicago: Implications of Two Models of Change." *Urban Education* 26: 8–24.

Perry, Constance M. 1999. "Proactive Thoughts on Creating Safe Schools." *School Community Journal* 9: 9–16.

Perry, Pamela. 2001. "White Means Never Having to Say You're Ethnic: White Youth and the Construction of 'Cultureless' Identities." *Contemporary Ethnography* 30: 56–91.

———. 2002. *Shades of White: White Kids and Racial Identities in High School.* Durham, N.C.: Duke University Press.

Peshkin, Alan. 1982. "The Researcher and Subjectivity: Reflections on an Ethnography of School and Community." In *Doing the Ethnography of Schooling,* edited by G. Spindler. New York: Holt, Rinehart and Winston.

———. 1991. *The Color of Strangers, the Color of Friends: The Play of Ethnicity in School and Community.* Chicago: University of Chicago Press.

Philips, Susan U. 1972. "Participant Structures and Communicative Competence: Warm Springs Children in Community and Classroom." In *Functions of Language in the Classroom,* edited by Courtney B. Cazden, Vera P. John, and Dell Hymes. Prospect Heights, Ill.: Waveland Press.

Phoenix, Ann. 1998. "Dealing with Difference: The Recursive and the New." *Ethnic and Racial Studies* 21: 859-880.

Pinderhughes, Howard. 1997. *Race in the Hood: Conflict and Violence among Urban Youth.* Minneapolis: University of Minnesota Press.

Pinkney, Alphonso. 2000. *Black Americans.* Upper Saddle River, N.J.: Prentice-Hall.

Pulido, Laura. 2000. "Rethinking Environmental Racism: White Privilege and Urban Development in Southern California." *Annals of the Association of American Geographers* 90(1): 12–40.

Quadagno, Jill. 1994. *The Color of Welfare: How Racism Undermined the War on Poverty.* New York: Oxford University Press.

Radin, Charles. 1997. "The New Face of Heroin." *Boston Globe,* 8 June, p. 14.

Reskin, Barbara. 2002. "Retheorizing Employment Discrimination and Its Remedies." In *The New Economic Sociology: Developments in an Emerging Field,* edited by M. Guillen, R. Collins, P. England, and M. Meyer. New York: Russell Sage Foundation.

Rezai-Rashti, Goli. 1995. "Multicultural Education, Anti-racist Education, and Critical Pedagogy: Reflections on Everyday Practice." In *Anti-racism, Feminism and Critical Approaches to Education,* edited by R. Ng, P. Staton, and J. Scane. Westport, Conn.: Bergin & Garvey.

Ridenour, Carolyn S., Thomas Lasley, and William L. Bainbridge. 2001. "The Impact of Emerging Market-Based Public Policy on Urban Schools and a Democratic Society." *Education & Urban Society* 34: 66–83.

Rist, Ray. 1974. "Race, Policy, and Schooling." *Society* 12: 59–63.

Rodriguez, Clara E. 1991. *Puerto Ricans: Born in the U.S.A.* Boulder, Colo.: Westview Press.

———. 1992. "Race, Culture, and Latino 'Otherness' in the 1980 Census." *Social Science Quarterly* 73: 930–937.

Rodriguez, Clara E., and Cordero-Guzman, Hector. 1992. "Placing Race in Context." *Ethnic and Racial Studies* 15: 523–542.

Roscigno, Vincent J., and James W. Ainsworth-Darnell. 1999. "Race, Cultural Capital, and Educational Resources: Persistent Inequalities and Achievement Returns." *Sociology of Education* 72:158–178.

Rosen, David M. 1977. "Multicultural Education: An Anthropological Perspective." *Anthropology & Education Quarterly* 8(4): 221–226.

———. 1980. "Class and Ideology in an Inner City Preschool: Reproductionist Theory and the Anthropology of Education." *Anthropological Quarterly* 53(4): 219–228.

Rosenfeld, Gerry. 1971. *"Shut Those Thick Lips!" A Study of Slum School Failure.* New York: Holt, Rinehart and Winston.

Sadker, Myra, and David Sadker. 1994. *Failing at Fairness: How America's Schools Cheat Girls.* New York: Scribner.

Saito, Leland T. 1998. *Race and Politics: Asian Americans, Latinos, and Whites in a Los Angeles Suburb.* Urbana: University of Illinois Press.

Saporito, Salvatore, and Annette Lareau. 1999. "School Selection as a Process: The Multiple Dimensions of Race in Framing Educational Choice." *Social Problems* 46: 418–439.

Schofield, Janet Ward. 1982. *Black and White in School: Trust, Tension, or Tolerance?* New York: Praeger.

———. 1986. "Causes and Consequences of the Colorblind Perspective." In *Prejudice, Discrimination, and Racism,* edited by J. F. Dovidio and S. Gaertner. Orlando, Fla.: Academic Press.

Schuman, Howard, Charlotte Steeh, Lawrence Bobo, and Maria Krysan. 1997. *Racial Attitudes in America: Trends and Interpretations.* Cambridge, Mass.: Harvard University Press.

Sellers, Robert M., Mia A. Smith, Nicole J. Shelton, Stephanie A. Rowley, Tabbye M. Chavous. 1998. "Multidimensional Model of Racial Identity: A Reconceptualization of African American Racial Identity." *Personality & Social Psychology Review* 2(1): 18–39.

Sewell, Tony. 1997. *Black Masculinities and Schooling: How Black Boys Survive Modern Schooling*. Straffordshire, England: Trentham Books.

Sewell, William H. 1992. "A Theory of Structure: Duality, Agency, and Transformation." *American Journal of Sociology* 98: 1–29.

Sigelman, Lee, Timothy Bledsoe, Susan Welch, and Michael W. Combs. 1996. "Making Contact? Black-White Social Interaction in an Urban Setting." *American Journal of Sociology* 101: 1306–1332.

Skiba, Russell, and Peter E. Leone. 2001. "Zero Tolerance and School Security Measures: A Failed Experiment." In *Racial Profiling and Punishment in U.S. Public Schools,* edited by Tammy Johnson, Jennifer Emiko Boyden, and William J. Pittz. Oakland, Calif.: Applied Research Center.

Skiba, Russell, and Reece Peterson. 1999. "The Dark Side of Zero Tolerance: Can Punishment Lead to Safe Schools?" *Phi Delta Kappan* 80: 372–376, 381–382.

Sleeter, Christine, and Carl Grant. 1988. "An Analysis of Multicultural Education in the United States." In *Facing Racism in Education,* edited by Nitza Hidalgo, Ceasar McDowell, and Emilie Siddle. Cambridge, Mass.: Harvard Educational Review.

Smith, Robert C. 1995. *Racism in the Post–Civil Rights Era: Now You See It, Now You Don't*. Albany: State University of New York Press.

Smrekar, Clair. 1997. *The Impact of School Choice and Community: In the Interest of Families and Schools*. Albany: State University of New York Press.

Solórzano, Daniel, Miguel Ceja, and Tara Yosso. 2000. "Critical Race Theory, Racial Microaggressions, and the Campus Racial Climate: The Experiences of African American College Students." *Journal of Negro Education* 69: 60–73.

Stanton-Salazar, Ricardo D. 2001. *Manufacturing Hope and Despair: The School and Kin Support Networks of U.S.-Mexican Youth*. New York: Teachers College Press.

Starr, Paul. 1992. "Civil Reconstruction: What to Do without Affirmative Action." *American Prospect* (Winter): 7–16.

Steele, Claude M. 1999. "Thin Ice: 'Stereotype Threat' and Black College Students." *Atlantic Monthly*, August, pp. 44–54.

Stone, Maureen. 1981. "The Education of the Black Child." In *The School in the Multicultural Society*, edited by R. Jeffcoate and A. James. London: Open University Press.

Suárez-Orozco, Marcelo M. 1995. "The Need for Strangers: Proposition 187 and the Immigration Malaise." *Multicultural Review* 4: 18–23, 56–58.

Swartz, David. 1997. *Culture & Power: The Sociology of Pierre Bourdieu*. Chicago: University of Chicago Press.

Takaki, Ronald. 1987. *From Different Shores: Perspectives on Race and Ethnicity in America*. New York: Oxford University Press.

———. 1993. *A Different Mirror: A History of Multicultural America*. Boston: Little, Brown.

Takeuchi, David T., David R. Williams, and Russell Adair. 1991. "Economic Stress in the Family and Children's Emotional and Behavioral Problems." *Journal of Marriage and the Family* 53: 1031–1041.

Tatum, Beverly Daniel. 1997. *"Why Are All the Black Kids Sitting Together in the Cafeteria?" and Other Conversations about Race*. New York : Basic Books.

Thompson, E. T. 1975. "The Plantation as a Race-Making Situation." In *Minorities: A Text with Readings in Intergroup Relations*, edited by B. Eugene Griessman. Hinsdale, Ill.: Dryden Press.

Thorne, Barrie. 1993. *Gender Play: Girls and Boys in School*. New Brunswick, N.J.: Rutgers University Press.

Tomasky, Michael. 1996. *Left for Dead: The Life, Death and Possible Resurrection of Progressive Politics in America*. New York: Free Press.

Traub, James. 2000. "What No School Can Do." *New York Times*, 16 January, sec. 6, p. 52.

Troyna, Barry. 1987. *Racial Inequality in Education*. London: Tavistock.

Troyna, Barry, and Richard Hatcher. 1992. *Racism in Children's Lives: A Study of Mainly-White Primary Schools*. New York: Routledge.

U.S. Bureau of the Census. *1990 Census of the Population*. Washington, D.C. Retrieved from govinfo.kerr.orst.edu

Valdes, Guadalupe. 1997. "Dual-Language Immersion Programs: A Cautionary Note Concerning the Education of Language-Minority Students." *Harvard Educational Review* 67: 391–423.

Valenzuela, Angela. 1999. *Subtractive Schooling: U.S.-Mexican Youth and the Politics of Caring*. Albany: State University of New York Press.

Valli, Linda. 1986. *Becoming Clerical Workers*. Boston: Routledge.

Van Ausdale, Debra, and Joe Feagin. 2001. *The First R: How Children Learn Race and Racism*. Lanham, Md.: Rowman & Littlefield.

Wacquant, Loïc. 2002. "From Slavery to Mass Incarceration." *New Left Review* 13: 41–60.

Weis, Lois, and Michelle Fine. 1993. *Beyond Silenced Voices: Class, Race, and Gender in United States Schools*. Albany: State University of New York Press.

———. 2000. *Speed Bumps*. New York: Teachers College Press.

Wellman, David T. 1993. *Portraits of White Racism*. New York: Cambridge University Press.

Wells, Amy Stuart, and Robert L. Crain. 1997. *Stepping over the Color Line: African-American Students in White Suburban Schools*. New Haven, Conn.: Yale University Press.

Williams, David R., and Chiquita Collins. 1995. "US Socioeconomic and Racial Differences in Health: Patterns and Explanations." *Annual Review of Sociology* 21: 349–386.

Williams, David R., Yan Yu, James S. Jackson, and Norman Anderson. 1997. "Racial Differences in Physical and Mental Health: Socio-economic Status, Stress and Discrimination." *Journal of Health Psychology* 2: 335–351.

Willis, Paul. 1977. *Learning to Labor: How Working Class Kids Get Working Class Jobs*. New York: Columbia University Press.

Wills, John S. 1994. "Popular Culture, Curriculum, and Historical Representation: The Situation of Native Americans in American History and the Perpetuation of Stereotypes." *Journal of Narrative and Life History* 4: 277–294.

———. 1996. "Who Needs Multicultural Education? White Students, U.S. History, and the Construction of a Usable Past." *Anthropology & Education Quarterly* 27: 365–389.

Wilson, William Julius. 1987. *The Truly Disadvantaged: The Inner City, the Underclass, and Public Policy*. Chicago: University of Chicago Press.

———. 1996. *When Work Disappears: The World of the New Urban Poor*. New York: Vintage Books.

Winant, Howard. 1995. "Book Review—Racial Faultlines: The Historical Origins of White Supremacy in California." *Contemporary Sociology* 24: 587–588.

Wright, Lawrence. 1994. "One Drop of Blood." *New Yorker*, July 25, pp. 46–55.

Yinger, John. 1995. *Closed Doors, Opportunities Lost : The Continuing Costs of Housing Discrimination*. New York: Russell Sage Foundation.

Zavella, Patricia. 1996. "Feminist Insider Dilemmas: Constructing Ethnic Identity with Chicana Informants." In *Feminist Dilemmas in Fieldwork*, edited by D. Wolf. Boulder, Colo.: Westview Press.

Zimmerman, Rick S., William A. Vega, Andres G. Gil, George J. Warheit, Eleni Apospori, and Frank Biafora. 1994. "Who Is Hispanic? Definitions and Their Consequences." *American Journal of Public Health* 84: 1985–1987.

Zuberi, Tukufu. 2001. *Thicker Than Blood: How Racial Statistics Lie*. Minneapolis: University of Minnesota Press.

Index

About the Author

Amanda E. Lewis is an associate professor of sociology and African American studies and a fellow at the Institute for Research on Race and Public Policy at the University of Illinois at Chicago. Her work on racial inequality and education has appeared in a number of books and journals.